TeenCoder™ Serie

TeenCoder™: Windows Programming

Student Textbook

Third Edition

Homeschool Programming, Inc.

TeenCoder™: Windows Programming

Third Edition

980 Birmingham Rd, Suite 501-128
Alpharetta, GA 30004

ISBN: **978-0-9887033-1-5**

Terms of Use

Disclaimer

Homeschool Programming, Inc, and their officers and shareholders, assume no liability for damage to personal computers or loss of data residing on personal computers arising due to the use or misuse of this course material. Always follow instructions provided by the manufacturer of 3rd party programs that may be included or referenced by this course.

Contact Us

You may contact Homeschool Programming, Inc. through the information and links provided on our website: http://www.HomeschoolProgramming.com. We welcome your comments and questions regarding this course or other related programming courses you would like to study!

Other Courses

Homeschool Programming, Inc. currently has two product lines for students: KidCoder™ and TeenCoder™. Our KidCoder™ Series provides easy, step-by-step programming curriculum for 4th through 12th graders. The Visual Basic series teaches introductory programming concepts in a fun, graphical manner. The Web Design series lets students create their own websites in HTML. Our TeenCoder™ Series provides introductory programming curriculum for high-school students. These courses are college-preparatory material designed for the student who may wish to pursue a career in Computer Science or enhance their transcript with a technical elective. Students can learn C#, Java, game programming, and Android application development.

3rd Party Copyrights

This course uses Microsoft's Visual C# 2010 Express as the programming platform. Visual Studio, Visual Studio Express, Windows, and all related products are copyright Microsoft Corporation. Please see http://www.microsoft.com/visualstudio/eng/products/visual-studio-2010-express for more details.

Instructional Videos

This course may be accompanied by optional Instructional Videos. These Flash-based videos will play directly from a DVD drive on the student's computer. Instructional Videos are supplements to the Student Textbook, covering every chapter and lesson with fun, animated re-enforcement of the main topics.

Instructional Videos are intended for students who enjoy a more audio-visual style of learning. They are not replacements for the Student Textbook, which is still required to complete this course! However by watching the Instructional Videos first, students may begin each textbook chapter and lesson already having some grasp of the material to be read. Where applicable, the videos will also show "screencasts" of a real programmer demonstrating some concept or activity within the software development environment.

This Student Textbook and accompanying material are entirely sufficient to complete the course successfully! Instructional Videos are optional for students who would benefit from the alternate presentation of the material. For more information or to purchase the videos separately, please refer to the product descriptions on our website: http://www.HomeschoolProgramming.com.

Table of Contents

Before You Begin

Please read the following topics before you begin the course.

Minimum Hardware and Software Requirements

This is a hands-on programming course! You will be installing Microsoft's Visual C# 2010 Express on your computer, which must meet the following minimum requirements:

Computer Hardware

Your computer hardware must meet the following minimum specifications:

	Minimum
CPU	1.6GHz or faster processor
RAM	1024 MB
Display	1024 x 768 or higher resolution
Graphics Card	Supports DirectX-10 or later
Hard Disk Size	3GB available space
DVD Drive	DVD-ROM drive

Operating Systems

Your computer operating system must match one of the following:

Windows XP (x86) with Service Pack 3 or above (except Starter Edition)
Windows Vista (x86 and x64) with Service Pack 2 or above (except Starter Edition)
Windows 7 (x86 and x64)
Windows 8 or Windows 8 Pro (excluding Windows 8 RT)

Conventions Used in This Text

This course will use certain styles (fonts, borders, etc) to highlight text of special interest.

```
Source code will be in 11-point Consolas font, in a single box like this.
```

Variable names will be in **`12-point Consolas bold`** text, similar to the way they will look in your development environment. For example: **`myVariable`**.

Function names, properties and keywords will be in **bold face** type so they are easily readable.

This picture highlights important concepts within a lesson.

Sidebars may contain additional information, tips, or background material.

Chapter Review sections will highlight key elements from each chapter.

Each chapter includes an activity that allows you to practice the concepts you have learned.

What You Will Learn and Do In This Course

TeenCoder™: Windows Programming will teach you the fundamentals of writing your own computer programs. You will be writing graphical Windows programs using Microsoft's C# programming language. This course is geared for high-school students who have expressed an interest in computer programming or who are looking for college-preparatory material.

Starting with the second chapter, you will complete a hands-on programming project at the end of each chapter. These projects will increase in complexity as you learn more about the C# language!

What You Need to Know Before Starting

You are expected to already know the basics of computer use before beginning this course. You need to know how to use the keyboard and mouse to select and run programs, use application menu systems, and work with the Windows operating system. You should understand how to store and load files on your hard disk, and how to use the Windows Explorer to walk through your file system and directory structures. You should also have some experience with using text editors and using web browsers to find helpful information on the Internet.

Software Versions

You will be using the *Microsoft Visual C# 2010 Express* software to complete this course. This program can be freely downloaded from Microsoft's website. Your course will contain links to download and install instructions in PDF format on our website, http://www.HomeschoolProgramming.com. Microsoft may from time to time change their website or download process or release newer versions of the product. Our website will contain updated versions of the instructions as needed.

Getting Help

All courses come with a Solution Guide PDF and fully coded solutions for all activities. Simply install the "Solution Files" from your course setup program and you will be able to refer to the solutions as needed from the "Solution Menu". If you are confused about any activity you can see how we solved the problem!

Course Errata

We welcome your feedback regarding any course details that are unclear or that may need correction. Please contact us using our online "Getting Help" form. You can find a list of course errata for this edition on our website, http://www.HomeschoolProgramming.com.

Chapter One: Introduction to Windows Programming

In this chapter you will review a brief history of the Windows operating system and learn about some of the more popular programming languages used to create software applications.

Lesson One: History of Windows

This course relies on the Windows operating system for our graphical programming environment. So, to begin, let's trace the origins of Windows from Microsoft's DOS up through today.

Disk Operating System (DOS)

Once upon a time, the computers of the world were text-based. It's hard to believe, but there was a time when a window was something you opened in the summertime to let in a breeze, and a mouse was something small and furry. We call this time: the 1980s.

DOS (short for Disk Operating System) was the main operating system on home computers in the 1980s. Unlike the Windows operating systems of today, there were versions of DOS produced by different companies. Microsoft created the MS-DOS version, but there were also popular versions from IBM (PC-DOS) and even free versions, like FreeDOS.

The DOS operating system used a series of text-based commands and a single-color text console to interact with the computer. DOS did not have many bells and whistles. Eventually, color video screens let you look at the text in one of up to 8 colors! To access a list of files on the hard drive, you had to know the right text commands. Here is a list of some of the more popular commands:

Command	Purpose
cls	Clears the screen. This was important, since text-based screens can get cluttered very quickly.
dir	This command would display the directories and files on the hard drive. If you had a lot of files, you would need to use modifiers, like /p , which would pause the list after every page of data.
cd	This command would change the current directory. You would need to follow this command with a valid directory name, like this: "cd \myFiles".
mkdir	This would make a new directory on your hard drive. To use this command, you would need to follow it with a name for your new directory, like this: "mkdir MyDir".

As you can tell, these commands were not exactly user-friendly – and there were TONS of them that you have to memorize in order to use your computer. It's no wonder that computer usage was limited to the brave and the super-geeky at this time.

In addition to being a bit difficult to use, the DOS operating system was only a 16-bit system. This means that it could only process 16 bits (or 2 bytes) of information at a time. It could also only use a maximum of 640 KiloBytes (KB) of memory (RAM). This is extremely small by modern standards.

In the mid-1980s, responding to pressure for a more graphical interface, Microsoft came out with "DOSShell". The DOSShell program ran on top of regular DOS and gave the user a slightly more graphical view of the files on the hard drive. DOSShell wasn't a true graphical operating system. Instead, it used text-based graphics (blocks and letters) to draw simple shapes on the screen. The most important (and at that time exciting) feature of DOSShell was the ability to use the mouse to point and click at the files on the screen. Still, it was a far cry from today's graphical operating systems.

Microsoft Windows

In the mid-1980s, Apple Computers came out with their "Lisa" computer. The "Lisa" had the first truly graphical operating system. This was an amazing breakthrough in the field of home computers. No more arcane commands to remember; just point and click! The original "Lisa" had several graphical programs: a calculator, a document viewer and a file manager.

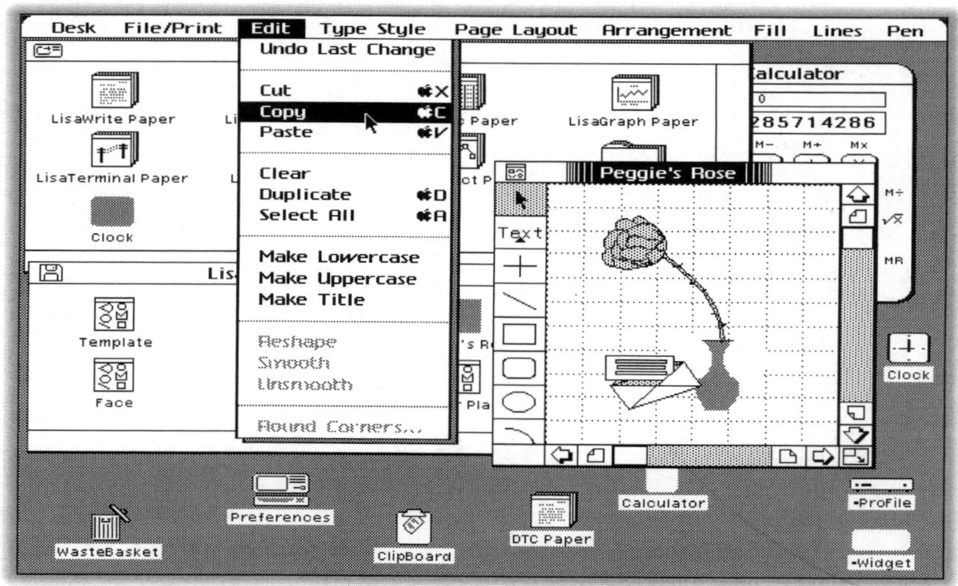

The "Lisa" Apple Computer – Courtesy GuidebookGallery.org

Where was Microsoft at that time? Actually, they were right there with Apple, working together on developing some of the software for Apple computers. Bill Gates, the founder of Microsoft, started to see a great potential for putting a graphical interface on an IBM-PC instead of DOS. Microsoft's first graphical operating system, called Windows 1.0, arrived in 1985. Windows actually ran on top of MS-DOS as an extension. As a first-generation product, it had quite a few problems! Windows 1.0 was slow, buggy and unpredictable. Needless to say, it was not a big-seller.

Bill Gates, however, kept working on Windows. In 1987 Microsoft released Windows version 2.0. This version of Windows still ran on MS-DOS, but it was slightly faster, much less buggy and more reliable. And perhaps the best improvement of all was the addition of two new, graphical programs: *Excel* and *Word*. Excel was a spreadsheet program and Word was a document-editing program. Microsoft had the clever idea to include a "runtime" version of Windows with these programs. This meant you did not have to own the full Windows operating system to run these programs. When you started Excel or Word a small version of Windows would start-up and run with the programs. When you finished with the programs, Windows would exit and you would go back to your DOS screen. This gave more people exposure to the world of graphical Windows software.

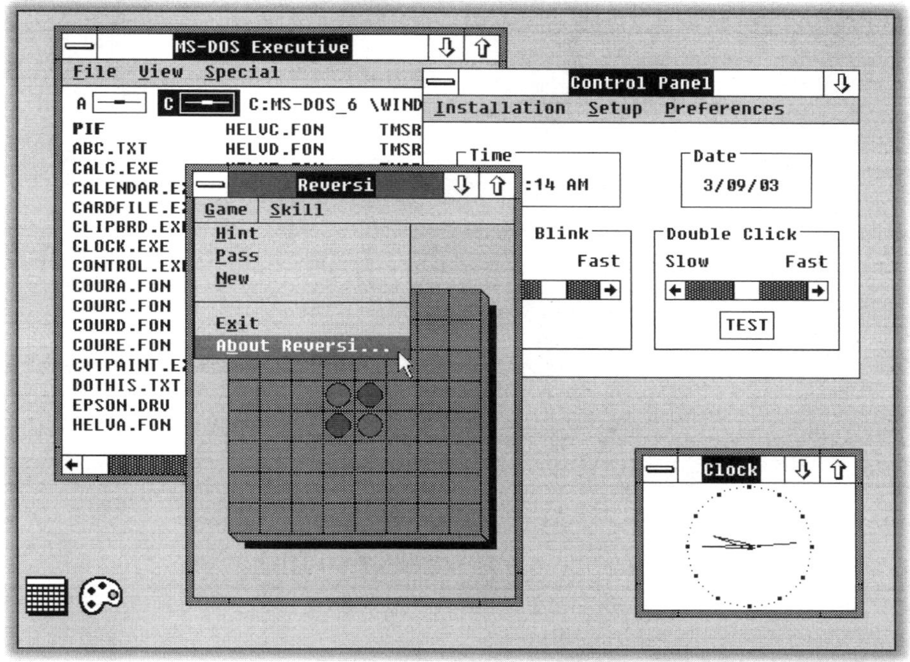

Windows 2.03 – Courtesy of GuidebookGallery.org

The second factor that made Windows 2.0 more popular was the advent of the first non-Microsoft software application that ran within Windows. The Aldus Company created a version of their popular *Pagemaker* publishing software just for the Windows operating system. This was the first time that an outside company invested in Windows products and it really boosted the Windows image.

There were some drawbacks to the new Windows 2.0 software. Most notably, you could not put one "Window" on top of another. You had to "tile" the windows on the screen. This was a very clunky implementation and was due to the fact that Apple had copyrighted the ability to overlap graphic windows on a video screen. In the late 1980s, Microsoft decided to test that copyright by releasing Windows 2.03, which included support for overlapped windows. Apple was not amused. Within months, Apple had brought 190 claims of copyright infringement against Microsoft, claiming that they had copied the "look-and-feel" of the Apple software. Luckily for Microsoft, however, all but 10 of these claims were thrown out of court. The final 10 claims were eventually dropped as well.

In 1990, Microsoft released another version of Windows, version 3.0. This version still sat on top of the MS-DOS operating system, so was limited by DOS's 16-bit structure. Windows 3.0 was a much more stable operating system and was becoming extremely popular. Around this time VGA cards and sound cards were becoming more common, and Windows took full advantage of these inventions. Suddenly, you could view graphics in 16 colors on the screen (a huge deal at the time) and you could listen to full stereo audio (also a big improvement over the PC speaker). This version of Windows became the first to provide a major source of income for Microsoft.

At the same time that Microsoft was working on Windows 3.0, they were also working with IBM on another operating system called "OS/2". OS/2 was a multi-tasking, graphical operating system. A multi-tasking operating system meant that a user could run two programs at the same time. This was a revolutionary concept at the time and for this reason, OS/2 was a powerful competitor in the 1980s and early 1990s.

Unfortunately, the IBM and Microsoft partnership hit some snags as Windows became more popular and more of a competitor to OS/2. Microsoft wanted to focus their development on further versions of Windows, and IBM wanted to stick with OS/2. This conflict led to a break-up of their partnership in the early 1990s. Since both companies had full access to each other's code at that time, they split the code up amongst themselves. Microsoft ported its version of OS/2 into a new product called "Windows NT" and IBM ported its code into the next release of OS/2. Unfortunately for IBM, the lack of OS/2 compatible software and the lack of interest slowly killed this operating system in the 1990s.

Windows 3.x and Windows NT

After their breakup with IBM, Microsoft re-doubled its development on the Windows product line. In 1992, Windows 3.1 was released, which contained many bug fixes for version 3.0. Very soon afterwards, a new version of Windows called "Windows for Workgroups" (WFW) 3.11 was released. This version of Windows included networking support. This was wildly popular in the business community, which was just starting to harness the capabilities of the local area network. The sales of WFW skyrocketed in the early 1990s.

Also at this time "Windows NT" was released. This operating system was targeted at businesses, which needed to manage the new networks and servers that were becoming very popular. NT was a multi-tasking operating system, due mainly to the inclusion of the old OS/2 code. It was also the first 32-bit operating system. This meant that NT could run programs more quickly and could take advantage of more memory (RAM). Unfortunately, NT included some advances that were initially developed by the Digital Equipment Corporation (DEC). These advances were brought over by a group of ex-DEC engineers that had been hired by Microsoft. Of course, DEC objected to this theft of ideas and actually won a lawsuit against Microsoft in the mid 1990s.

Windows 95 and NT 4.0

In 1995, Windows released a dramatically different version of Windows: "Windows 95". Windows 95 combined the best features of NT 3.51 and WFW. This was also a 32-bit operating system, which was faster and allowed for the use of more RAM on a computer. Windows 95 was only a hybrid 32-bit system because it still had to support the older 16-bit software. Unfortunately, this significantly slowed down the speed of the operating system.

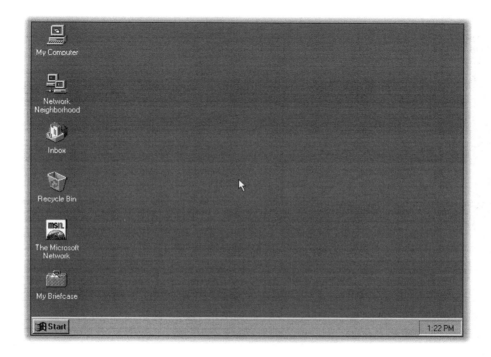

Windows 95 – courtesy of Microsoft Press

Windows 95 was a true breakaway product in the Windows line of software. This was the first time that Windows had stepped completely away from the DOS model. This means that the Windows software was not running on top of the DOS operating system, the Windows software *was* the operating system. This maneuver quickly made all other hybrid versions of DOS in the market fade away. The Windows 95 software was completely re-designed to make it easier for anyone to use, regardless of their computer skills. Windows 95 was also a multi-tasking operating system, allowing users to run more than one program simultaneously.

At the same time Windows 95 was released, Microsoft also released "Windows NT 4.0". This version of NT was re-designed to have the same look-and-feel of Windows 95. Windows NT 4.0 software did not maintain the hybrid 16-bit compatibility support and was therefore a faster operating system.

Windows 98

In 1998, Microsoft released Windows 98. This version of Windows was mainly a bug-fix improvement over Windows 95, although 98 also supported larger sizes of memory and hard drives. This version also included the Internet Explorer software for free, allowing users to browse the Internet. Due to Microsoft's dominant position in the personal computer market, the free Internet Explorer rapidly gained significant market share against other browsers from 3rd party companies like Netscape.

Windows XP

In 2001 Microsoft released a major re-work of Windows, called Windows XP. This version marked the final merging of the NT and Windows product lines. It also marked the almost complete obliteration of the old DOS. The Windows product was called "XP Home" and the NT version was called "XP Professional". These versions of Windows were full 32-bit operating systems, with better support for memory and larger hard drives. They were relatively stable and bug-free, but opened up serious security risks. The increasing popularity and usage of the Internet opened a whole host of security problems in the XP software. One study claimed that within hours of installing XP and connecting to the Internet, a PC was infected with at least one virus. Microsoft released additional bug and security fixes in the form of "service packs".

Windows Vista

In 2006 Microsoft released a new version of Windows called "Vista". This new version included some new graphics applications, DVD authoring software and better versions of the Windows Media Player and Internet Explorer. Vista also included many new security updates in response to the security issues in the XP product line.

Windows 7

Windows 7 was released in 2009 and fixed some of the security and usability features of Windows Vista. This version included support for a faster boot-up, better power management for laptops and portable computers, and support for multi-touch devices. Windows 7 also comes in a 64-bit version which allows it to make use of more memory and faster processor (CPU) designs.

Windows 8

The newest release of Windows at the time of this writing is called "Windows 8". Windows 8 includes a significant re-design of the long-standing Windows graphical user interface. Microsoft is attempting to make the user experience more like the popular smart-phones and tablets, with an emphasis on touch screens.

Lesson Two: The Evolution of Windows Programming

A Windows program could be simply defined as any program designed to work with the Windows operating system. However, like most simple definitions, this is vague and not very useful. So what makes up a true Windows program? In this lesson, we will look at some common traits that most Windows programs share.

Graphical Programs

The most common trait of a Windows program is a graphical interface. Some sort of graphical representations are used for objects in the program. The Windows Explorer software, for example, might use a folder image to represent a directory and a sheet of paper to represent a simple file. Most software will use an image of an old floppy disk to represent the concept of "saving" your information. (This is a bit amusing, since most new computer users have never seen a real floppy disk – they haven't come standard on new computers in years!)

Graphical programs also share a common input device: the mouse. The mouse is useless in a text-based program, but is essential in a graphical program. The development of the mouse was a very important and significant achievement enabling easy use of graphical applications. It's usually much easier and faster to navigate through controls by point-n-click instead of trying to select items using the keyboard.

Common Graphical Elements

In addition to being a graphical program, a Windows program usually contains certain *common graphical elements*. In fact, the phrase "common look and feel" is a key selling point for many applications. It's important for users to have a consistent experience across many applications. Otherwise they have to re-train themselves to use each application. For example, most people know to click the "X" in the upper-right corner of a program to close it. If you want to save your information, what menu option would you choose? Chances are you would click on "File" and then "Save", and the "File" menu is the first item on the menu bar. No matter what Windows application you are using, there is always a "File" and "Save" option. This common look-and-feel gives a seamless quality to different applications within the Windows environment.

A common look and feel is so important that in recent years Microsoft has released a series of standards for Windows programs called "Windows Logo" or "Windows Certification Program". These requirements govern how a program should look in order to be a Microsoft-sanctioned product.

Have you ever noticed how all Windows programs tend to look alike? When you want to save your work, you click on "File" and "Save" – no matter what program you are running! This is part of the common look-and-feel of Windows.

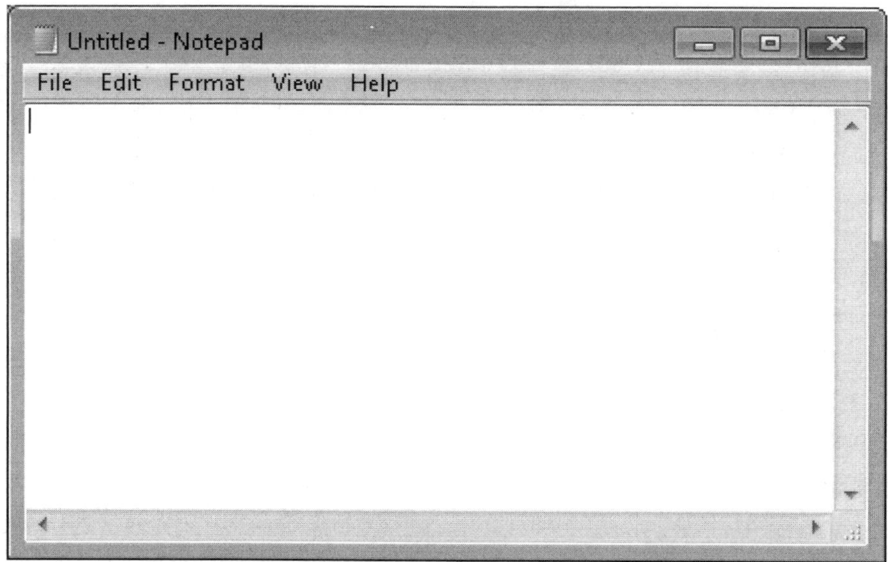

The Notepad program, showing common menu items, a title bar and status bar.

In addition to common menu systems, Windows applications tend to have the following common elements:

- A rectangular shape – windows are square or rectangular and can be re-sized anywhere on the screen
- A title bar at the top of the screen with the application title, and minimize, maximize and exit buttons
- A menu bar under the title bar with at least "File", "Edit", and "Help" items
- A status bar at the bottom of the screen, which gives additional information about the program, such as page numbers in documents or file counts in an Explorer application

How a Windows Program Works

Now that you know what a Windows program looks like, let's talk a little bit about how they work. Windows programs are mostly "event-driven". The programs respond to events that are caused by a user clicking buttons, typing text or moving the mouse on the screen. This is a dramatic difference from "console" applications which tend to execute in a more predictable sequence with tightly controlled user input. Event-driven applications will execute as dictated by events generated by the user.

How to Program a Windows Application – Old Style

In the early days of Windows programming, it would take several pages of code just to display a simple window on the screen. After all of this code, you would have a window on the screen, but you would not be able to interact with the window. To interact with your window, you will need to receive "messages" about the events that are occurring on the screen.

Windows programs are very chatty! The operating system will send a "message" about every event to the program. It doesn't matter if a user clicks a button, types a sentence or moves the mouse; the operating system will send a message!

The operating system will generate a "message" for every event that occurs in a Windows program. Button-clicks, mouse movements and key presses are all events that create messages. The programmer would have to write special handling code to route the messages to the correct piece of logic that would handle the event.

Altogether, writing early Windows programs was an extremely complex process that scared many would-be programmers away. Thankfully, you will not need to perform these tasks to create your programs now! Modern programming languages have made the process of programming Windows applications much easier.

Modern Object-Oriented Approaches

In the last five to ten years, the world of Windows programming has become much easier. Most of the hard work required to build a graphical window or process events is safely wrapped up in pre-built code libraries. Programmers can concentrate on the unique features of each program instead of re-inventing the wheel each time. Today's Integrated Development Environments (IDEs) allow you to design a screen as if you were painting on a canvas. You can set the size, color, text, and other properties of windows and controls by pointing, clicking and dragging the items with the mouse. With a few mouse clicks you can create event-handling methods without worrying about the internal plumbing necessary to make messages from a control arrive in the right place.

The introduction of object-oriented programming means programmers have increasingly useful libraries of code to handle many common programming tasks. We will discuss event-driven programs and object-oriented programming in more depth later in this book. For now, you should understand that these technologies will make your programming experience far more enjoyable than it was for the programmers of yesteryear!

Lesson Three: Windows Programming Languages

There are many different programming languages that have been used to create Windows programs. In this lesson, we will cover some of the more common languages that have been used in the past and that are still in use today.

C/ C++/ Visual C++

One of the first programming languages for Windows programs was the "C" language. This language has been around for many decades and was used almost exclusively in the early years of Windows programming. The C language is very powerful, but lacks some of the modern niceties of later languages.

The C++ language (also called "C with Classes"), added some object-oriented concepts to the original C language. These concepts allowed programmers to create and re-use large libraries of common code. Object-oriented programming reduced the need to re-create code for common methods like displaying a window on the screen.

The Microsoft Visual Studio C++ Integrated Development Environment (IDE) provides a graphical way to design screens in an application. It also provides a large library of pre-built classes called the Microsoft Foundation Classes (MFC) to make working with most aspects of Windows programming easier. In old style C and C++ programming, a window was designed in a painstaking iterative process. A programmer would write code to display a window at a specific location and size on the screen using numeric values (in pixels).

When the program was run, the programmer would look at the screen, note any changes and then close the program. Then they would go back to the source code, change the values slightly and run the program again. This was a very clunky, tedious process. The Visual Studio IDE allowed a programmer to review and adjust a screen at design-time. They could click and drag buttons and other objects onto a window and adjust the size and placement *without* running the program - a great improvement!

In the early days of Windows, programmers had to do a lot of guessing when trying to place buttons and controls on a Window. They could not see the actual window until the program was run. Now they can design a window before they ever run the program!

The C++ language was the primary programming language for Windows programs for many years. Lately, however, this language has lost some popularity to more modern languages like Java and C#.

Java

In the early 1990s, a company called Sun Microsystems created a new programming language called "Java". Java was created from the ground up as a purely object-oriented language. The Java language was easier to use than C++ in many respects, which made it instantly popular with new programmers.

Java also allowed programmers to write a program one time and then run on many different operating systems, not just Windows. In the early 1990s, the Internet was becoming more popular and the Java language was able to fill the programming needs of this environment. For many years, Java was the king of Internet programming languages.

The name "Java" came from a design meeting at Sun Microsystems in the early 1990s. Scores of designers and programmers were brainstorming about possible names when someone yelled out "Java"! The name was unique and non-technical – and it stuck!

Visual Basic

The Visual Basic programming language grew out of the wildly popular BASIC language. The original BASIC programming language was created to allow non-programming students to write simple programs for their computers. The Visual Basic language is a Windows version of this popular language. One of the best benefits of this language is that it is an extremely simple language to learn.

The Visual Basic IDE was one of the first to allow a programmer to design the screen before the program was tested. In the time it took for a C++ programmer to lay the basic foundation for their Windows program, a Visual Basic programmer could have a program up and running. For this reason, the Visual Basic language was often used for "rapid application development" or RAD. The most common use of RAD programs is prototype programming. Prototype programs are programs which are often used as "proof-of-concept" programs. This means that when a company has an idea for a new program, instead of dedicating a lot of time and resources to creating the program with a complicated language, they will create a quick version with Visual Basic. If the program looks promising, they will then re-develop the program in a more robust language like Java or C++.

Visual C#

In this course, we will be using a programming language called C# (pronounced "C-sharp"). C# was developed by Microsoft in order to compete with Java and take advantage of lessons learned during the evolution of earlier languages. C#, like Java, is an object-oriented language with a large library of pre-built objects to make programming easier. The libraries tend to be more Windows-specific, allowing programmers to fully utilize the power of the Windows operating system. C# was first released 2002 and has gained popularity for a wide range of applications. We will discuss C# in more depth in the next chapter.

Chapter Review

- DOS (Disk Operating System) was a text-based operating system.
- The first graphical operating system was on the Lisa computer, created by Apple in the early 1980s.
- Windows 3.0 was the first widely popular version of Windows.
- OS/2 was IBM's graphical, multitasking operating system in the 1980s and 90s. This operating system was co-authored by Microsoft, but eventually died after the partnership between IBM and Microsoft ended.
- Windows 95 was the first 32-bit version of Windows for the consumer market.
- The Windows XP operating system united the Windows and Windows NT product lines.
- Windows 8 is the most recently announced version of Windows.
- A graphical program will use images to represent major aspects of a program.
- Graphical programs allow the user to use the mouse to interact with the program.
- Microsoft's "Windows Logo" and "Windows Certification" programs were created to ensure Windows programs maintain a common look and feel.
- One of the first programming languages used to create Windows programs was the "C" language.
- Modern programming languages like C++, Java, and C# have simplified Windows development tasks.
- The Java language was created by Sun Microsystems in the early 1990s.
- Visual Basic is an advanced version of the original BASIC programming language.
- Visual Basic is an extremely easy language to learn, but is not as powerful as C++ and Java.
- The C# language was created by Microsoft as an answer to the Java programming language.

Activity: Install Visual C# 2010 Express

In this activity you will be installing the course files, the Microsoft Visual C# 2010 Express software and the MSDN Help Library on your computer.

Course files	The files that come with this course include material for the student (chapter sample programs, activity starters, instructional documents) and for the teacher (activity solutions, tests, answer keys, etc).
Visual C# 2010 Express	This software is a free student version of the professional Visual Studio product. Visual Studio is a popular example of an IDE, or Integrated Development Environment. This is a very important piece of software for any programmer! An IDE is the central place where you will create, compile, run, and debug your program.
MSDN Help Library	The MSDN Help Library is an integrated reference system that allows programmers to quickly pull up help on functions and programming concepts from within the IDE.

Installing the Course Files

The files for this course are installed by a single setup executable that came with your course. The setup file is called "TeenCoder_WindowsProgramming.exe". Ensure that you are running a Windows account with administrative privileges on your machine when you launch the setup executable.

The setup executable will offer you the choice of installing the Student Files and/or Solution Files. You may install these components on the same computer (if the student should have free access to the solutions) or on different computers (so the teacher can maintain control over the solutions). For a better understanding of the setup process and the files present in the course material, please refer to the "Getting Started Guide" on our website at http://www.HomeschoolProgramming.com.

Go ahead and perform this setup process now. We recommend installing to the default "C:\TeenCoder\Windows Programming" directory as we will refer to that directory structure throughout the textbook. You may choose a different location if you want. The setup program will automatically create a "My Projects" directory under the target installation – this is where all of the student projects will go!

Once installation is complete you will have a new "TeenCoder" group on your Windows Start Menu. Underneath "TeenCoder" is a "Windows Programming" folder. Within that folder are one or two menus for the Student and Solution files (depending on your choices during setup). The look and feel of the Windows Start Menu may change between versions of Windows, but your final Start menu should contain folders and links as shown to the right (assuming both Student and Solution files installed).

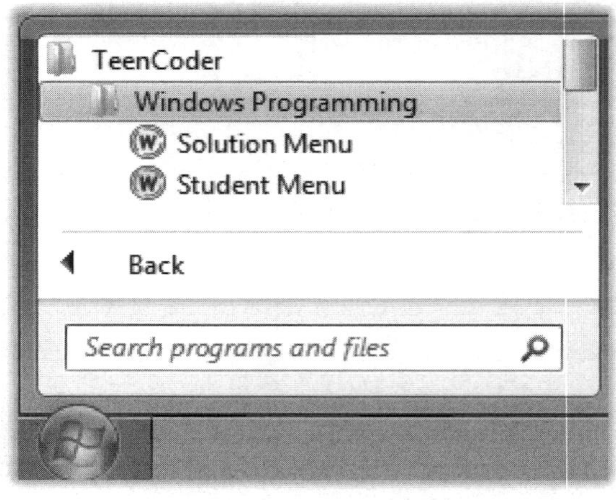

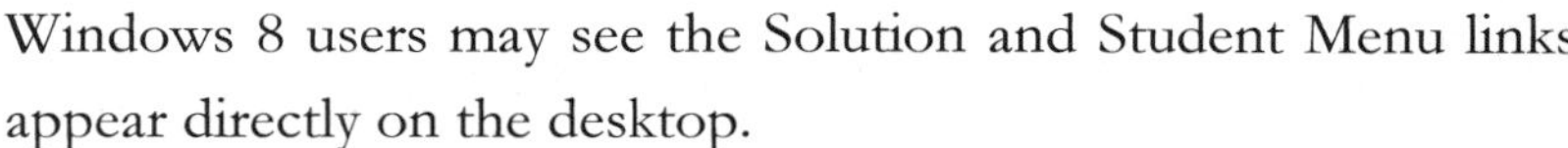

Windows 8 users may see the Solution and Student Menu links appear directly on the desktop.

You can run these menus for convenient, graphical access to all of the instructional documents (PDFs), activity solutions, and other material distributed with the course. You may also simply run Windows Explorer and navigate to your target install directory ("C:\TeenCoder\Windows Programming") and launch these files on your own! Use of the Menu systems is optional. Here is an example screen shot from Windows Explorer that shows the directory structure and files in your target directory (details may vary).

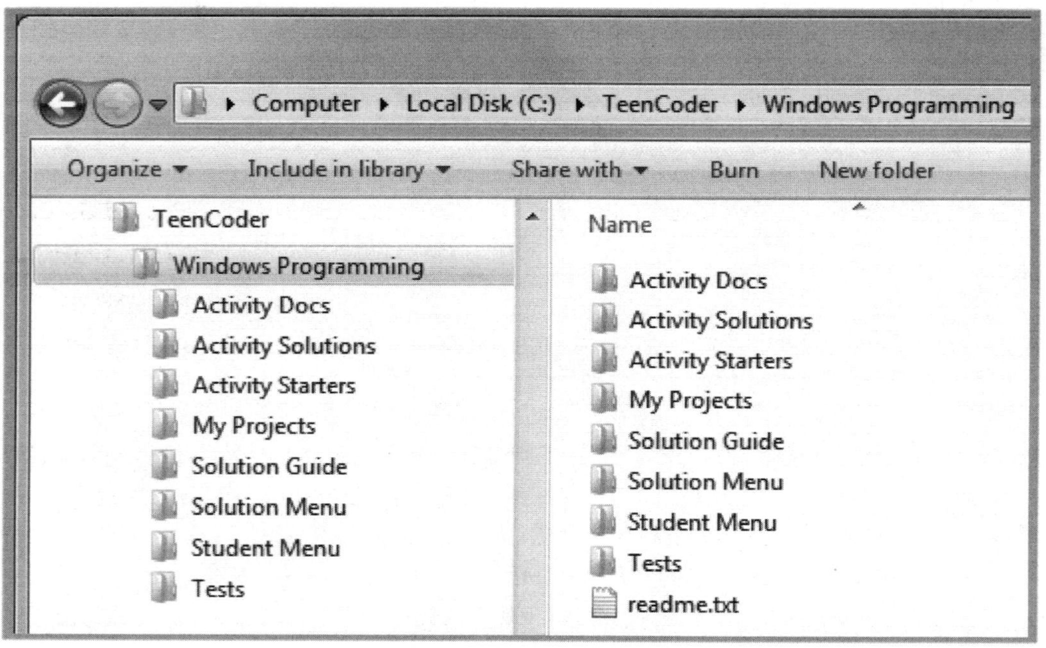

All course descriptions of directory structures will refer to the default installation path. If you choose to install elsewhere, remember to map our instructions to your new location.

Supplemental course documents are in PDF format. A ".PDF" file is a common document format that requires the free Adobe Acrobat program to read. Your computer should already have the Acrobat Reader installed. If you cannot view the PDF documents, you will need to install Acrobat Reader first from http://get.adobe.com/reader/.

Installing Visual C# 2010 Express

Your next major job is to install the Microsoft Visual C# 2010 Express software on your computer. You will need to be connected to the Internet during the download and installation process. Always ask your teacher before doing any activity online! Now, let's get started!

Your Student Menu contains a tab called "Software Install Instructions". Click on that tab and you will see a button called "Get Online Documents". Click that button and you will be directed to a page on our website that contains PDF documents with the current download and installation instructions.

The first document titled "Visual C# 2010 Install Instructions" ("Visual_CS_2010_Install_Instructions.pdf") contains complete, step-by-step instructions on downloading and installing the software. Please use the links from your Student Menu to find and open the Visual C# Install Instructions document now. Follow the instructions to install the IDE on your computer. You can also directly access all install documentation from our website, http://www.HomeschoolProgramming.com.

Within 30 days of installation you also need to register the software with Microsoft (a free process), so we recommend you do that now. Our online document page contains "Visual C# Registration Instructions" ("Visual_CS_2010_Registration_Instructions.pdf"). Open that document now and complete the instructions to register your software with Microsoft.

Getting Help for C#

Very often you will want to get help on an error, or function description, or some other part of Visual Studio or the Visual Basic programming language. The MSDN (Microsoft Developer Network) Help Library, a great reference tool, can be installed on top of Visual Studio. Then, to get help on any topic, just position the mouse in the IDE on the item in question (like a compiler error number or function name) and hit the F1 key. If help files are not installed locally the help library can go online to get help for you.

On our online documents page, please find the document titled "Visual C# 2010 MSDN (Help Library) Install Instructions" ("Visual_CS_MSDN_Install_Instructions.pdf"). Follow those instructions now to install the MSDN Help Library.

You can also use many online resources to help find solutions to error messages or understand the meaning of certain Visual C# topics. Any of the major search engines will lead you to dozens of topics on programming and Visual Studio. Some well-established sites such as Wikipedia (http://www.wikipedia.com) also offer good articles on many programming concepts.

The Working Directory for Student Projects

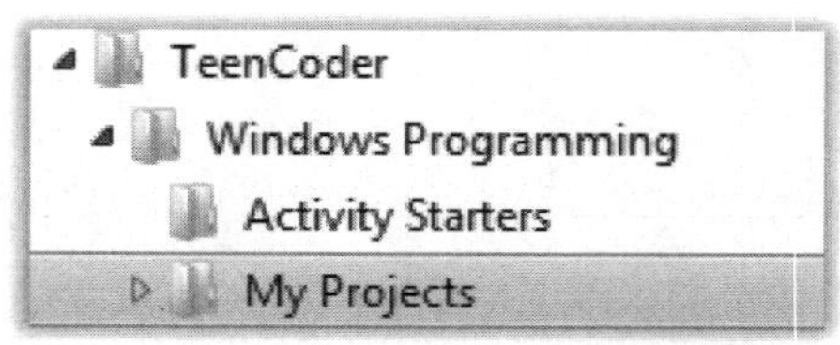

After installing the course files, a "My Projects" directory was automatically created for you. This directory will be the location where you will save all of your projects for this course. The default directory structure is "C:\TeenCoder\Windows Programming\My Projects". Each project you create should be placed in a new sub-folder within your working directory. You may select a different working directory or even create additional working directories on your own; just remember your directory location when you want to save and load your projects. Multiple students may use the same computer for this course by creating different working directories! Use the Windows Explorer program to create new directories.

Chapter Two: Fundamentals of C#

In this chapter we will discuss the C# programming language in more detail. You will learn the steps involved in transforming source code to an executable program. You will also become familiar with the Visual C# 2010 Express Integrated Development Environment (IDE) and write your first C# program!

Lesson One: Introduction to C#

This course will use the C# (pronounced "C-Sharp") language to create Windows programs. Microsoft originally called this language "COOL" which stood for: **C**-like **O**bject **O**riented **L**anguage, but the name was later changed in order to obtain a clear trademark. The final C# name was chosen to mean that this language is a "note above C", or a better version of the C language.

The C and C++ languages were very popular and they are still widely used today. However, there are some major drawbacks to these languages. The most important drawback is the degree of difficulty involved in learning the languages. The languages allow you to do many low-level, powerful things, but lack a variety of nice features like automatic memory management, built-in string classes, and strong management of data types. When compared to more modern, object-oriented languages, both C and C++ can seem pretty clunky.

C# was created to fix the issues that programmers have with the C and C++ languages. C# is easy to learn and simple to use. The C# language is inherently object-oriented which allows for more modern, organized, and robust designs and program implementations. C# also provides full access to the Microsoft .NET Framework, which is a comprehensive set of libraries and objects providing powerful, easy-to-use interfaces into the Windows environment.

The .NET Framework

In the many years since the first programming language emerged, programmers have implemented the same things over and over again in different languages. Every language has its own way to perform common tasks like displaying information in a Window, printing to a printer, and saving information to a file. Today's programs are more complex than ever before, requiring more advanced features like network communication and security. As these features become commonplace in many applications, it takes more effort to re-invent them from scratch for each application and for each programming language.

The developers at Microsoft decided on a solution: they would create a giant library of pre-built methods and components that would work with multiple languages. They decided to call this library the ".NET

Framework" (pronounced "dot net framework"). The .NET Framework would be free to download and install and would support any Windows platform (XP, Vista, Server, Mobile, etc.). A programmer could use this framework with Visual Basic applications, C# applications, C++, JScript, and other languages.

Now you may be wondering how you can use the same pre-built methods and components in different programming languages. The answer to that is found in *how* the programs are "compiled" (turned into an EXE) and run. When a C or C++ program is compiled, it is completely translated into machine code. Machine code is the native language of all computers and is represented as a series of 1s and 0s. This translation into machine code will result in a program that is tailor-made for a specific operating system and processor. If you need to create the same program for a different operating system, you would have to change the settings in your compiler and re-compile the program to produce a different executable.

A .NET Framework program will compile very differently. Instead of compiling straight into machine code, it will compile to an intermediate "bytecode" form called the "Common Intermediate Language" (CIL). All languages based on the .NET Framework (Visual Basic, C#, etc.) will compile source code into this form. The CIL contains no dependencies on any particular operating system or processor. To run a CIL on a specific operating system and processor, another piece of the .NET Framework called the "Common Language Runtime" (CLR) kicks in. The CLR will translate the independent CIL format into the machine code for a specific operating system and processor. This means that the same program can execute on different platforms without any changes or need to re-compile!

Here is a diagram of this process:

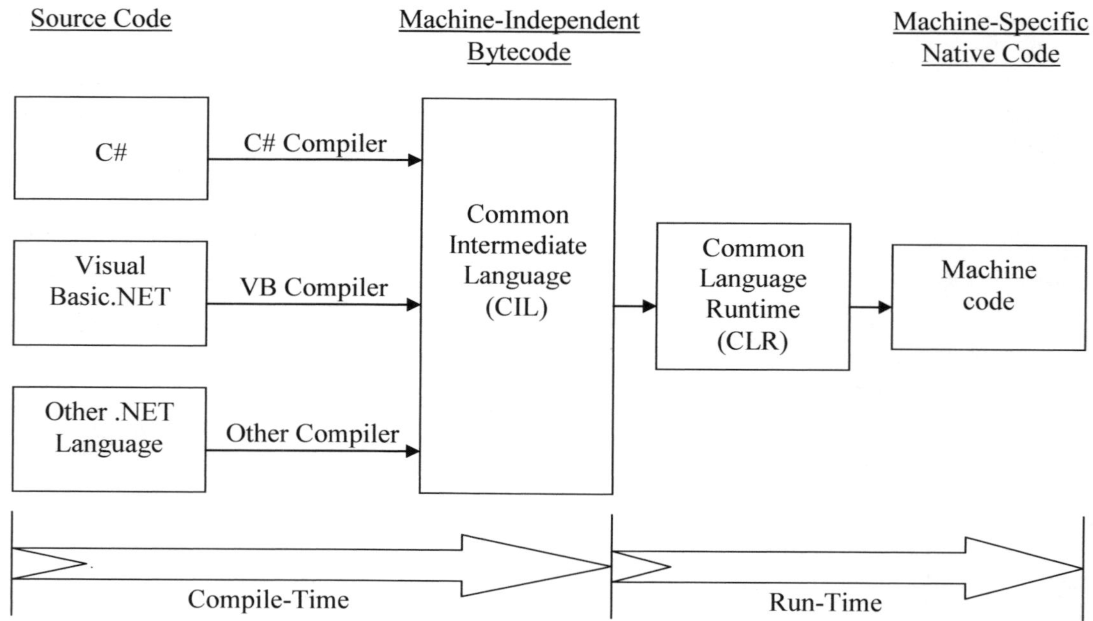

Of course, this means that any computer that wants to run a .NET Framework application must have the .NET Framework installed for the CLR to be available. Many installation programs can automatically distribute the .NET Framework as part of a larger application install process.

The original version of the .NET Framework was, unsurprisingly, 1.0. Over time newer versions were released as more features were added and previous bugs fixed. You can check to see what version you have installed on your computer by doing the following:

1. Open up the Control Panel program on your computer from the Windows Start bar.
2. Open the "Add/Remove Programs" or "Programs and Features" button and scroll down until you find one or more entries that look like this: "Microsoft .NET Framework X". (Do not actually click on Change/Remove or perform any actions on the entry!)

   The following example shows the .NET Framework installed on a Windows 7 system:

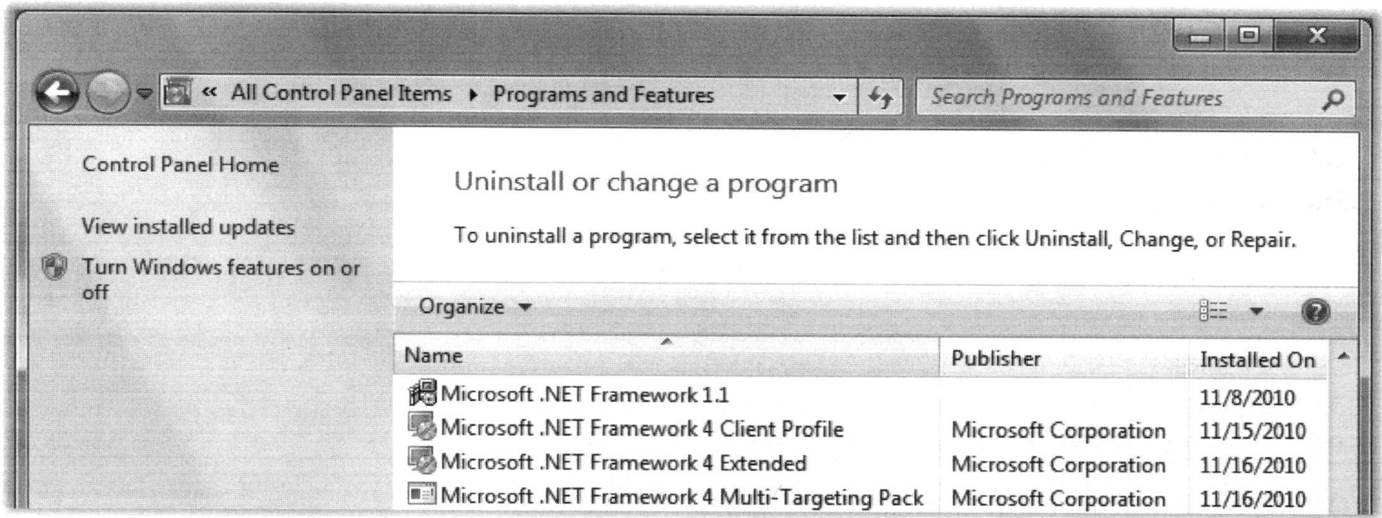

The "X" numbers represent the version of .NET Framework on your computer. You may actually have multiple versions installed. This course requires version 4 or later for the programs we will write. Version 4 should have been installed automatically when you downloaded and installed the Visual C# 2010 Express software at the end of the last chapter.

Lesson Two: Visual C# 2010 Express Software

The main software package that we will be using in this course is called "Visual C# 2010 Express". In this lesson we will discuss how to use the software to create your own programs.

Using the IDE

Microsoft Visual C# 2010 Express is a great example of an IDE (Integrated Development Environment). In the early days of programming, a programmer would write their program code in one application, compile and run it in another application, and test it in yet another application. Today, programmers have Integrated Development Environments. The IDE is a single place where you can create your screens, type in your code, and run and debug your program. Everything you need as a programmer can be found in your IDE.

Let's take a look at your Visual C# IDE, which you installed at the end of the last chapter. To start this application, click on your Windows Start button, and then click on "All Programs". You should see an icon for "Microsoft Visual C# 2010 Express" under a "Microsoft Visual Studio 2010 Express" folder. This is the Visual C# IDE, so go ahead and run it!

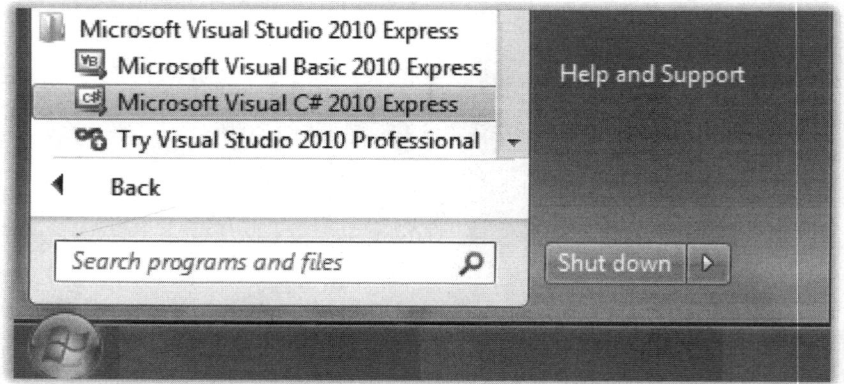

The exact layout of the Windows Start menu and the names of the items may be slightly different on your computer, depending on your version of Windows and your own personal customizations.

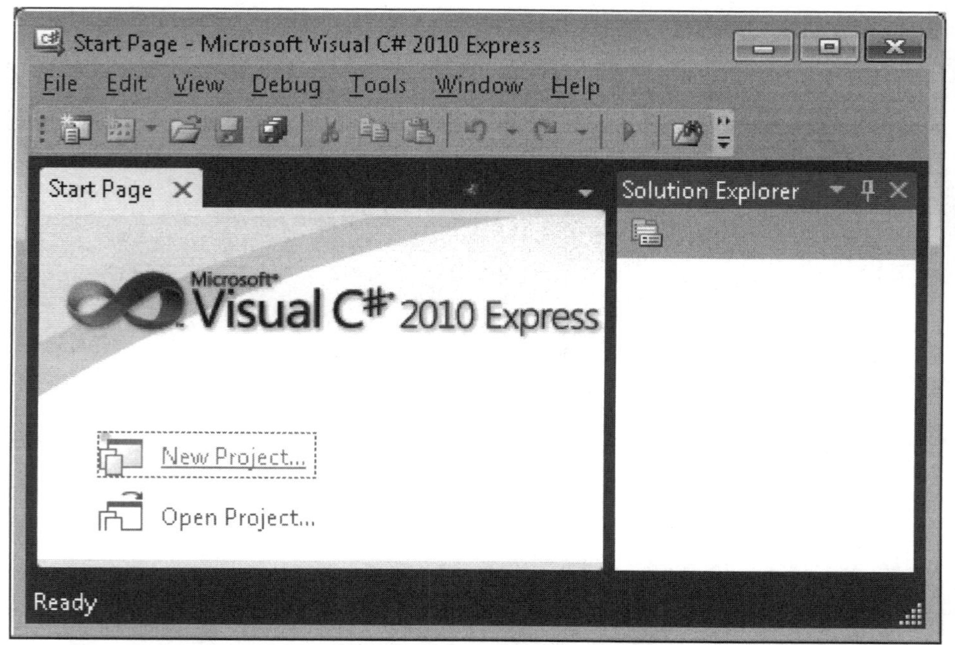

In this lesson, we will walk you through the important screens in the IDE. Follow along in your own software to start learning the program!

Run the Visual C# IDE and you should see the "Start Page" screen. The "Start Page" lets us create new projects and open existing projects.

The first thing we will do is create a new "project". Projects are a way to group together all the screens and files necessary for an application. Each of the activities in this course is a separate project.

To create a project, click on the "New Project..." link in the middle of the Start Page. Or, you can click on the "File" menu option and then click on "New Project". Go ahead and do this now. You should see the following screen:

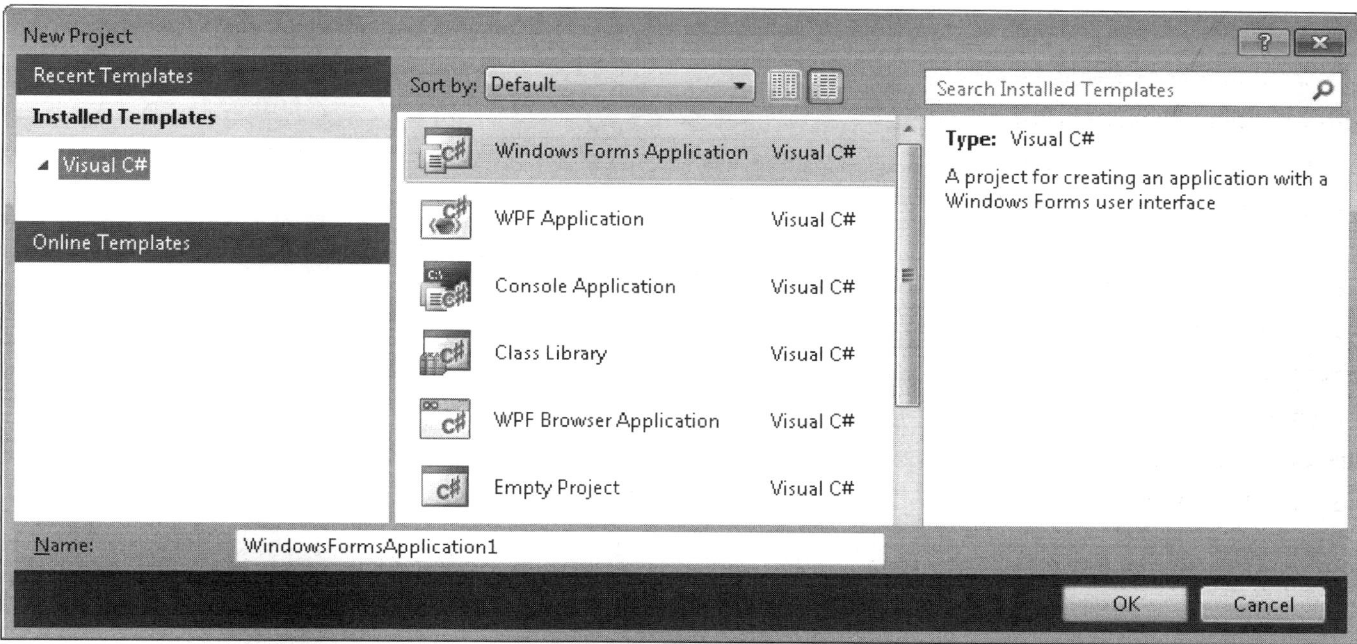

The top-left section of this screen lists "Installed Templates". A template is a definition of a general kind of program you can create. The middle area lists different types of programs that you can create with Visual C#. For this course, we will be using the "Windows Forms Application", so click on this line to highlight it.

The "Name" text box at the bottom of the screen is for the name of your new project. The default name is "WindowsFormsApplication1". It is important for every project to be given a separate, meaningful name, so you should change this field. Note that the project name should not contain any special characters like apostrophes or commas! Just use a combination of letters, numbers, and spaces.

Replace the default entry with "MyProject" and click on the "OK" button. The software will bring up the main IDE window.

Here is the main IDE screen you will see after creating a new project called "MyProject". We will go through the areas on this screen one at a time.

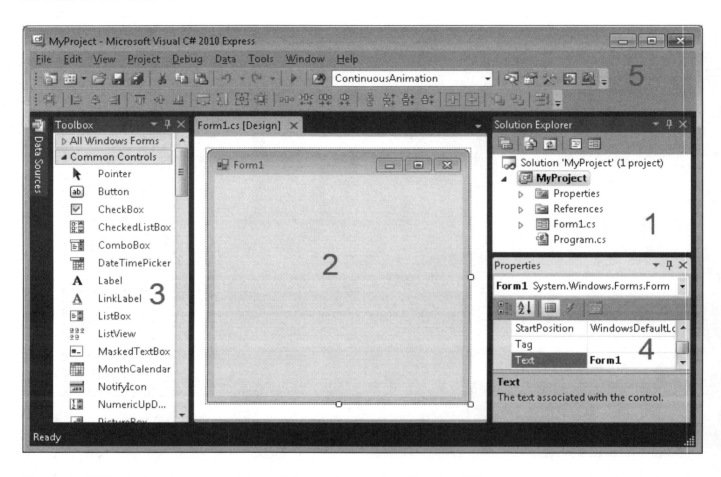

The main IDE window is separated into different frames, just like the different panes on a house window. In the picture above we have labeled each pane with the numbers 1 – 5 for easy reference, though those numbers do not show up in the actual application. It is possible to move or re-arrange the location of these frames on the screen to your liking and show and hide individual frames depending on what you are doing. So, as you progress through a project, you may find the layout and the types of visible panes will change from time to time. If you are missing a frame don't worry, it's always possible to find a button or menu command that will show it again!

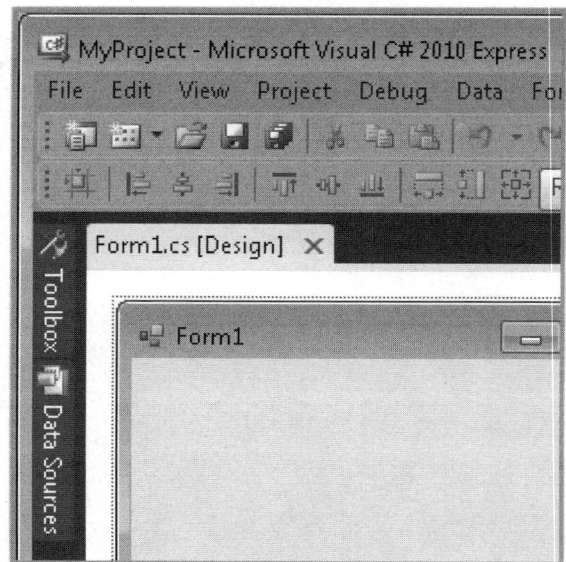

You may also find some frames collapsed to the side of your screen on a tab. As shown to the right, the Toolbox frame may be represented as a little tab. Just click the tab to expand and restore the frame! You can also click a little button at the top of the frame that looks like a thumb-tack to keep the frame visible.

Solution Explorer

The first frame (#1) that we will look at is the Solution Explorer. If you don't have this frame, look for the icon that looks like this on the toolbar: . The Solution Explorer button will show or hide this frame in the IDE window. You can also view or hide any of the other important windows we will discuss from the "View" menu at the top of the screen.

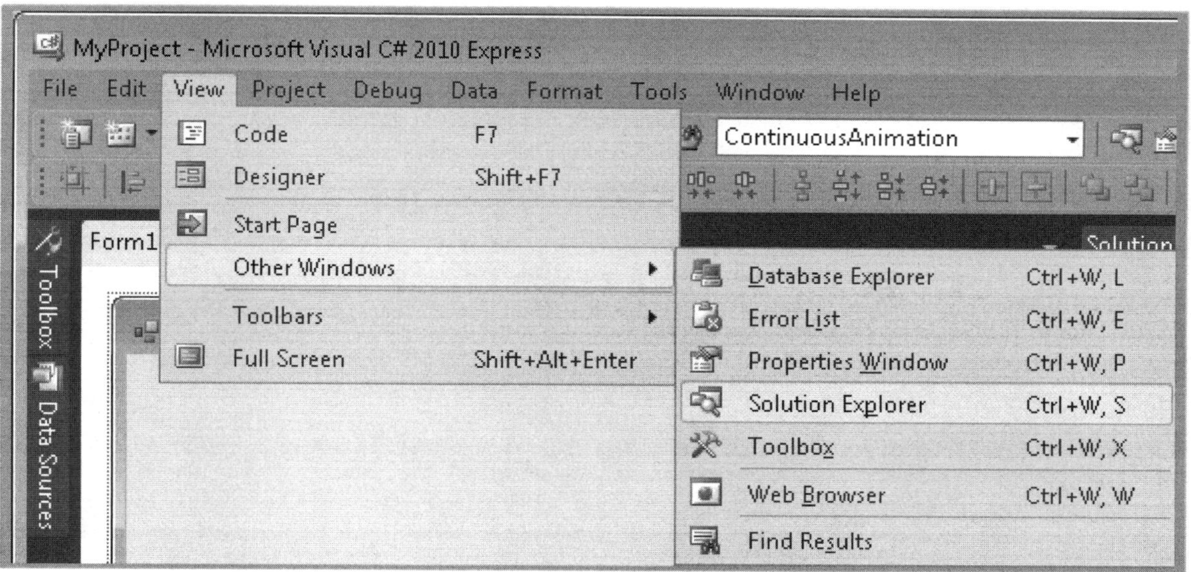

The Solution Explorer frame is where you can view and access all the forms or files for your project.

In your current Solution Explorer you should see the name of your project, "MyProject", and four entries underneath.

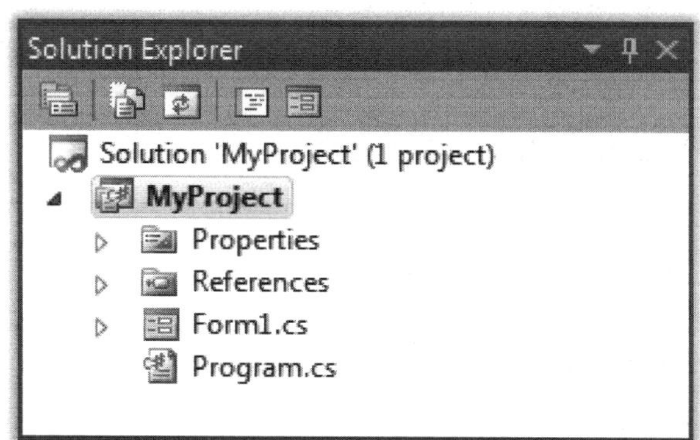

Let's briefly look at each of these entries to understand what they mean!

Properties	Underneath this entry are settings for the project that are important for the compiler, but not too interesting for the programs we will be writing. You can safely ignore the things under this section and shouldn't have to change them.
References	The references section contains a list of .NET Framework objects available for use in your application. Everything you need in this course will be automatically added to this list, so you don't have to worry about it. If you ever needed to add a 3rd party library containing new objects that were not part of the .NET Framework, this is the area where you would attach those objects to your application.

Form1.cs	This is the default form (window, or screen) and source code created for your project. All of the source code you write will go into the "Form1.cs" file. It's one of the most important files and will be described in detail later!
Program.cs	The "Program.cs" is a small bit of code auto-generated for you when the program was created. You generally won't have to change it. The **Program** class is simply responsible for launching your Form when the program starts.

Main Window

The main window frame in the middle of your IDE (#2) contains a tabbed selection of source files or forms that you have opened in your project. Each of the tabs is usually either

- A Form Design page ("Form1.cs [Design]")
- A source code editing page ("Form1.cs")

The Form Design page will let you resize, color, add controls, and set other visual properties of your Form. This is the canvas that you will use to create your window screen! If you don't see this tab, you can click on the icon in the Solution Explorer or right-click on "Form1.cs" and select "View Designer".

The source code editing page is where you will write the code to make your program work! You can click on the icon in the Solution Explorer or right-click on the "Form1.cs" name and select "View Code". Go ahead and switch back and forth between the Form Design and source code windows so you can see the difference between them.

Controls ToolBox

The next frame (#3) holds the Controls Toolbox, which should be visible when you are looking at a Form Design page. If you don't see this window, click on the button to show or hide the Toolbox. You can also select "View → Other Windows → Toolbox" from the menu. The Controls Toolbox contains all the visual controls or widgets that you might need to build your form. These controls are added by simply dragging and dropping the control from the toolbox to the form with your mouse. Try this now: left-click on the "Button" and drag it onto your form in the Form Design page.

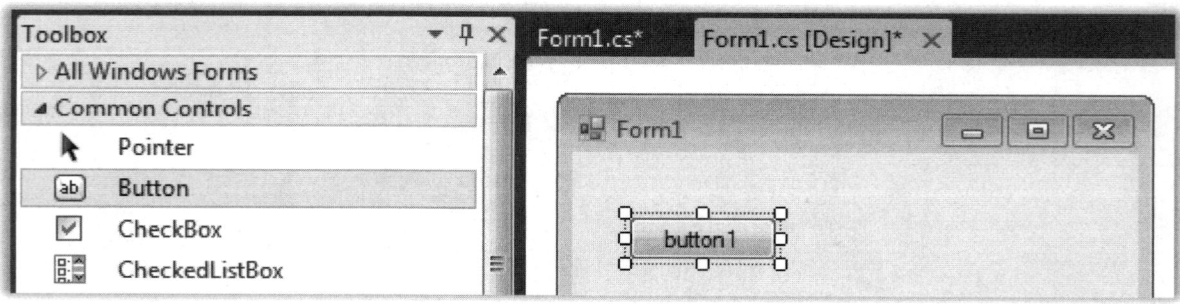

Properties Sheet

The next important frame (#4) is the Properties Sheet. If you don't see this frame, click on the icon or hit the F4 key to show it (don't forget your trusty "View → Other Windows" menu option also)! The Properties Sheet is used to set all of the options for the individual controls. For example, if you wanted to change the color, text, or name of a control, you would do it on the Properties Sheet.

Try changing the text on your newly added button now:

- Click on the button you just added to the form and look at the properties available for this control.
- Find the "Text" property and type "Click" where the property says "Button1".
- Notice how the text on your button changes!

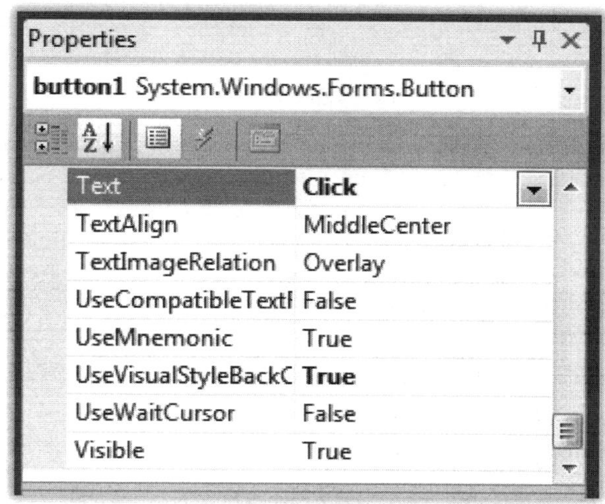

Menu and Toolbar

The last sections (#5) of the IDE are the menu bar and toolbar. You are probably familiar with these types of menus and toolbars, since many Windows applications have them. These buttons and menu options are used to control every aspect of the IDE program. You can open and save new projects and forms, run programs, show or hide frames, close the IDE, and so on.

Solutions, Projects, and Source Files

The IDE uses the concept of a "project" to help organize all of the elements needed to create one executable program. A project can contain source files (*.cs) and other resources (icons, images, sounds, etc.). All of the configuration and details about a project are stored in a project file that has a ".csproj" extension. As you work through the activities in each course chapter, you will usually create new projects for each activity. When you compile, build, and run a project you are focused on one executable program.

The IDE also allows you to group multiple projects together into a "solution". Notice in your Solution Explorer frame at the top it says something like "Solution MyProject". The IDE always has only one "solution" open at a time. Each solution may have only one project, or it may have many projects. Putting more than one project in a solution lets you quickly navigate to different projects and compare source code, or build a bunch of related programs at the same time. For our purposes, we will be creating a separate solution for each project in this course. Each of these solution files will have a ".sln" file extension.

When you save your solution, it will give you the option to "Create a directory for the solution". This means that you will end up with all of your solution and project files placed into one directory (which will have the same name as the solution). We have done this for all of the "Activity Starter" programs that are available in your Student Files. This is usually a good way to organize your projects, so we highly recommend selecting this option when you save your solutions.

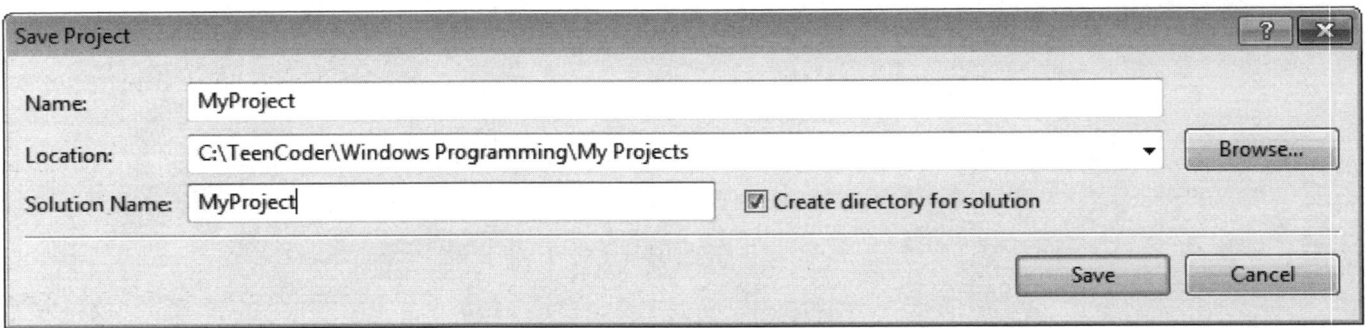

Change the "Location" field to match your main your student working directory, "C:\TeenCoder\Windows Programming\My Projects" and then click "Save". Once you save your new project and build the application into an EXE, you will see a directory structure similar to the one shown below.

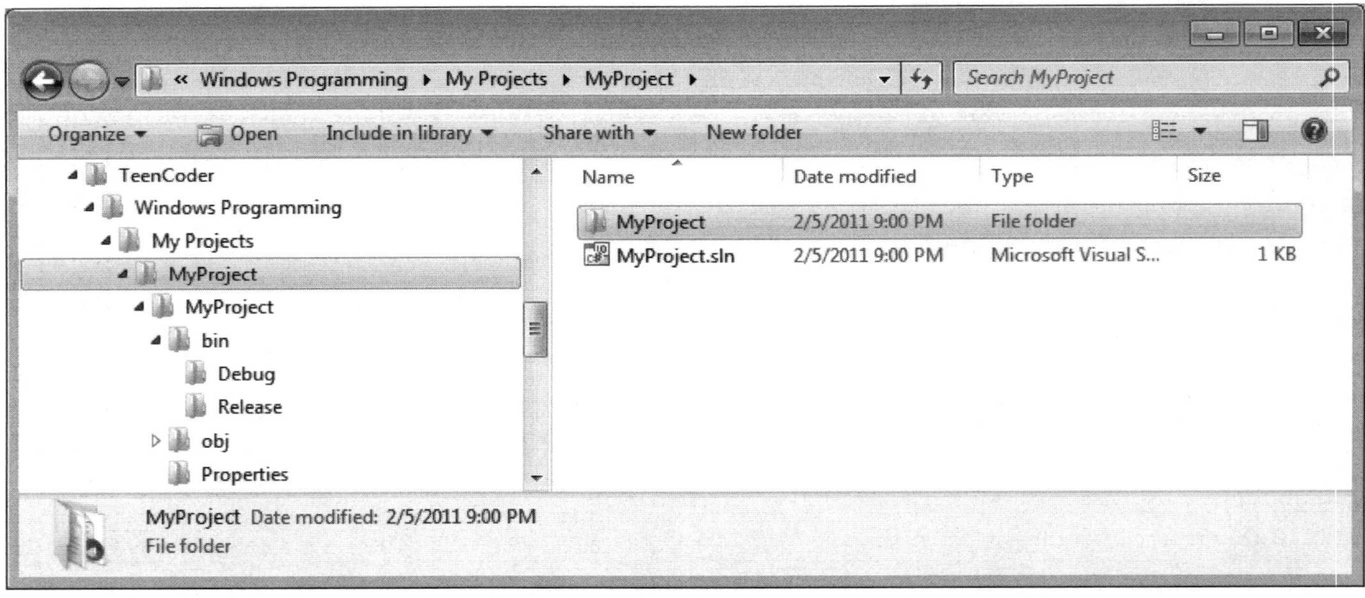

The top "MyProject" folder contains just the solution file (.sln), while the underlying "MyProject" sub-folder contains the "MyProject.csproj" project file and all of the other related files, including your source code!

Source files contain the code that you write from the built-in text editor within the IDE. In this course, our source files will have the ".cs" extension (short for "c-sharp"). The Visual Studio IDE knows that all files saved with a ".cs" extension contain C# source code.

Un-Hiding File Extensions

By default the Windows operating system will hide the file extensions in Windows Explorer. This is pretty annoying for programmers who need to be able to tell files like "MyProject.sln", "MyProject.csproj", "MyProject.cs", and "MyProject.exe" apart from each other. If your own Windows Explorer is hiding file extensions on your computer, take some time to change this behavior. We'll describe how to do this on the Windows 7 operating system, and other versions should be similar.

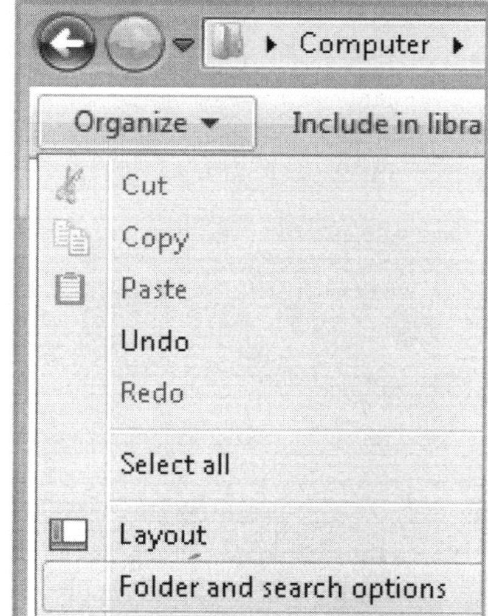

First, open Windows Explorer. Then click on the "Organize" button near the top-left and scroll down to click on "Folder and Search Options".

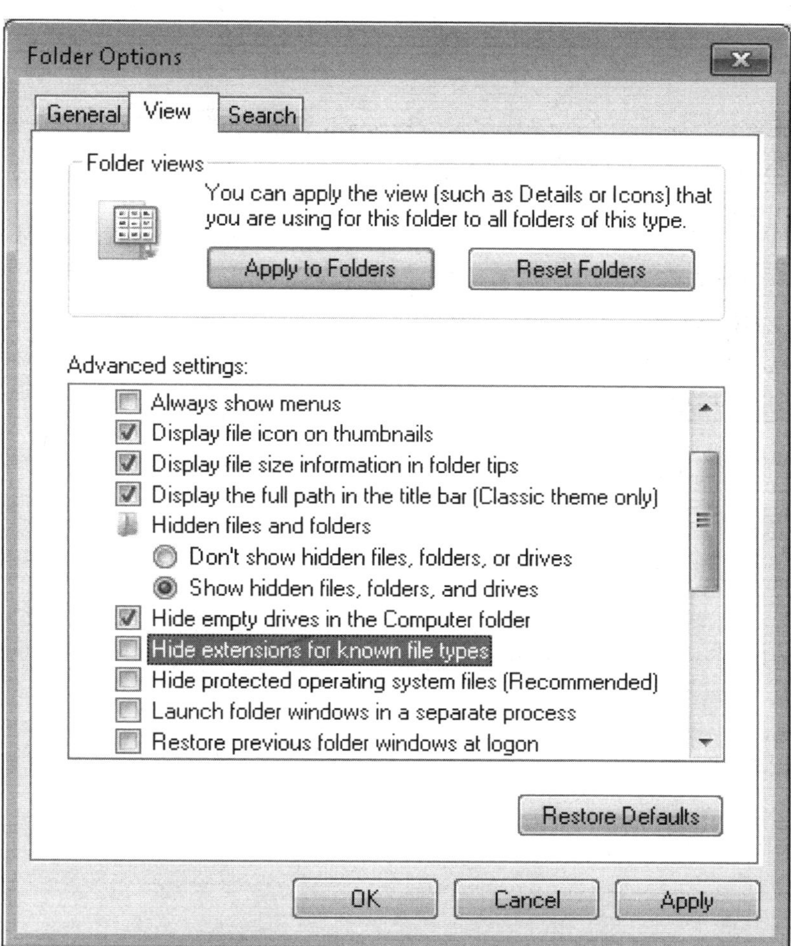

You will then see a "Folder Options" dialog with three tabs: "General", "View", and "Search". Click on the "View" tab, and you should see an "Advanced Settings" list containing many checkboxes. Scroll down until you see one that says "Hide extensions for known file types" and uncheck this box. Then click the "Apply to Folders" button to make this change for all folders on your hard drive. Finally, click "OK" to close the dialog. Now you should be able to see the file extensions directly in Windows Explorer. No more guesswork!

Other Files and Directories

When you build and run a project, Visual Studio will create a variety of other temporary or internal files that you should mostly not have to worry about. When you see files like *.ncb, *.suo, *.obj, just leave them alone. The output you are most interested in is the ".exe" file, which is the executable program you have created!

The second "MyProject" folder also contains many items, including these important files:

Form1.cs	This file contains your form's source code and is what you will spend most of your time writing!
Form1.Designer.cs	This file contains your form screen definition and is very important!
Form1.resx	This file contains information about outside resources you have added to the project such as graphics, sounds, or other languages.
MyProject.csproj	This file contains your project settings. You will not normally need to change any project settings, but if you do the changes will be handled through the IDE.
Program.cs	The **Program** class will automatically run your Form when the program starts.

If you are ever concerned about saving your source code, or sending it to someone else for review, the above files are the most important files to copy! You can also "zip" up your entire project directory to send someone all of your files in one convenient package.

There are three more sub-folders under the "MyProject" folder: "bin", "obj", and "Properties".

The "bin" folder is created the first time you build your program. This is where the Visual Studio will place the executable (EXE) or fully-compiled version of your program. For this project, the executable file will be called "MyProject.exe". The "Debug" folder will contain the executable version that is run when you launch the program from the IDE. If you simply build the program in the IDE (without running it) then the executable is placed in the "Release" folder.

The "obj" folder is also created the first time you build your program. This folder contains some temporary files that are output when Visual Studio builds your program. You will not need to understand or use these files directly. These files are all maintained and handled by the Visual Studio software.

The "Properties" folder is automatically created as you are writing your program. The files in this folder contain information about how your project looks in IDE. You will not need to understand or use these files directly. These files are all maintained and handled by the Visual Studio software.

Making a Copy of Your Project

You may want to make a copy of your project, especially if you just completed something important and want to make a backup copy. The easiest way to do this is using Windows Explorer, not the Visual C# IDE!

To make a backup copy of your project, simply run Windows Explorer and find your project directory (e.g. "My Projects\MyProject"). Then copy that entire folder to a different folder name such as "My Projects\MyProject Backup". That's it! You now have two copies of your project…one in "MyProject" and one in "MyProject Backup". You can change and run each of these projects without messing up the code you have in the other project.

Lesson Three: Hello World

In this lesson we will be creating our first C# program. To create this program, we will again be using the Visual C# Express IDE. Go ahead and open up the IDE now.

Once the IDE is open, click on "File" and "New Project". You should see the New Project screen below:

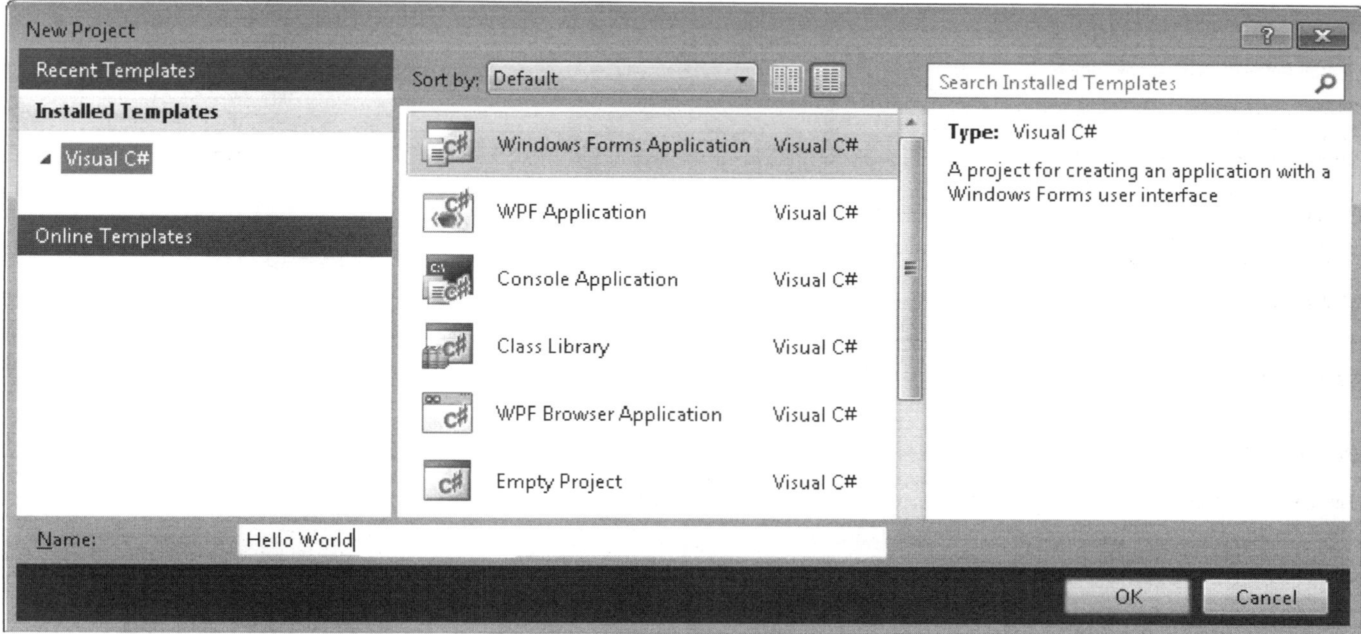

Make sure the Windows Forms Application icon is highlighted and name your new project "Hello World". Click on the "OK" button to finish creating the new project.

You should now see the main IDE window, which should look like the image shown below:

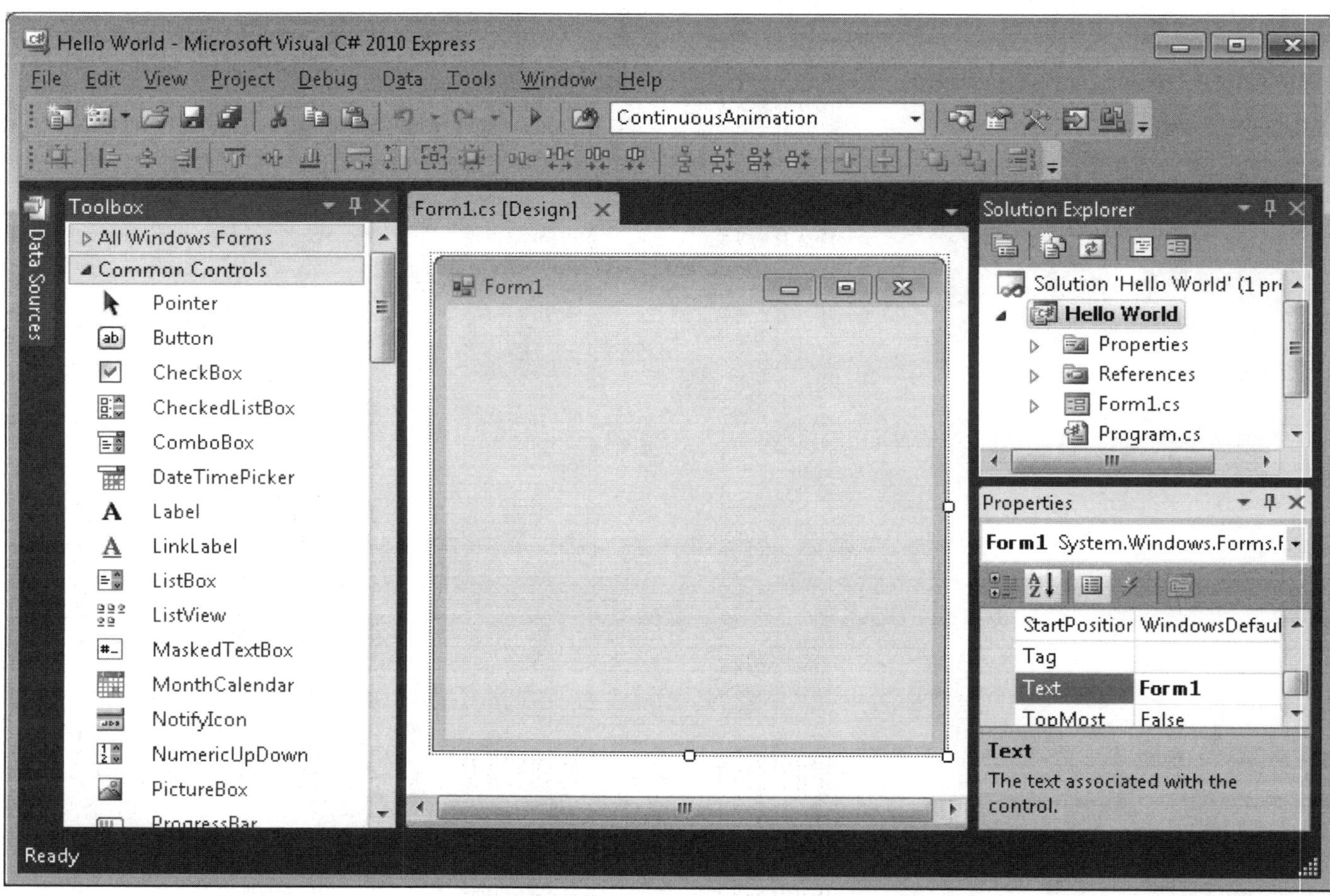

The default name for the form is "Form1". The first thing we will do is change that name to something more meaningful. Renaming won't have any visible effect on your form, but keeping your source files well-organized with unique, meaningful names is important once you start creating a bunch of projects!

Click anywhere on the form to highlight it and then look at the Property Sheet in the lower right corner. In the list of properties, find the property called "**(Name)**" (this should be near the top of the list). You will notice that in the spot next to **(Name)**, you see the current name "Form1" in bold type. Click on "Form1", and you will see a cursor appear on that line. Go ahead and delete the word "Form1" and put in "HelloForm". Congratulations! You have changed your first form property. The **(Name)** property is important when you have more than one form in your program. For now, it's just good practice.

Another good practice is to rename the form's code file to something more meaningful than "Form1.cs". In the Solution Explorer, you should see the name of this file ("Form1.cs"). If you right-click on the filename and then choose "Rename", you can easily rename the file. In this case, rename the file to "HelloWorld.cs". Just like the **(Name)** property, this step is important when you have more than one form in your program, and for now, it's just good practice.

If you look at your form in the main window, you will see that it still has a caption (or title) of "Form1". The next thing we are going to do is make that caption a little more interesting.

To change the caption, we need to find the property called **Text**. Look through the list of properties in the Property panel until you find this item (the list is alphabetical, it will be near the bottom). You will notice that in the spot next to **Text**, you see the current caption "Form1" in bold type. Click on "Form1", and you will see a cursor appear on that line. Go ahead and delete the word "Form1" and put in "Hello, World!". Once you are finished, click back on the form and you will see the caption change!

Now we are going to add a control to our form. For this program, we will add a Label control. A label is just a simple control that allows you to add some text or words to the screen. To add this control, first find the **Label** in the Controls Toolbox. Once you find the **Label**, just click on it and drag it over to your form.

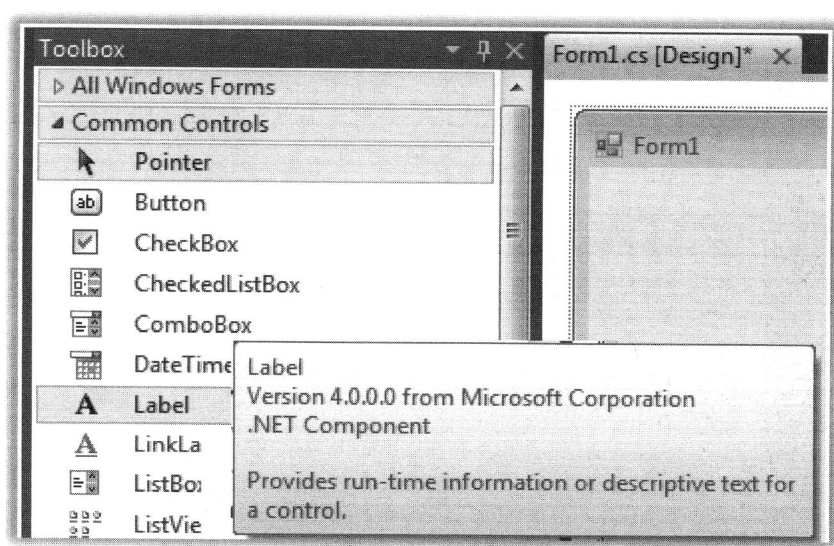

Now your form should look like this:

That's a good start, but let's makes it even better. Click on the label to highlight it, and look at the property sheet. You should be looking at the properties for **`Label1`**. We are going to change the text for this label just like we changed the caption text. Find the property called **Text** that has the value "Label1". Click on the word "Label1" and change the text to "Hello, World!" Now click on the form again and *voila!* The label now says "Hello, World!".

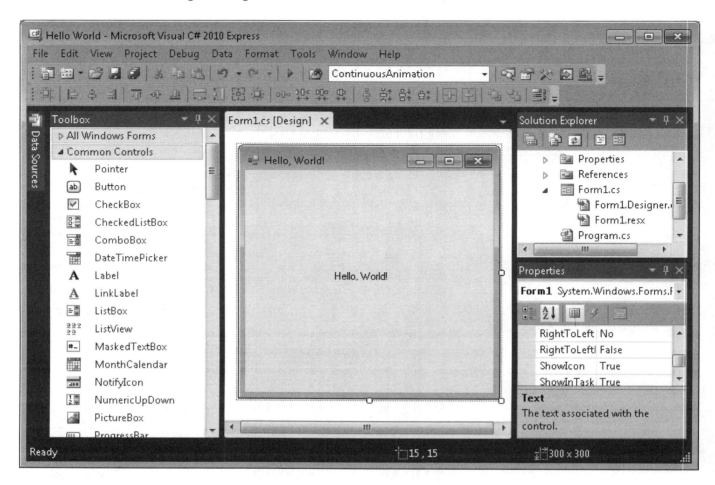

Now, let's run our program! To do this, find the button on the main toolbar that looks like the play button on a DVD player: ▶. Click on this button and you should see your program run. You can also just hit the "F5" key to start your program.

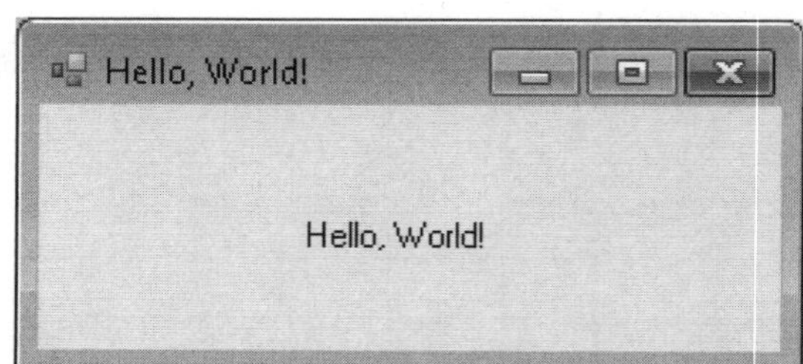

To exit your program click on the "x" in the upper right corner of the screen, just like in any other Windows program. Congratulations! You have just created your first program in Visual C#.

Saving and Loading Your Project

You should always save your project before you exit the Visual C# IDE. To do this, click on File and "Save All". You can then come back to work on your project later by re-loading it into the IDE. Always remember after reloading your project…if you don't see your source code or Form Design screen in the main center area, your work has not vanished! You can always show those screens by selecting your Form's .cs file in the Solution Explorer, right-clicking, and selecting "View Code" or "View Designer".

The first time you save your project, the IDE will pop-up this window:

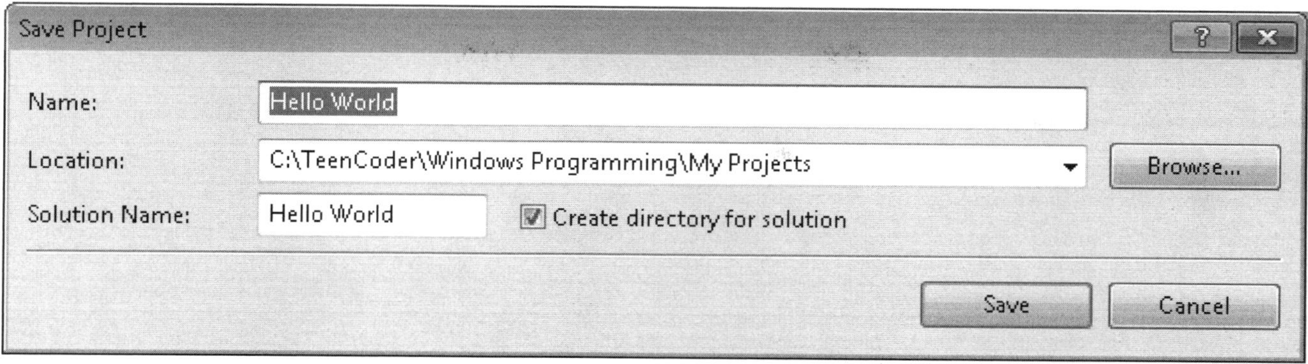

Make sure that the **Location** is pointing to your working directory (e.g "C:\TeenCoder\Windows Programming\My Projects"). Then change the **Solution Name** to "Hello World" and click the **Save** button. Notice that we have the option **Create directory for solution** checked. This means that all of your files will be kept in a directory called "C:\TeenCoder\Windows Programming\My Projects\Hello World".

Now when you want to go back to this project, just click on "File" and "Open Project".

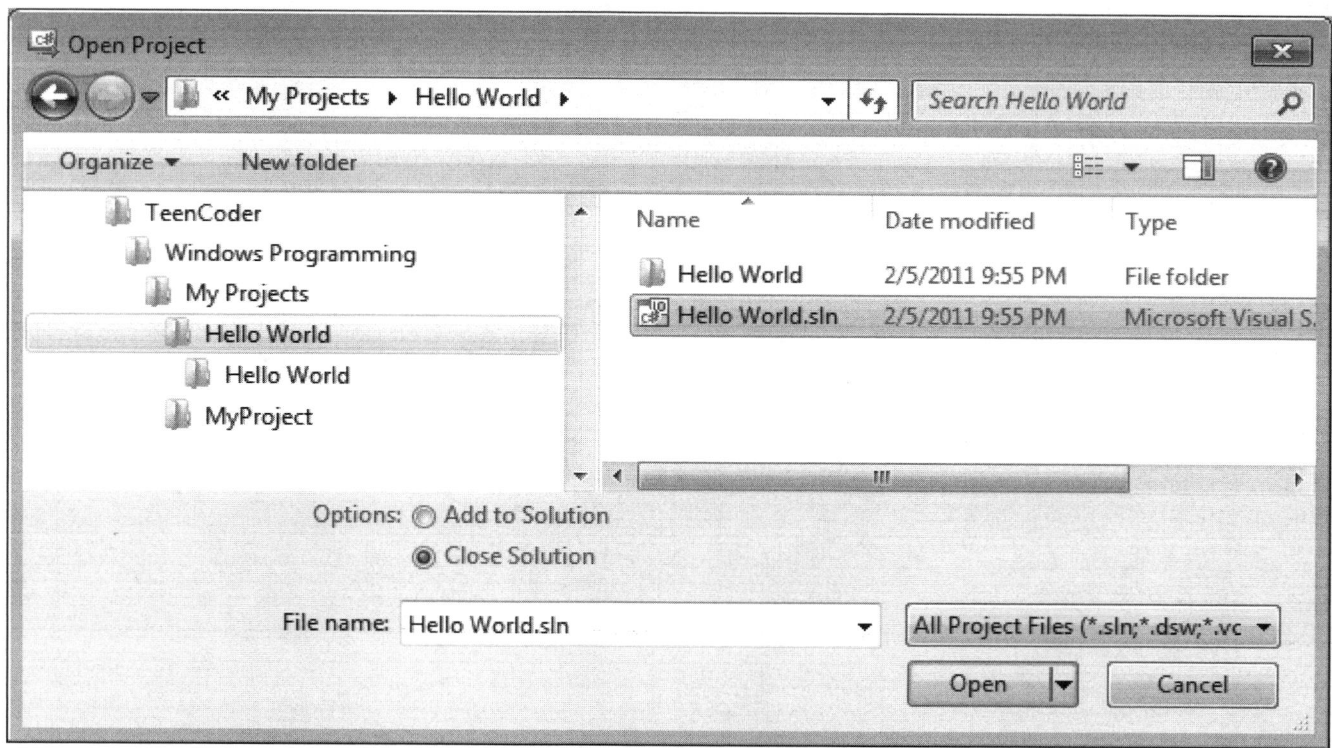

From here, you can navigate to the directory where you saved your project. If you followed the default directory structure when installing your Student Files, you should find your solution in "C:\TeenCoder\Windows Programming\My Projects\Hello World\Hello World.sln". If you choose this file and click the **Open** button, your solution containing the Hello World project will open into the IDE.

Chapter Review

- The C# language has many improvements over the C and C++ languages.
- The .NET Framework is a giant library of common, re-usable code.
- A C# program is not compiled to machine code. It is compiled to an intermediate format called Common Intermediate Language (CIL). From there, the program is compiled to machine code on the user's computer by the Common Language Runtime (CLR). This allows the same program to run on many different operating systems.
- Any computer trying to run a C# program must have the .NET Framework installed.
- An IDE (Integrated Development Environment) is a piece of software where a programmer can write, build, run, and test a program.
- A project is a way of organizing the different files that belong to a program. A solution is a way of organizing a group of projects.
- Form and control properties are changed by setting values in the IDE's Property Sheet.
- A **Label** is a control that allows you to display non-editable text on the screen.
- Set the **(Name)** property of a control to give it a variable name that you can access from within your source code.
- You can view your form's design screen or source code by selecting the form on the Solution Explorer, right-clicking, and selecting "View Code" or "View Designer".
- Make backups of your project by using Windows Explorer to copy the entire project directory to another location.
- A project folder contains a solution (*.sln) file and a sub-directory with your project file (*.csproj), source code (*.cs), and other resources.

Activity: Enhance Hello World

In this activity, you will open the "Hello World" project and get some practice adding controls and changing the properties of forms and controls.

Your activity requirements and instructions are found in the "Chapter_02_Activity.pdf" document located in your "TeenCoder\Windows Programming\Activity Docs" folder. You can access this document through your Student Menu or by double-clicking on it from Windows Explorer.

Complete this activity now and ensure your program meets the requirements before continuing!

Chapter Three: Windows Programming Concepts

In this chapter we introduce several important building blocks for Windows programs. You will learn about forms and controls used to build a screen, C# syntax, how to handle events, and how to use .NET Framework objects.

Lesson One: Common Windows Elements

The most obvious element in any Windows application is the graphical window itself. C# Windows applications are built around a .NET Framework object called a **Form**. A form represents one screen or dialog window within the application. You simply add your controls (buttons, text boxes, list boxes, etc) by dragging-and-dropping them from the Toolbox onto the form. Designing your own window is as easy as creating a picture in a drawing program!

Windows Forms

The form is the most important graphical element in C#. All of the programs that we will write in this course will be based on forms. Every time we create a new project, the IDE will create a basic form, which we will modify to fit our program's needs. The code for each form is made up of two main files: the source file for all of the code that you will write and the source file that defines the graphics that will exist on your form.

The source file for your program code typically starts out as "Form1.cs". As we mentioned earlier, it is good practice to change this file name to the name that you have given your form. For example, if your form is called **`CalculatorForm`**, the file name should be "CalculatorForm.cs". This file will contain all of the code that executes when a user performs actions on your form.

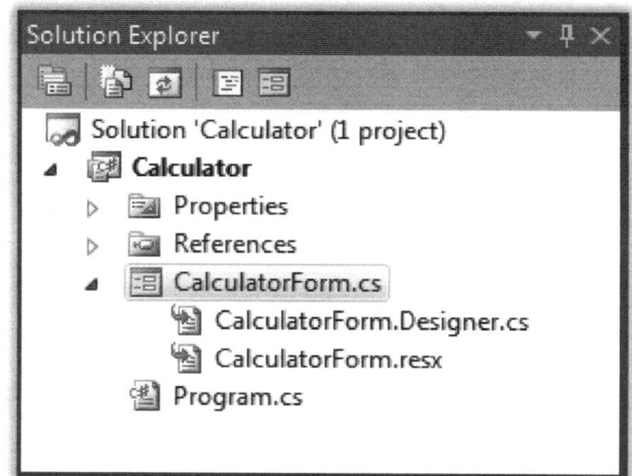

The source file for the form graphics is called "<Form Name>.Designer.cs". This file will hold information about the buttons, menus, colors and shapes on your form. You don't need to change this file by hand, because it is automatically updated as you make changes in the Form Design screen.

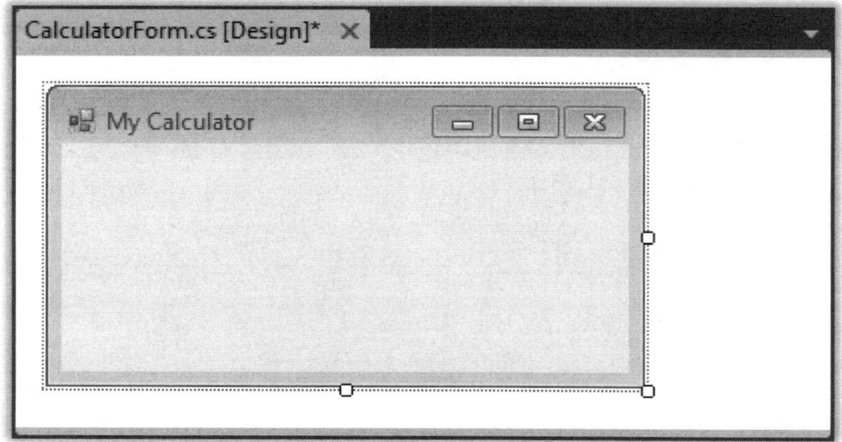

Now, let's take a look at the Form Design window in the IDE. To view this window, find the tabs at the top of the screen and click on the tab called "<Form Name>.cs [Design]". This will show you a graphical representation of your form. If you do not see this tab, just click on "View" on the top menu and then choose "Designer".

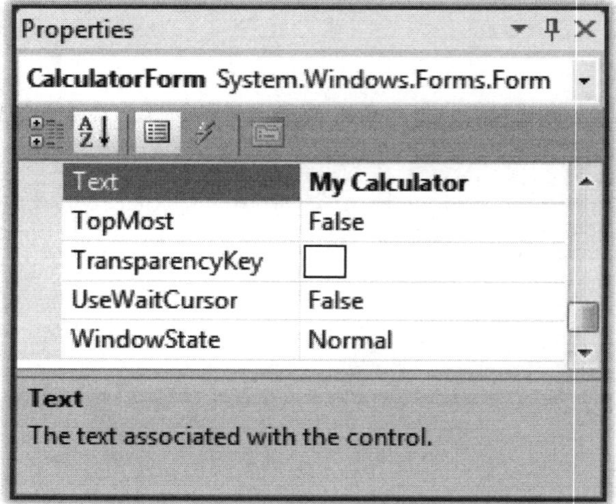

You should also see a panel on the right of your screen called "Properties". If this panel does not show up on your screen, just click the "View" menu and then click "Other Windows → Property Window". The Properties panel will show you all of the available properties for the current control that is selected on your form. If you click on the form itself, you will see the properties for the form. If you click on a button that is on your form, the Properties panel will display the properties for that button. This is an easy and fast way to change the look and feel of your form and its components.

A Windows application can contain one or more forms. Each form must be given a unique name. When the program is first created, the IDE will give you a *starter* form that is named "Form1". For the sake of clarity, you should change this name to something that is more meaningful. You can easily change the name of a form by clicking on the form and then taking a look at the Properties panel. Find the property called **(Name)** and change the text in this field from "Form1" to your chosen form name.

Controls

Controls are graphical widgets that you can place on the form for a person to use. C# contains over 60 basic controls in the Controls Toolbox. From the Toolbox you can easily add buttons, toolbars, menus, text boxes, printing controls, pictures, checkboxes, etc.

Controls are added to a form by simply dragging and dropping the control from the Control Toolbox to the form. Once you place a control on the form, you can change the color, shape, text, and other aspects by changing its properties in the property sheet. You can quickly modify your control by just pointing and clicking -- no need to write any code! To access the property sheet for a control or form, right-click on the control and select "Properties" from the menu. The property sheet should become visible in a frame.

Let's look at some of the more common form controls:

A very common control is the button. Buttons exist in just about every Windows program. They let the user save work, accept changes, open files, etc. Most actions that can be taken in a program are activated when the user clicks on a button.

Another popular control is the text box. Text boxes allow a user to enter text such as names, addresses, or passwords into a program.

Just as the text box is useful for allowing a user to enter text, a label control is useful when the program needs to display textual information to the user. Labels are most often used to identify certain controls so that the user knows what information is needed. For example, if you have a text box on the screen, you can use a label control to tell the user to enter their name, address, user ID, etc.

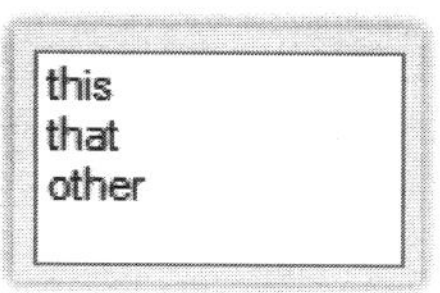

List box controls are useful for showing a user a group of items. A plain list box control is just a box that has one item per line. If there are more items than can be shown in the box, a scroll bar will appear. The user can then scroll up or down to see all of the list entries. A user can select one or more items at a time.

The combo box control is a combination of a list box and a text box control. A user can type a new item into the list, or click on the arrow button on the right of the list box to show a list of available items. A combo box control will only take up one line of space on a form. The user must click on the arrow button to show the full list of items. This can save space on a crowded form. A variation of the combo box is a "drop-down list box". This control is identical to the combo box, except that the user is prevented from entering new items into a list.

Another type of control is the option control. Option controls enable a user to make a choice between several options. There are two main types of these controls: radio buttons and check boxes.

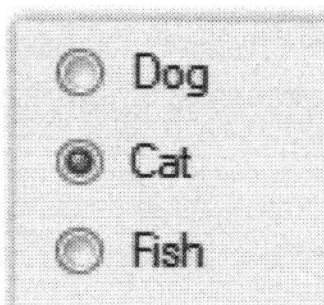

Radio buttons offer user a choice between *one* of several options. Each radio label is preceded by a white circle. When the user selects a label by left-clicking the mouse cursor on the circle, a dot will appear in the circle. Only one option can be selected in a group of radio buttons.

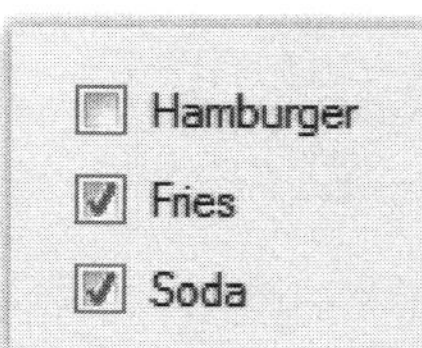

A checkbox also offers the user a choice of options, but this time they can select zero, one or more of these options. Each checkbox label is preceded by a white box. When the user selects a label by left-clicking the mouse cursor on the white box, a check will appear in the box.

There are many other types of controls that you can add to your form – tree controls, numeric pickers, and more – too many to cover in one lesson!

All of these controls have their own properties. These properties are used to set information like the control's size, location on the screen and the text that appears on the control. All of these properties are found in the property sheet on the main IDE screen.

The most important property for any control on the screen is the control's name. A **(Name)** property exists for each and every control that is on your form. This is the name that you can use to access this control in your code, so it is very important to give each control a unique name. Just like the form itself, a control is given a default name like "Label1" or "Listbox2" when you add it to your design. The first thing you should do after you add a control to your form is change the name!

Let's say we add two buttons on our screen: one to "Print" and one to "Exit". The first button will automatically be named "Button1" and the second "Button2". If we do not change the names of these buttons, our code can become difficult to read.

```
Button1.Text = "Print";  // Hope this is the right button!
Button2.Text = "Exit";   // Not sure about this one either!
```

Any programmer who was trying to read our code would have a difficult time figuring out exactly what **Button1** and **Button2** are supposed to do. Instead, if we changed the names to **PrintButton** and **ExitButton**, we could write the following:

```
PrintButton.Text = "Print";  // Now it's obvious!
ExitButton.Text = "Exit";    //
```

Now we know what this section of the program is doing just by glancing at the code. This is why giving the controls on your form meaningful names is so important!

Lesson Two: C# Syntax

Each computer programming language has rules about how a program can be written. These rules are called the format or *syntax* of the language. If you do not follow the language syntax rules, your program will not compile or run. If you are familiar with the C or C++ language, you will find the C# syntax is very similar.

Comments

Comments are lines of text that programmers use to tell anyone reading their program what the program is doing. These are plain text lines and contain no program code at all. The C# language uses the "//" characters to identify a comment line. There are no syntax rules for the text you type within a comment. Comments can appear by themselves on a line. You can also add a comment at the end of a line of code.

```
// This is a comment by itself on a line.
int sample = 42;        // this is a comment at the end of a source line
```

There is one other way to create a large comment across multiple lines. Instead of using the "//" sequence on each line, you can surround the entire multi-line comment with "/*" to start the comment block and "*/" to terminate the comment block.

```
/*    This is a comment block
      All of the text between these symbols
      are considered comments.
*/
```

The compiler knows that anything that comes after a "/*" is a comment, including a return. The compiler only sees the end of the comment when you end it with the "*/" combination. This is extremely helpful when you have a large group of comments and you don't want to keep typing "//" at the beginning of every line. Just remember to end any comments started with "/*" with the "*/"!

It is always a good idea to start out every source file with a small block of comments that tell the name of the programmer (you) and what the program is supposed to do. This is helpful for anyone else that reads the file later or for yourself if you don't remember earlier programs.

For your programs, we suggest using a comment block similar to this at the top of each source file:

```
/* TeenCoder:  Windows Programming
   HelloWorld Application
   <your name>
   <the date, e.g. March 30th 2013>
*/
```

The Using Keyword

The .NET Framework objects in C# are carefully organized into groups called "namespaces". We will discuss how these namespaces work in a later chapter. For now, you should know that you can add them to your program through the **using** keyword at the top of your source file. The **System** namespace is the most common namespace in the C# language.

```
using System;    // allows access all objects in the System namespace
```

When the IDE creates projects for you, it will automatically add several **using** statements at the top of each source file to give access to the necessary form and other objects.

Statements and White-space

A statement is a piece of code that performs some specific action. For example, this is a single statement:

```
length = 8;
```

You could type multiple statements (or even your entire program!) together on the same line of text. The compiler doesn't need code to look pretty; it just insists that you obey the rules for correctly forming statements.

```
length = 8; width = 11;
```

However, as a human being, you would like the code to be formatted in such a way that it's easy to read. We use white-space to make the code easier to read. White-space refers to characters you type in like spaces, tabs, or carriage returns and line-feeds (what you get in the text file when you press Enter to go to the next line). These characters do not add any meaning to the program; the compiler ignores them completely. For instance, if you have two statements in your program, you can separate them on different lines by adding white-space (pressing Enter) between the statements:

```
length = 8;
width = 11;
```

All the space between the end of the first statement and the beginning of the second statement (including the return), would be considered white-space. You could have one return between the two statements or a hundred, the compiler doesn't care. White-space is just there to make things easier to read.

If the compiler ignores white-space, including returns, how does it know we have reached the end of our statement? The C# language (like the C language) uses semicolons (;) to end statements. Semicolons are to code statements what periods are to sentences. They tell the compiler that the statement's end has come. So if the compiler understands that the semicolon is the end of the statement, could you just start your next statement right after the semicolon? Yes, but don't! No one wants read a paragraph that spans 10 pages and no one wants to read code that is all jumbled together. That's what white-space is for!

Lesson Three: Event-Driven Programming

In console applications, the program flow starts at the beginning of the code and executes each statement in an orderly and predictable manner. This is called structured programming and works great for console applications or background applications like those that run on servers and websites. Windows programs, however, work entirely differently.

In Windows programming, a user is typically presented with a form which has many different options on it. There may be any combination of buttons, text boxes, list boxes, etc. that the user can utilize. There is no way to predict exactly which action the user will choose to perform. This makes it difficult to execute the program in an orderly and structured manner. Instead, your program becomes *event-driven*, which means that certain functions within your code will execute when specific events occur.

Some of the more common events in Windows programming occur when the user clicks a button, moves the mouse or types in a control on the screen. In this lesson, we will demonstrate the use of a button-click event by creating a different kind of "Hello World" application.

Go ahead and open up the Visual C# Express Edition IDE. Once it has opened, create a new project called "Hello World2". Remember not to put any commas or special characters in the project name. When your new project is open, first change the form's caption to "Hello, World". Highlight the form by clicking on it and then find the **Text** property in the Property Sheet frame. Change the text from "Form1" to "Hello, World". Also change the **(Name)** of your form to "HelloForm2". Highlight the form by clicking on it and then find the **(Name)** property in the Property Sheet frame. Change the **Text** from "Form1" to "HelloForm2".

Next, look at the Controls Toolbox and find the **Button** control. Create a button on your form by dragging and dropping it onto your form. Your form should now look something like the example shown to the right.

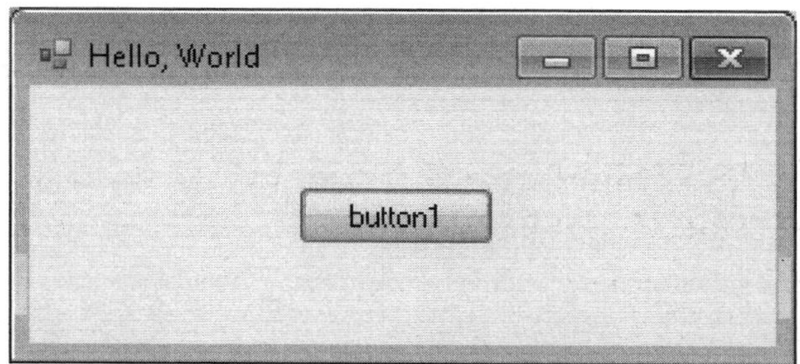

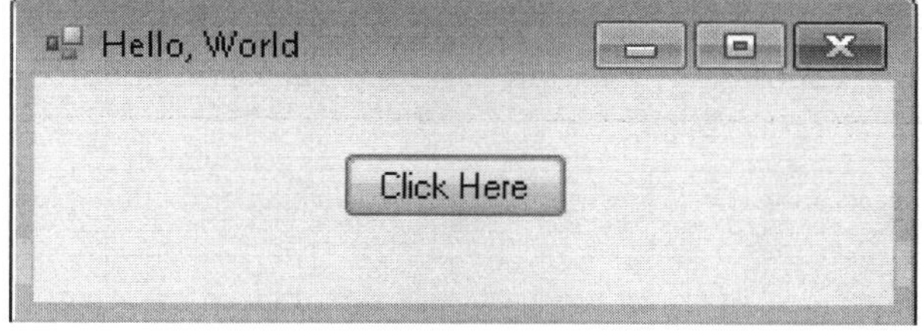

The button controls have some of the same properties as the form control. For starters, we are going to change the **Text** property of our button. To do this, click on the button and then look for the **Text** property in the Property sheet. Change "Button1" to "Click Here". We will also change the **(Name)** of our button. Look for the **(Name)** property and change it from "Button1" to "MyButton". Now your form should show your new button text.

Once you have created your button, it's time to make it do something! We want our button to respond to a *button-click* event. To do this, just double-click on the button in your Form Design screen.

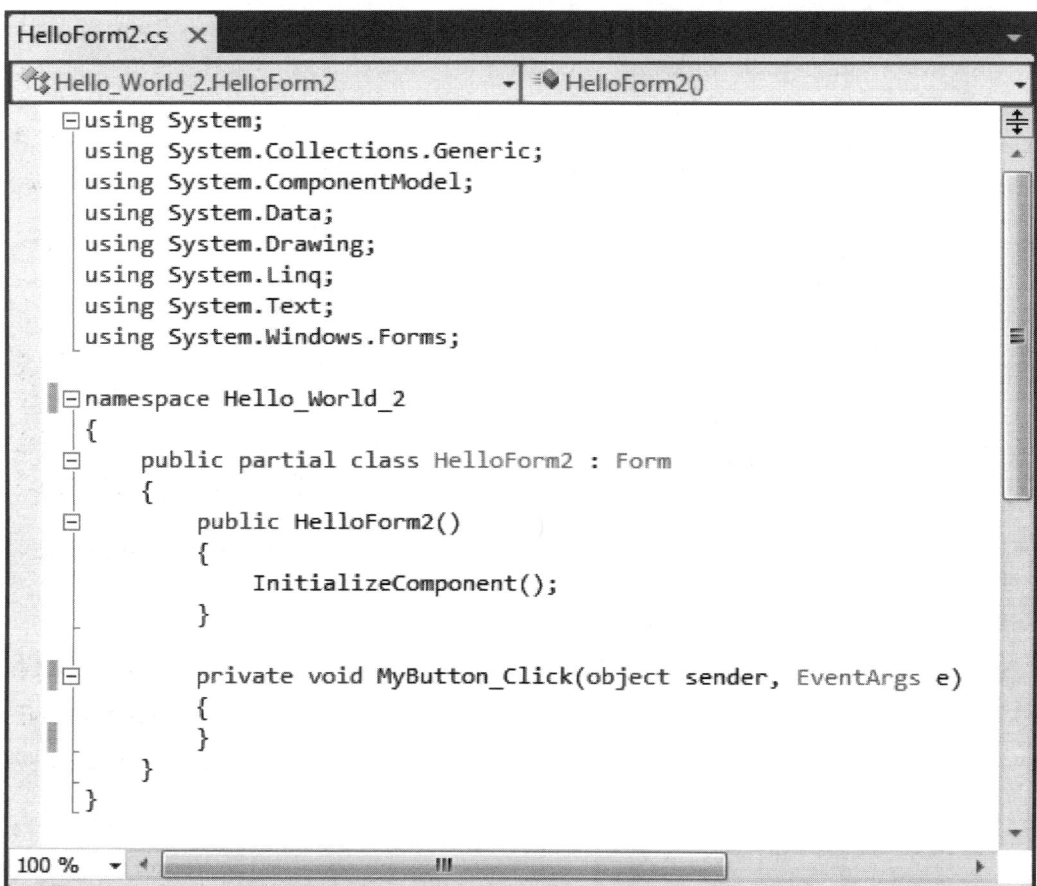

Your form's source code window will now appear as shown to the left.

What you see is the code window for your form. The code already here is automatically created by the Visual C# IDE!

The first thing you will notice is the long list of namespaces at the top of the window. Visual C# will always add these common namespaces to a program when it is created. Do we need them all? Not really. In fact, for this program, we will only use the first and last namespace (**System** and **System.Windows.Forms**). If you wanted to, you could delete out the other using statements, but they don't harm the program, so we will leave them here.

After the **using** statements, you will see the beginning of the namespace for your program: "Hello_World_2". This namespace will hold all of your code for this program. The next statement begins the definition of our form: "HelloForm2". All code between these opening and closing curly brackets belong to the form object:

```
public partial class HelloForm2 : Form
{
}
```

You'll learn much more about objects later, but for now it's important to know that most of your code will appear in between the opening and closing curly braces that mark the beginning and end of the form object.

The next group of statements is also created by the Visual C# IDE and is executed when the form is first created. If you need to initialize anything when the program starts, this is a good place to do it:

```
public HelloForm2()
{
        InitializeComponent();
}
```

Finally, we see the function **MyButton_Click()**, followed by a set of curly braces ({ }). When a user clicks on our button, the program will execute any statements that exist between these braces.

```
private void MyButton_Click(object sender, EventArgs e)
{
}
```

The things listed between the parentheses ( ) after **MyButton_Click()** contain information about the button-click event; you can ignore them for now.

Of course, right now there are no statements in our click function, so let's add some! We are going to add code to pop-up a message box that says "Hello, World!" To do this, we will use an object called **MessageBox**. This is a common .NET Framework object which will show a small window with a message.

```
MessageBox.Show("Your text here");
```

What we are doing above is calling the **Show()** function on the **MessageBox** object. The **Show()** function tells the program to show the pop-up text on the screen. The parentheses are used to enclose the parameters, or information that we are passing to this function. There is only one piece of information this function needs: the text string to display. For our button, we will be displaying the text "Hello, World!"

To add this code to our program, put your cursor between the curly braces for the **MyButton_Click()** function. Hit Enter to get a new line, the Tab key to indent your new code and then type the following line:

```
MessageBox.Show("Hello, World!");
```

Something strange probably happened as soon as you started typing this line. The IDE popped-up a "helper" window to suggest things you might be trying to find. After you finish typing "MessageBox." the window will change and show you the functions on the **MessageBox** object.

When you continue typing "Show(" it will display a description of the **Show** function and the parameters you can use with it.

```
MessageBox.Show(
▲ 1 of 21 ▼ System.Windows.Forms.DialogResult MessageBox.Show(string text)
            Displays a message box with specified text.
            text: The text to display in the message box.
```

These pop-up windows are helpful tools for programmers who need to know how to use this function. For now, however, just ignore the helper windows and type in your line as shown above.

Your finished code should look like this:

```
private void MyButton_Click(object sender, EventArgs e)
{
        MessageBox.Show("Hello, World!");
}
```

Now we are ready to test our program! Find the Start button on the toolbar and click on it, or you can just hit the "F5" key. Your program "Hello World2.exe" should now run and show the form with the "Click Here" button.

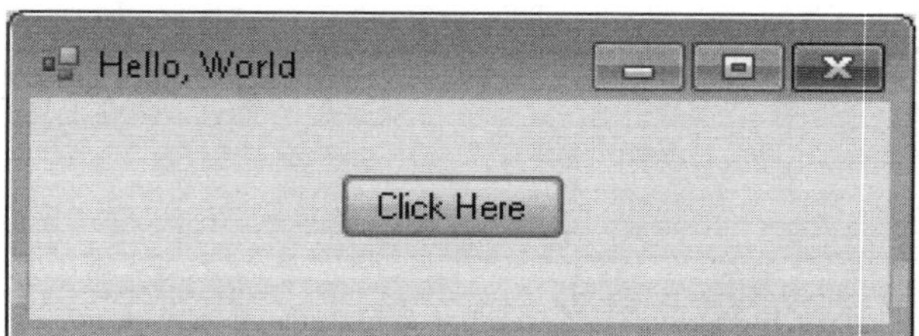

Click on that button and you should see your message box!

Congratulations! You just wrote your first C# code statement!

Don't forget to save your project when you are finished! To save your project, click "Save All" from the File menu. Make sure the Location contains your working directory and give it a Solution Name of "Hello World2". Avoid adding any commas or special characters to the name.

Lesson Four: Namespaces

In a last chapter, we introduced you to the .NET Framework and how all of its objects are carefully organized into namespaces (or groups). Now we will discuss these groups in more detail.

Understanding Namespaces

All C# objects belong to a group called a *namespace*. Each namespace is identified by a string which is typically a descriptive name for the group. These groups or namespaces are hierarchical, which means one namespace can contain another. All of the objects in the .NET Framework belong to a well-defined namespace hierarchy. For instance, the main namespace is called **System**. The **System** namespace contains numerous sub-groups or namespaces like **Windows**. In turn, the Windows namespace contains sub-groups like **Forms**. Each namespace is separated with a period. So if we needed to reference the **Forms** namespace, we would use the following string:

```
System.Windows.Forms
```

The **System** is the parent namespace, the **Windows** namespace is a child of **System**, and the **Forms** namespace is a child of **Windows**.

To access the objects in a specific namespace, add the **using** keyword that was described in a previous lesson. All **using** keywords must be at the top of the source file.

```
using System.Windows.Forms;

Application.Run(new Form1());
```

The **Application** object that we used in the code above is an object which is found in the **System.Windows.Forms** namespace. If we did not include the line "**using System.Windows.Forms**", we would have to use the *fully qualified* name for **Application**, which includes the entire namespace:

```
System.Windows.Forms.Application.Run(new Form1());
```

As you can see this requires a great deal more typing than just declaring the namespace with the **using** keyword.

Creating Your Own Namespaces

You can (and will!) create your own namespaces in programs to categorize all of the objects you write. Everything in C# is defined in some namespace. Typically, you will just use the name of your program as a namespace to cover all of the source code in your program. The IDE will automatically create a namespace for you when it creates a project, so you don't need to do it by hand.

Here is an example of a namespace you might create yourself:

```
namespace HelloWorld  // define the HelloWorld namespace
{                     // everything inside this bracket belongs to HelloWorld
    static class Program
    {
        static void Main()
        {
        }
    }
}                     // closing bracket ends the HelloWorld namespace
```

This will define a **Program** object in the **HelloWorld** namespace.

You can also create a namespace within a namespace as follows:

```
namespace outer
{
    namespace inner
    {
        class MyClass1
        {
        }
    }

    class MyClass2
    {
    }
}
```

Here we have defined two objects: **MyClass1** and **MyClass2**. **MyClass1** is in the "**outer.inner**" namespace and has a fully qualified name of **outer.inner.MyClass1**. **MyClass2** is in the "**outer**" namespace and has a fully qualified name of **outer.MyClass2**.

If you wanted to use these classes from another program, you just add the **using** keyword at the top of your program like this:

```
using outer;
using outer.inner;
```

.NET Framework Namespaces

As we have mentioned before, the .NET Framework library is enormous. There are a huge number of namespaces that contain useful components for your programs. If you go to a bookstore, you could probably find a whole shelf full of reference books that are devoted to the definitions of all of these objects.

The following table lists some common .NET namespaces. We will use objects from some of them later on.

Namespace	Description
System	Defines exceptions, variable data types, mathematical operations, and other central language elements.
System.Collections	Defines **Lists**, **Maps**, and other data structures used to hold groups of objects
System.Data	Contains classes that let you access databases and other types of structured data
System.Drawing	Enables you to draw on forms
System.IO	Supports reading and writing of data to files and other Input-Output (IO) devices
System.Media	Contains methods to play sounds and music
System.NET	Lets you send and receive Internet messages using many standard protocols such as HTTP
System.Text	Contains different ways to manipulate text strings
System.Timers	Defines the **Timer** object, which is useful in graphical applications to make things happen at regular intervals
System.Web	Defines objects that perform web browser methods including web requests and response parsing, cookie management, etc.
System.Windows	Gateway into the Windows Presentation Framework (WPF) classes, which is what you use to write windows-based graphical applications
System.Windows.Forms	Specific elements relating to creating dialog-based forms, controls, etc.

If you need to add any **using** statements to the top of your programs other than the defaults created for you, those statements will be listed in the activity description.

Chapter Review

- A "window" in C# programming is called a "form".
- A form is an important element in any graphical Windows application. This is the canvas on which a programmer draws the visual controls in a program.
- A form can contain many different types of "controls". Controls are graphical items that enable a user to interact with a program.
- Comments are a way to narrate or explain a program to anyone reading the source code. A single-line comment is always started with the double-slash "//". A group of comment lines can be enclosed between "/*" and "*/" characters.
- White-space refers to the characters you type into a program like spaces, tabs, or carriage returns and line-feeds, which make the program easier to read. These characters are ignored by the compiler.
- Event-driven programs respond to events like button-clicks and mouse movement. Graphical Windows programs are event-driven programs.
- You can double-click on a button from the Form Design screen to automatically create an event handler function that will be called when the user clicks the button.
- You can use the **MessageBox** object to display a message on the screen.
- Namespaces allow you to hierarchically organize your components into descriptive groups.
- All C# objects are defined with a namespace.
- You can create your own objects and namespaces, or use some pre-built namespaces such as those found in the .NET Framework.
- Add a **using** statement with a namespace to the top of your code for easy access to objects in that namespace.

Activity: A More Personal Hello

In this activity, you will practice creating message boxes using the **MessageBox**.**Show**() function.

Your activity requirements and instructions are found in the "Chapter_03_Activity.pdf" document located in your "TeenCoder\Windows Programming\Activity Docs" folder. You can access this document through your Student Menu or by double-clicking on it from Windows Explorer.

Complete this activity now and ensure your program meets the requirements before continuing!

Chapter Four: Data Types and Variables

In this chapter you will learn how to name and use the data your programs will need to complete their tasks.

Lesson One: Value Data Types

Most programs require data to work. A calculator application needs numbers to calculate, an MP3 player needs music files to play, and an image editor needs pictures to load. Clearly, data can come in various forms or types. In this lesson we will introduce some of the *data types* commonly used in C# programming. All of the data types described in this lesson are *value* data types, meaning the computer will reserve enough memory to hold the entire data type each time you declare an instance of the type in your code.

Numeric Data Types

The simplest data types are numeric. There are many different types of numbers (large, small, decimal, positive, negative, etc) and C# defines a data type for each kind. When storing numeric data in your program it's important to select the right data type for the numbers you will be using.

Computers store all data in *binary* form - meaning a series of digits that can have two values: 1 or 0. Each binary digit is called a "bit". In memory these bits are held together in groups of 8 called "bytes". Some example bytes in binary form are: 00000000, or 11111111, or 01010101.

Numeric data types have one or more bytes depending on the *range* - the minimum and maximum possible numeric values to be stored in the data type. The following chart of C# integer data types shows the name of the data type, the corresponding **System** object name, how many bytes the type contains, and the range.

Integer Data Type	.NET Framework Object	Bytes in Memory	Range
byte	**System.Byte**	1	0 to 255
sbyte	**System.SByte**	1	-128 to 127
short	**System.Int16**	2	-32,768 to 32,767
int	**System.Int32**	4	-2,147,483,648 to 2,147,483,647
uint	**System.UInt32**	4	0 to 4,294,967,295
long	**System.Int64**	8	-9,223,372,036,854,775,808 to 9,223,372,036,854,775,807
ulong	**System.UInt64**	8	0 to 18,446,744,073,709,551,615

All C# numeric data types have a short name (e.g. **int**) and a longer corresponding .NET Framework name (e.g. **System.Int32**). When writing code you will typically use the short form to describe your data. You can use the .NET Framework object name for some advanced features (more on that later).

The integer data types that start with the letter "u" are called "unsigned" data types. This means that these data types do not hold any sort of positive or negative sign. In another words, they cannot contain any value less than zero. This may seem like a limitation, but what this really does is allow the range of positive numbers go higher than any of the signed data types. If you need to hold a larger positive number, an unsigned data type is a great option.

The **byte** data type is an exception to the unsigned data type naming rule. Even though its name does not start with a "u", it is an unsigned data type. If you need to use a signed byte, use the **sbyte** data type.

An additional group of C# data types can be used to hold "real" numbers, meaning numbers that have some decimal or fractional part.

Real Data Type	.NET Framework Object	Bytes in Memory	Range
float	**System.Single**	4	-3.402823 x 10^{38} to 3.402823 x 10^{38}
double	**System.Double**	8	-1.79769313486232 x 10^{308} to 1.79769313486232 x 10^{308}
decimal	**System.Decimal**	16	-7.9 x 10^{28} to 7.9 x 10^{28} with 28-29 significant digits

Real numbers can be described in terms of the precision (how many numeric digits) and range (how large or small). Both precision and range take some memory to represent. Therefore, the **float** data type which has the fewest bytes of memory has the smallest precision and range. When you go from the 4-byte float to the 8-byte **double**, your precision and range both become much larger. The **decimal** data type is the largest of all in terms of precision -- it can hold 28 or 29 significant digits! However the overall range isn't quite as high as the other two. You would use a **decimal** if you need to store a very precise number that doesn't have a huge range.

There are two additional built-in value data types that are not numeric: **char** and **bool**. A **char** represents one letter, numeric digit, or keyboard symbol such as "a", "3", or "*". A **bool** is short for "Boolean" which is a **true** or **false**.

Data Type	.NET Framework Object	Bytes in Memory	Range
char	**System.Char**	2	One text character
bool	**System.Boolean**	1	**true** or **false**

Each **char** data type is two bytes because it stores characters in a "Unicode" format. This format supports not just English characters, but a huge range of characters and symbols from other languages. Later on we will describe how to build larger strings (lines of text) from characters.

.NET Framework Data Types

Since the C# language is inherently object-oriented, each of the data types is also represented by an object in the .NET **System** namespace. This means that you can use the system object name or the data type name – they are completely interchangeable! The following code illustrates this concept:

```
int myInt1;
System.Int32 myInt2;

 myInt1 = 42;
 myInt2 = myInt1;
```

The first two statements create variables with the exact same data type. You can even assign one variable equal to the other variable. You can use either the object name or the data type name to declare a variable, although the use of the data type name is more common.

Each **System** data object has some special functions (also called methods) and properties. Two of the more common properties are:

- **MaxValue** – This property holds a constant value with the biggest number the data type can hold.
- **MinValue** – This property holds a constant value with the smallest number the data type can hold.

These properties are very helpful in determining if you will be able to store a certain value into your variable. The following code demonstrates the use of the **MaxValue** property:

```
// set myInt1 to the maximum possible value for the data type
int myInt1 = System.Int32.MaxValue;
```

One of the more useful methods on every **System** data type is the **ToString()** method. This method is used to translate a numeric value into a **string**. The following code demonstrates this method:

```
string myString = myInt1.ToString();
```

We will discuss the **string** data type in more detail later in this chapter. For now just keep in mind that you can always convert a number to a **string** by calling the **ToString()** method.

"Enum" as Your Own Data Type

You may want to define a data type that contains a small number of possible values that are very specific to your program. For instance, let's say you were creating a fishing program, and wanted to identify different types of fish. You can define items using the **enum** keyword, giving a name for your data type, and then listing the possible values between a pair of brackets. You need to separate each value with a comma.

Let's define some fishy values!

```
enum FishType
{
   TROUT,
   BASS,
   FLOUNDER,
   GUPPY
}
```

Now you have a new data type called **FishType** that can hold one of the four possible values listed! Your **enum** data type is a "value" data type and can be declared and initialized just like an **integer** or any other number. You pick a particular value by using the enumeration name, a period (dot), and then the value:

```
FishType myFish = FishType.GUPPY;
```

Keep in mind that when you declare a variable of an enumerated type, the variable can only hold one of those values from the enumeration. There are many pre-defined enumerations within the .NET Framework that you will discover later!

Lesson Two: Variables

In addition to telling the C# compiler what kind of data type to use, we need to tell the compiler what name we will use to refer to the data in our program. When you create an instance of a data type and give it name, that instance is called a *variable*. Variables are places where you store data in your program. You can change a variable's contents while running the program (hence the name "variable").

Variable Declaration

To create a new variable you *declare* it. Each variable declaration starts with a data type followed by a name:

```
bool isAccepted;              // declare a boolean called isAccepted
char myChar;                  // declare a char variable called myChar
double myDoubleNumber;        // declare a double called myDoubleNumber
float myFloatNumber;          // declare a float called myFloatNumber
decimal myDecimalNumber;      // declare a decimal called myDecimalNumber
```

Each of these lines of code would create a variable in a program. The first line will create a **boolean** variable named **`isAccepted`**, the second line would create a **char** variable named **`myChar`** and the third line would create a **double** variable named **`myDoubleNumber`**. The last two lines declare **float** and **decimal** numbers called **`myFloatNumber`** and **`myDecimalNumber`**. After you declare a variable, the compiler has reserved enough space for you to place data into the variable. You refer to the variable later using the name.

Assigning Variables

Now that you have declared your variable, you can initialize it with a value. To assign data to a variable, use an *assignment statement* with the equals sign. The left of the statement must be a variable name and the right of the statement can be any expression that results in a single data value. This data must match the variable's data type. In other words, you can only assign an integer to an **int** data type, a character to a **char** data type, etc.

```
isAccepted = true;          // boolean values are either true or false
myChar = 'A';               // use single quotes around individual characters
myDoubleNumber = 1.02;      // fractional numbers by default are double values
myFloatNumber = 1.02F;      // use the "F" suffix to specify a float value
myDecimalNumber = 1.02M;    // use the "M" suffix to specify a decimal value
```

Notice that when you type in any number with a decimal point, by default the compiler will treat it as a **double** data type. You must add the 'F' suffix to make it a **float** or the 'M' suffix to make it a **decimal**!

You can also initialize the variable with a value at the same time that you declare it.

```
bool isAccepted = false;
char myChar = 'A';
double myDoubleNumber = 1.02;
float myFloatNumber = 1.02F;
decimal myDecimalNumber = 1.02M;
```

You can, of course, change the value of the variable later using a normal assignment statement.

Constant Variables

A *constant* variable is a variable whose value never changes during the course of a program. A good example of this type of variable is mathematical PI, whose value is always a constant starting with 3.14159.... This value should not ever be changed by a program. To make a variable constant, you just add the **const** keyword in front of the data type.

```
const double PI = 3.14159;
```

A constant variable must be initialized with a value when it is declared. Traditionally, a constant variable is named with all upper case letters, but this is not a requirement. You can use constant variables to hold fixed values you may want to easily change while designing the program, but not once the program starts running. For instance, let's declare some constants holding the number of rows and columns in a board game:

```
const int NUM_ROWS = 8;
const int NUM_COLS = 8;
```

Later, if you want to make your game board 10 x 10, you can just change the constants before rebuilding your program. So long as you used the constant variables everywhere in your program instead of hard-coding the number 8, the change should be just that easy!

Rules for Naming Variables

You have seen that variable names are just a string, or series of characters. There are some rules to follow to ensure the variable name is valid and accepted by the compiler -- you can't use just anything! Valid characters for variable names are any combination of letters, numbers and underscore characters (_). However the name must start with either a letter or an underscore. A variable name can never start with a number.

Let's take a look at some examples of good and bad variable names:

```
int CAPITAL;        // capital letters are fine
int lowercase;      // lowercase letters are fine
int MixedCase;      // mixed case names are fine
```

The underscore character is often used in declarations. Often this is used to visually separate words used in the name, but can also be used as a leading or trailing character.

```
int _score;         // leading, trailing, or embedded underscores are ok
```

Numbers are also acceptable in the names of variables as long as they don't begin the name. They can be either embedded in the middle of the name, or at the end of the name.

```
int score42;        // embedded or trailing numbers are fine
int 42score;        // ERROR:  can't begin with a number
```

All variable names must be one continuous string of letters and symbols, and cannot contain spaces.

```
int no spaces;      // ERROR:  can't contain spaces or other whitespace
```

All declarations must have unique names. You cannot use the same name for two different variables.

```
int same;           // once is ok
int same;           // ERROR:  can't declare the same variable twice
```

You cannot use reserved words for your variable names. The C# compiler has a list of words with specific meaning to the compiler. The compiler will not allow you to use reserved words as your variable name.

```
int return;         // ERROR:  can't use a reserved keyword as a name
```

C# is a *case-sensitive* language. This means that a variable named **myInteger** is different from the variable called **MyInteger**. The case for each letter is just as important as the letter itself!

```
int same;           // this is one variable
int SAME;           // this is a completely different variable
```

Variable Casting

Sometimes you need to convert variables of one data type to another. This may happen with numeric data because you have an integer that needs to be used as a real number or vice-versa. The compiler will let you assign data from one variable to a variable of another data type if the assignment is "safe", meaning there is no chance you will lose or truncate data while making the conversion. For example, it's safe to convert an integer to a double because the double can always exactly represent an **int** like 42 as the **double** 42.0.

```
int myInt = 42;                // start with integer 42
double myDouble = myInt;       // convert it to a double 42.0
```

However, other conversions are not necessarily safe so the compiler won't let you do them automatically. Consider the reverse of the above:

```
double myDouble = 42.3;        // start with double
int myInt = myDouble;          // ERROR:  converting decimal to an integer
```

The compiler will be worried that the integer data type can't hold the fractional part of the double, so will respond with an error similar to this:

"Cannot implicitly convert type "double" to "int". An explicit conversion exists (missing a cast?)"

You can, however, override the compiler's natural caution and force the conversion by *casting*. Casting means you explicitly tell the compiler to convert the source data type to the target data type, doing whatever is necessary to make the data fit. To cast, use the target data type in parentheses right before the source data, and the compiler will force it to the target data type.

```
double myDouble = 42.3;        // start with double
int myInt = (int)myDouble;     // cast it to an integer
```

As a general rule of thumb, only cast when *you are sure* the conversion is safe even if the compiler is unsure. So if you have a real number that you are certain actually holds an integer, cast away! Or, if your intent as part of the program features is to truncate the fractional part of a real number, you can cast it to an integer also.

You may also have to cast one numeric type to another if the target data type is smaller than the source. The compiler will be worried about losing data when storing potentially very large **long** number into a smaller **int**:

```
long myLong = 42;              // start with a long
int myInt1 = myLong;           // ERROR:  assign long to an integer
int myInt2 = (int)myLong;      // OK:  cast long to integer before assignment
```

Variable Scope

We've shown you many different variable declaration and initialization examples without really talking about *where* these lines of code go. This is important too! Where you declare your variables will determine which parts of your program can see and access those variables as well as how long they "live" before being discarded by the computer program. The concept of variable lifespan and visibility is called *scope.*

All variables must be declared within some set of opening and closing curly braces. These braces will mark the beginning and ending of the variable's scope. If you declare the variable just inside a "class" definition, then the variable will be visible to all of the funcitons within that class, and will live for as long as the class itself does. Let's consider a class **HelloForm** which could be created as part of a new project:

```
public partial class HelloForm : Form
{
    // this variable is declared within a class but outside any function
    int myClassInt = 1;

    public void function1()
    {
       // myLocalInt is declared locally inside function1
       // we can also use all class-level variables such as myClassInt
       int myLocalInt = myClassInt;
    }
    public void function2()
    {
       myClassInt = 2;  // yes we can see class-level variables here too
       myLocalInt = 2;  //  ERROR: can't see local variables from other functions
    }
}
```

We have declared two variables: **`myClassInt`** is at *class-level* scope within the class curly braces but outside any function. This variable can be seen and used by all functions and will live as long as the class does. On the other hand, **`myLocalInt`** is declared within the **function1**() curly braces. This means the variable is *local* in scope to that function and will only live until the last statement in **function1**() has finished. At that point the variable is destroyed, and it cannot be seen or used by any other function.

It's a common programming error to attempt to access a variable from a scope where it is not visible. If you do so, the compiler will display an error message similar to the one generated by our example code:

" The name 'myLocalInt' does not exist in the current context. "

Lesson Three: Reference Data Types

In the last two lessons we learned about the kinds of "value" data types. When you declare a value data type variable, you automatically get a spot in computer memory reserved for that value. There is data in that space right away (though it might not be what you want until you initialize the variable). This means that you can use the variable as soon as it is declared, although you should really initialize the variable before you use it.

In this lesson, we will learn about "reference" data types. These data types are called "reference" types because declaring them as variables does not create space for the data in memory. Instead the variable name is merely a "reference" to wherever the data actually resides. When you first declare a variable for a reference data type, the variable's value is **null**, which means "nothing". The variable literally refers to nothing and has no data at all associated with it.

You declare a reference variable just like a value variable; use the data type first and then the variable name.

```
<AnyReferenceDataType> myData;    // myData contains null by default
```

If you try to use a reference variable that contains **null**, you will cause an error in your program. So how do you set a reference variable so that it refers to actual data? In order to create a new instance of your reference data type, you must use the **new** keyword followed by the data type name, open and closing parentheses, and then the statement-ending semicolon:

```
<AnyReferenceDataType> myData = new <AnyReferenceDataType>();
```

This creates a new place in memory that will hold the value for the variable. The reference variable will not hold these values itself; instead it will hold a link to the place in memory where these values reside. Think of a reference variable as a card in an address book. When you first add the card, it is a blank. It does not hold any information or reference. Now let's say you want to put your best friend's house address on the new card. You do not put the physical house on the card, you just write down where the house is located. A reference variable works the same way. It holds the address where the data object is located but not the actual value.

Notice we added a set of parentheses after the data type when using the **new** keyword. When you create a new instance of a data type, you can sometimes add parameters just like a function to help initialize the data type.

Another way to set a reference variable is to assign the variable equal to some other reference that has already been initialized with a valid data object.

```
myData = <some existing object>;  // myData now refers to valid data
```

As long as the existing object refers to valid data, the variable **myData** will be valid after this statement. This does not mean that we are copying the data that is in the existing object, just that we are pointing our new reference variable to the same data. If we go back to our address book example, this would be like adding another card in the address book and then writing down the same home address for your friend. You now have two cards or references to the same thing.

In this same way, two or more reference variables can point to the same data in memory:

```
<AnyReferenceDataType> myData1 = <some existing object>;
<AnyReferenceDataType> myData2 = myData1;
```

Now, both **myData1** and **myData2** refer to the same data in memory! It's like having two names or an alias for the same person.

Since a reference variable can possibly contain **null** instead of a valid reference, you should ensure in your program that your reference variables are not **null** before you use them. You may, on occasion, want to remove the variable reference to some object. In this case simply assign the variable to **null** and it will no longer refer to anything.

```
myData = null;          // myData reference variable is now null
```

So far we haven't given any concrete example of a reference data type. That's coming up next when we talk about strings!

Lesson Four: Introducing Strings

The C# language has a built-in **string** data type. A string is a series of characters that form a line of text. It can be a short string like someone's name, or a very long string like an entire book. The **string** data type is a reference data type like we described in the previous lesson. To create a string variable, you would declare it just like any built-in data type:

```
string myString;
```

In this example, we declare a string, but do not initialize it to any value. This means that our **myString** variable will start out with a value of **null**. In order to use this variable in a program, we will have to initialize it by assigning a text value to it.

```
myString = "You're a better man than I am, Gunga Din!";
```

Now we can use the string variable in our program! Notice that we did not have to use the **new** keyword to create a new string. The string is a special exception among the reference data types because it is so heavily used. To initialize a string, you only need to assign a value within double-quotation marks. You must use straight double quotes (") instead of the fancy curly quotes (“ ”) sometimes added by word processors. Of course, you can declare and initialize a string at the same time:

```
string myString = "Greetings";
```

Now our **myString** variable is created, initialized and is ready to use in a program. The **string** data type is heavily used in C# and has many special helper functions to make it easy and convenient.

String Equality

To compare two strings to see if they are equal, you can use the **Equals**() method on the **string** object. Let's look at some examples:

```
// initialize three string with different values
string myString1 = "hello";
string myString2 = "jello";
string myString3 = "Hello";

// compare them to see if equal
bool isEqual1 = myString1.Equals(myString2);
bool isEqual2 = myString1.Equals(myString3);
bool isEqual3 = myString1.Equals(myString3,StringComparson.OrdinalIgnoreCase);
```

We first declare three strings with three different values. Notice the first and third string differ only by the case of the first letter. Now, the first call to **Equals**() compares the first two strings, which are clearly different. So the first result in **isEqual1** is **false**. The second comparison between the first and third string also returns **false** because **Equals**() is by default case-sensitive. If we want to do a case-insensitive comparison we can pass in the optional parameter **StringComparson.OrdinalIgnoreCase** as shown above. Then the third result will be **true** because the strings are equal except for case differences.

String Concatenation

Concatenation is the process of putting together two pieces. For strings you can put together two smaller strings to make a larger string. Because this is such a common task, C# allows you to "add" two strings together using the plus sign (+).

```
string myString = "hello" + "goodbye";
```

The above example will place the value "hellogoodbye" into the **myString** variable. Notice that there is no natural space between words because we didn't have one inside the quotes. This is important to remember when you are combining text. C# will not place a space in between the two strings, you must do this yourself if needed.

If you have a variable with some string contents already, and you want to add more to the end, you can use the plus-equals operator (+=) like this:

```
string myString = "hello";
myString += " there"; // myString now contains "hello there"
```

Notice that we placed a space before the word "there". The final string thus contains the phrase "hello there".

The += operator is a shortcut way of writing the full assignment statement. This statement would have done exactly the same thing:

```
string myString = "hello";
myString = myString + " there";   // myString now contains "hello there"
```

Accessing String Characters

So how is a **string** data type implemented in C#? It actually consists of a series of **char** elements. Each character in a string can be accessed by a numeric index value in square brackets. The first character in the string has an index value of [0] and the last character has an index value of [length of the string minus 1].

For example, "giraffe" has 7 characters so the index ranges from 0 to 6. In our code we could read the first character with the index [0] and the last character with the index [6].

g	i	r	a	f	f	e
0	1	2	3	4	5	6

```
string myString = "giraffe";
char c1 = myString[0];    // c1 = 'g'
char c2 = myString[6];    // c2 = 'e'
```

As you can see in the above example, you can access the individual characters in the string by using the index value of the character. However, you should always be careful not to try and access an index value that does not exist. For example, if we tried to access index value [7] of **myString**, we would generate an error, since the only valid index values in that string are 0 through 6:

```
char c3 = myString[7];    // ERROR: giraffe only has 7 chars with index 0 - 6
```

This error would not show up when you compile the program, but would cause a runtime error. Always remember that the index value start at 0, not at 1!

You can easily access the individual characters in a string by using an index value in square brackets. Just remember that the first character in the string is index 0, not index 1!

You can also find the number of characters in a **string** by reading the **Length** property, like this:

```
string myString = "rhino";
int len = myString.Length;   // the len variable now contains 5
```

String objects are quite powerful and we have only scratched the surface of the functions available to you. We'll devote an entire chapter to strings later, but for now you can start using them in your programs.

Blank Strings and Null Strings

A valid string may not contain any characters. These "empty" strings are simply written as two double quotes back-to-back with no spaces in between. A **null** string, however, is very different! A **null** string literally means no string of any size. It's somewhat like the difference between holding an empty bag with nothing in it, and not having any bag in your hand at all.

```
string myEmpty = "";  // this string is empty
string myNull = null; // this string is null
```

Chapter Review

- Value data types have memory allocated for them by the compiler when they are declared, and can be used right away. Each variable of a value data type contains its own copy of the data.
- There are different numeric data types depending on the type of number you want to use
- A **char** data type is used to store a single character.
- A **bool** data type is used to hold a logical **true** or **false**.
- A variable is a named instance of a data type.
- A constant variable is a variable whose data will not change while the program is running.
- You can *cast* variables of one data type to another.
- *Scope* refers to the visibility and lifespan of a variable declared within a set of curly braces.
- Reference data types refer to a data object located elsewhere in memory.
- Reference data types do not contain the value of the data itself.
- Reference data types are initialized with the **new** keyword.
- The **string** data type is a reference data type.
- Since the **string** is so common, you do not have to use the **new** keyword to initialize a string variable.
- To initialize a string, just set it equal to some text contained within quotation marks.
- Strings can be compared with the **Equals**() method.
- Two or more strings can be joined together by using the plus (+) or plus-equals (+=) operators.
- Strings are made up of individual characters that can be accessed by a numeric index.
- The valid numeric index values for a string range from 0 to N – 1, where N is the length of the string.
- Blank strings are represented by two double quotes with nothing inside ("").

Activity: Experiment with Data Types

In this activity, you will create a program that declares and initializes several different types of variables and displays them to the user with a **MessageBox**.

Your activity requirements and instructions are found in the "Chapter_04_Activity.pdf" document located in your "TeenCoder\Windows Programming\Activity Docs" folder. You can access this document through your Student Menu or by double-clicking on it from Windows Explorer.

Complete this activity now and ensure your program meets the requirements before continuing!

Chapter Five: Basic Flow Control

In this chapter you will learn how to test data against certain conditions, and then make decisions in your program based on the results. The way that a program responds to certain decisions is called *flow control.*

Lesson One: Logical Expressions

Logical expressions are parts of a statement that evaluate to **true** or **false**. Logical expressions are very important because they allow your program to make decisions about what code to run. For instance, let's say we had a list of students and we only wanted to print out those students who were older than 10. We would use a logical expression (age > 10) to decide whether or not to print each student's name. This type of decision is part of program flow control, since the result of the expression could change which set of statements the program will execute

Comparison Operators

All logical expressions involving two or more components require a *comparison operator.* These symbols are used in logical expressions to compare two values. The result of evaluating two values (operands) with a comparison operator is always **true** or **false**. Let's explore the C# comparison operators now!

The first conditional operator is the *equal to* (==) operator. The result of this operator is **true** if both sides of a logical expression are equal. For example:

```
1 == 2    is a false statement since 1 does not equal 2.
2 == 1    is a false statement since 2 does not equal 1.
1 == 1    is a true statement since 1 equals 1.
```

The next conditional operator is the *not equal to* (!=) operator. This result of this operator in a logical expression returns **true** if the two sides of the expression are not equal to each other. The result is **false** if they are equal to each other. For example:

```
1 != 2    is a true statement since 1 is not equal to 2.
2 != 1    is a true statement since 2 is not equal to 1.
1 != 1    is a false statement since 1 is equal to 1.
```

Next, the *less than* (<) operator will return **true** if the left side of the expression is smaller, or less than the right side. The statement is **false** if the left side of the equation is not less than the right side. For example:

```
1 < 2       is a true statement since 1 is less than 2.
2 < 1       is a false statement since 2 is not less than 1.
1 < 1       is a false statement since 1 is not less than 1.
```

The next operator is the *greater than* (>) operator. The result of this operator in a logical expression is **true** if the left side of an expression is larger than right side. The result is **false** if the left side is not greater than the right side. For example:

```
1 > 2       is a false statement since 1 is not greater than 2.
2 > 1       is a true statement since 2 is greater than 1.
1 > 1       is a false statement since 1 is not greater than 1.
```

The next conditional operator is the *less than or equal to* (**<=**) operator. The result of this operator in a logical expression is **true** if the left side of an expression is smaller than or equal to the right side. The result is **false** if the left side is not smaller or equal to the right side. For example:

```
1 <= 2      is a true statement since 1 is less than 2.
2 <= 1      is a false statement since 2 is not less than nor equal to 1.
1 <= 1      is a true statement since 1 is equal to 1.
```

Next, we have the *greater than or equal to* (>=) operator. The result of this operator in a logical expression is **true** if the left side of an expression is larger than or equal to the right side. The result is **false** if the left side is not larger than or equal to the right side. For example:

```
1 >= 2      is a false statement since 1 is not greater than nor equal to 2
2 >= 1      is a true statement since 2 is greater than 1.
1 >= 1      is a true statement since 1 is equal to 1.
```

These relational operators are very important in the use of flow control, since they help the program to make decisions about what statements to execute.

Mathematical vs. Logical Expressions

While logical expressions always return **true** or **false**, mathematical expressions can evaluate to any number. Because both mathematical and logical expressions tend to involve two operands and a operator, they are easily confused. Remember that a logical expression like (1 < 2) results in **true** or **false**, while a mathematical expression like (1 + 2) results in another number!

Logical Operators

Comparison operators are not the only operators that can evaluate to **true** and **false**. *Logical operators* also return **true** or **false** based on operands that are **true** or **false**.

There are four logical operators: **and**, **or**, **exclusive or**, and **not**.

Logical Operation	C# Symbol	Example	Description
and	&&	a && b	Returns **true** if both "a" and "b" are **true**, or **false** otherwise
or	||	a || b	Returns **true** if either "a" or "b" are **true**, or **false** otherwise
exclusive or	^	a ^ b	Returns **true** if either "a" is **true** and "b" is **false**, or vice-versa
not	!	!a	Returns **true** if "a" is **false** or **false** if "a" is **true**

The "a" and "b" operands may be Boolean values originally, or they may be logical expressions that evaluate to **true** or **false**. You can therefore use the logical operators to join together two or more logical expressions. The resulting compound expression still evaluates to **true** or **false.**

The logical OR statement is made by using two of the "bar" keys on your keyboard. This key is located just above the Enter key on most keyboards. The bar is the shifted "\" key and looks like this when typed: "|".

Let's go back to our student list example. If we want to print out a list of students that are over the age of 10, and are named "Bob", we could write the following expression:

```
(age > 10) && (name.Equals("Bob"))
```

The logical expression above will evaluate to **true** if both **age** is greater than 10 **and** **name** is equal to "Bob". The next logical expression would be **true** for all students that are 10 **or** 11 years old:

```
(age == 10) || (age == 11)
```

Variables in Logical Expressions

Any of the simple numbers we demonstrated above when talking about expressions can be replaced by variables instead. All of the basic numeric variable types can be used freely in logical expressions. For example, if **age** was a numeric data type, the expressions listed below are valid.

```
age > 18
age == 18
age != 18
```

You do not want to use comparison operators to compare two reference variables! Reference variables only point to areas in memory that hold some data. Comparing reference variables will only let you know if the variables are pointing to the exact same copy of the data, but will not tell you if the data itself is the same in two different areas! So a comparison like this would not work as expected:

```
myReference == yourReference   // Not what you expect!
```

If your references pointed to two exact copies of the same data, the comparison operator "==" could still return **false** because the address of the data in memory is different for each reference! C# has a special rule for **string** references because they are so commonly used. Comparison of **string** references will actually compare the data in the strings, but it's still clearer to use the **string.Equals**() function as described earlier.

Do NOT use comparison operators to compare two references! Only for strings will the comparison operators work as expected, and it's generally clearer to use the string.Equals() function to compare strings.

Using Parentheses for Clarity

If you look at a small expression such as "**a** && **b**", it's easy to predict the results. But when we start joining together more complex expressions, the behavior can be harder to predict. Consider this example, where both "**a**" and "**b**" happen to be **true** and "**c**" is **false**.

```
bool result = a || b && c;
```

We're not really sure if C# will evaluate "**a** || **b**" first or "**b** && **c**" first! In one case the overall result would be **false** and in the other case, **true**. There are C# rules to govern this behavior, but most people don't like to untangle this sort of mess based on mysterious rules.

Fortunately, you can use parentheses to guide how expressions are evaluated. Use parentheses to wrap up individual expressions that you want evaluated first. The results are then combined into a larger expression. By adding parentheses below, we know exactly how the expression will work, with "**b** && **c**" evaluated first.

```
bool result = a || (b && c);
```

Lesson Two: Using the "if" Statement

Normally your program statements will execute one by one in the order they appear in your source file. The term *flow control* refers to making decisions based on conditions to change the normal execution order. There are several statements that can make flow control decisions. In this lesson we will focus on the **if()** statement.

The if() Statement

The **if()**statement will execute a block of code if a logical expression evaluates to **true**.

```
if (<logical expression>)
{
        // this code executes if the logical expression is true
}
```

The **if** keyword is always followed by a logical expression in parentheses. The logical expression can be very simple or very complicated, but it must evaluate to either **true** or **false**. If the logical expression is **true**, the code contained within the curly braces below the **if** statement is executed. If the expression is **false**, the code in the curly braces is skipped, and the program continues on the next line below the ending curly brace.

If you do not use any curly braces, the **if()** statement will only execute the *very next* statement when the condition is true!

```
if (<logical expression>)
        // this statement executes if the logical expression is true
// any other statements afterwards will execute regardless of the results
```

You can use as many **if** statements in your program as you like:

```
if (<1st logical expression>)
{
        // this code block executes if the 1st logical expression is true
}

if (<2nd logical expression>)
        // this code statement executes if the 2nd logical expression is true
```

The if(), else if(), and else Statements

You can use the **else if** keywords to evaluate an expression only if the previous **if** expression was **false**. You may add a final **else** keyword as well. This **else** statement will not use a logical expression. Instead, it will designate statements to be executed if none of the prior **if** or **else if** statements are **true**.

```
if (<1st logical expression>)
{
        // this code executes if the 1st logical expression is true
}
else if (<2nd logical expression>)
{
        // this code executes if the 1st logical expression is false
        // AND if the 2nd logical expression is true
}
else
{
        // this code executes if all of the above expressions are false
}
// this is the next line in the program, independent of the flow above
```

The above sample code shows a series of decision making statements. If the first logical expression is **true**, the code in the first set of curly braces will be executed. Once this code is executed, the program will drop all the way down past the **else** statement block and will continue the program execution at the next line.

If the first logical expression is **false**, the program will drop down and test the second logical expression. If this second expression is **true**, the code in the second set of curly braces will be executed. Once this code is executed, the program will drop down past the **else** statement and program execution will continue at the next line in the program.

If both logical expressions are **false**, the program will drop down to the last **else** statement. This statement is a catch-all statement that will execute if no other expression has evaluated to **true**. Once this set of statements has executed, the program will continue at the next line in the program. Once you start an **if** expression, you may follow it with any number (0 or more) of **else if** expressions. The final **else** is optional.

In C# the expression in the parentheses must be a logical expression and not a mathematical or assignment statement. Only expressions that evaluate to **true** or **false** are accepted. Consider the examples below, where we have made some mistakes within our **if()** expressions.

```
if (a = 5) // ERROR:  assignment statements are not logical expressions
{
}
if (a + 5)// ERROR:  mathematical equations are not logical expressions
{
}
if (a == 5) // OK!  This is a logical expression
{
}
```

What's wrong with some of these expressions? Well, in the first statement, you are not checking to see if "**a**" equals 5, you are actually assigning the value **5** to the variable "**a**". The second statement adds 5 to the value of "**a**", which results in another number and not **true** or **false**.

In some languages the numbers 1 and 0 are synonymous with **true** and **false**. C++ programmers are fond of using numbers and letting the compiler automatically cast them to **true** and **false**. C# will not allow you to cast a number to a Boolean **true** or **false** however. You need to use a comparison operator instead to determine the Boolean value.

```
int value = 1;
if (value) { }      // ERROR: 'value' is an integer
if (value == 1) { } // OK:  comparison operator results in Boolean
```

If you have a Boolean variable that already holds a **true** or **false** result from some earlier calculation, then you can use that directly in your **if()** statement expression.

```
bool value = true;
if (value) { }      // OK: 'value' is a Boolean
```

Lesson Three: For() Loops

Loops are often used in a program to execute a series of statements over and over again. One common loop type is a "**for**" loop. This loop is used to execute a set of statements a fixed number of times.

"For" Syntax

All **for**() loops are based on an integer index, which is a numeric variable (e.g. **int**). The index starts at some specified number and is then increased or decreased each time through the loop until a test logical condition becomes **true**. The syntax of a **for**() loop looks like this:

```
for (<initialization statement>; <test statement>; <assignment statement>)
{
     // statements to be executed within the loop go here
}
```

Let's look at this syntax in depth. The loop always starts with the keyword **for** and then three statements inside parentheses, separated by semicolons. The *body* of the loop is between the opening and closing curly braces. The loop body is the group of statements you would like executed each time through the loop.

The *initialization statement* is simply an assignment statement that sets your index variable to an initial value. We can declare our **index** variable somewhere outside of the **for**() loop, and then use it inside. An initialization statement starting the index at 0 would look like this:

```
int index;
for ( index = 0;
```

Notice that each parameter in this **for** statement is ended with a semicolon. These are individual statements and must be ended this way for the code to compile. You may optionally declare the index variable at the same time you initialize it instead of declaring it outside the loop. In that case the variable is *local* in scope to the **for**() loop itself and will disappear when the loop exits.

```
for ( int index = 0;
```

The test statement that comes next is a logical expression that evaluates to **true** or **false** based on the current value of the loop index variable. The loop will continue to execute the body statements while the test expression is **true**. For example, we could continue the loop while the index was less than 10 like this:

```
for ( index = 0; index < 10;
```

The test condition will be evaluated at the start of every loop. Once the statement is **false** (index is greater than 9 in this example), the program will skip to the next line of code after our statement block.

The assignment statement is the third and final statement within the parentheses. This statement will update the loop's index variable. The assignment will happen after the body of the loop has executed each time, but prior to the test condition evaluating the next time through the loop. If we wanted to increase the index by one each time through the loop, we could use the following assignment statement:

```
for ( int index = 1; index < 10; index = index + 1)
```

Since adding one to a variable is such a common operation, you can use a special shortcut to write this more simply. Instead of "**index** = **index** + 1" you can simply write "**index**++" to do exactly the same thing. We'll discuss the "++" operator in more detail later, but you may see it frequently used in loops.

```
for ( int index = 1; index < 10; index++)
```

Notice that you do not need a semicolon after the last assignment statement – just between the three statements. Your assignment statement can do whatever you like to the index variable each time through the loop – typically increment or decrement by 1, 2, or some other amount. But you must do *something*, otherwise your test condition never has a chance to go **false** and you will be stuck in an infinite loop!

It is common practice to shorten the names of loop variables to just a single character like "i" (for index). While this runs against normal good-programming practice to use descriptive names, the shortened names are well-understood by anyone else looking at your code.

Example for() Loops

Here is a complete example using a **for**() loop to show a pop-up message box with the numbers 0, 1, 2, and 3:

```
// declare a for loop with index "i" starting at zero,
// incrementing once each time through the loop, and
// continuing so long as i < 4
for (int i = 0; i < 4; i++)
{
    MessageBox.Show(i.ToString());
}
```

We can change the example to start at the number 4 and count backwards (decrement) by 2 each time:

```
// declare a for loop with index "i" starting at 4,
// decrementing twice each time through the loop,
// and continuing so long as i >= 0
for (int i = 4; i >= 0; i = i-2)
{
      MessageBox.Show(i.ToString());
}
```

This code will show three pop-up messages: one when "**i**" = 4, one when "**i**" = 2, and one when "**i**" = 0.

Breaking Free!

Sometimes you may want to terminate your **for**() loop early, no matter what the index variable or test conditions say. You can use a "**break**" statement to immediately exit any loop you might be within at the moment. For example, say we wanted to find the first space in a string. We might write a **for**() loop to look over all of the characters in the string. Once we find the first space there is no point in looking at the rest of the string, so we can exit the loop right away.

```
string target = "Paper or plastic?";
int firstSpace = -1;

// walk over each character in the target string
for (int i = 0; i < target.Length; i++)
{
      // check to see if this character is equal to space
      if (target[i] == ' ')
      {
            // save the index of the first space
            firstSpace = i;
            // exit the loop, we're done!
            break;
      }
}
```

Here the **for**() loop will result in the **firstSpace** variable being set equal to the index of the first space character in the target string (5 in this example). If we didn't have the **break** statement our **for**() loop would continue until the end and we'd actually find the last space instead (at index 8). The **break** statement can be used in all loop types, not just the **for**() loop, and it has exactly the same effect!

Lesson Four: While() Loops

A second type of program loop is called a "**while**" loop. This type of loop is used to execute a set of statements ***while*** a condition is **true**. You may not know in advance how many times the loop will execute, but you know the conditions under which it should continue executing. For instance, you may want to examine some user input looking for a specific value. Since you don't know what the user will enter, or how long it will take to find the right value, you will not know ahead of time how many inputs you will be processing. This is where a **while**() loop comes in handy.

"While" Syntax

A **while**() loop is based on a logical expression that evaluates to either **true** or **false**. As long as this expression evaluates to **true**, the loop will continue to execute.

The **while** loop syntax looks like this:

```
while ( <logical expression> )
{
      // statements to be executed within the loop go here
}
```

Let's take a closer look at this syntax. The loop is begun with the **while** keyword followed by a logical expression in parentheses. Just like the **for** loop, the body of the **while** loop is defined by curly braces surrounding the statements to be executed in the loop. The logical expression is evaluated in order to determine whether or not to run the statements within the loop body. If the logical expression is **false** at the very beginning, the loop body will never execute at all!

Within the loop body you *must* have some statements that will affect the logical expression, usually by modifying one or more variables involved in the expression. Otherwise the logical expression will never change and you will have an infinite loop!

Your logical expression may be simple or complex, with multiple logical expressions combined with the AND ("&&"), OR ("||"), or NOT("!") operators. Be sure to use parentheses to make it clear how the individual expressions will combine. For example:

```
while ( ( A < B) || ( (C + D) > 42))
```

This loop will execute while A is less than B, OR the sum of C + D is greater than 42.

Example While Loop

Here is an example using a **while**() loop that will calculate the factorial of 5 (5! = 1 x 2 x 3 x 4 x 5 = 120)

```
int counter = 5;
int result = 1;

while (counter > 1)     // while not done
{
      result = result * counter;  // multiply result by current counter
      counter--;        // IMPORTANT - decrement the value of the counter
}
```

We will make 4 passes through this loop, where the value of the counter in each pass is 5, 4, 3, and 2. Once the counter reaches 1 the logical expression is **false** and the loop body is skipped. At the end of the while loop, the value of **result** would be 120 – which is the factorial value of 5.

Common Mistakes with While Loops

The most common programming mistake with loops is the *infinite* loop. This condition is caused by failing to change the logical expression within the loop body. If your **while** logical expression is **true**, and you do nothing in your loop body to ever make the expression **false**, your program will be stuck in that loop forever!

This example **while**() loop will never end.

```
while (1 < 2)
{
      // this is an infinite loop because 1 is always less than 2
}
```

You are responsible for changing the result of your logical expression in your while loop body. If you never change the result of this expression, the while loop will never stop running. This is called an infinite loop, since the loop executes infinitely, or forever!

Do-While Loops

The last type of loop we will discuss is called the "**do-while**" loop. This loop is very similar to the **while()** loop, except that the logical expression is not tested until the *end* of the loop body. This means that our loop body will *always* execute at least one time.

A **do-while** loop is based on a logical expression that evaluates to either **true** or **false**. As long as the expression is **true**, the loop will continue to execute. The **do-while** syntax looks like this:

```
do
{
        // loop statements here
}
while (<logical expression>);
```

Let's look at the syntax in depth. The first statement is the **do** statement. This is a simple keyword-only statement and marks the beginning of the loop body. As in previous loops, the loop body is contained within the curly braces.

The last part of the loop is the **while** statement. This is the same syntax as the simple **while** statement we discussed earlier. The **while** keyword is followed by a logical expression (simple or complex) within a set of parentheses. Once again, remember the logical expression MUST be changed within the loop code. Otherwise, you will end up with an infinite loop! After the closing parenthesis you must have a semicolon to mark the end of the **while** statement.

Let's re-work the prior example where we calculated the factorial of 5. Since we know that the calculation will perform at least one pass of our while loop, we can use a **do-while** loop to accomplish the same thing:

```
int counter = 5;
int result = 1;

do
{
        result = result * counter;  // multiply result by current counter
        counter--;       // IMPORTANT - decrement the value of the counter
} while (counter > 1);    // while not done
```

Again, we will make 4 passes through this loop, where the value of the counter in each pass is 5, 4, 3, and 2. Once the counter reaches 1 the logical expression is **false** and the loop body is skipped. This **do-while** loop also produces a result of 120.

Chapter Review

- A logical expression is an expression that will always result in either **true** or **false**.
- Relational operators are symbols used to compare numeric values.
- Compound expressions are two or more logical expressions combined with the logical operators "&&" (and), "| |" (or), or "^" (exclusive or).
- Use parentheses to guide the evaluation order of small parts within a larger expression.
- **If**() statements use logical expressions to decide the flow of a program.
- The **if**() statement can be combined with an **else if** or an **else** statement to test for additional conditions.
- **For**() loops are used to execute a block of code a specific number of times.
- Infinite loops are a common pitfall when coding loops. An infinite loop is a loop that never ends because the test condition never becomes **false**.
- You can use a **break** statement to immediately exit whatever loop you might be inside at the moment.
- A **while** loop will execute while a certain condition is **true**. When that condition becomes **false**, the program will exit the **while** loop.
- The test condition for a **while** loop must be eventually altered within the loop such that it becomes **false**. A **while** loop will not automatically increment or decrement an index value.
- The test condition for a **while** loop will be tested at the top of the loop.
- The test condition for a **do-while** loop will be tested at the end of the loop.
- A **do-while** loop will always execute at least once, since the condition is not tested until the end of the loop.

Activity: Jeepers, Beepers!

In this activity you will create a program that will play a beep sound a specified number of times. You will use the **Console.Beep()** function to cause the computer to beep.

Your activity requirements and instructions are found in the "Chapter_05_Activity.pdf" document located in your "TeenCoder\Windows Programming\Activity Docs" folder. You can access this document through your Student Menu or by double-clicking on it from Windows Explorer.

Complete this activity now and ensure your program meets the requirements before continuing!

Chapter Six: User Input

In this chapter, we will take a more in-depth look at the different controls that are used to retrieve user input. You will learn about text boxes, list and combo boxes, and radio buttons and check boxes.

Lesson One: Text Boxes

A common user input control is the text box, which allows the user to enter a line of text into a program. The text box control is found in the Toolbox pane of your IDE when you are looking at the Form Design tab. Look under the heading "Common Controls" to find the "TextBox" item.

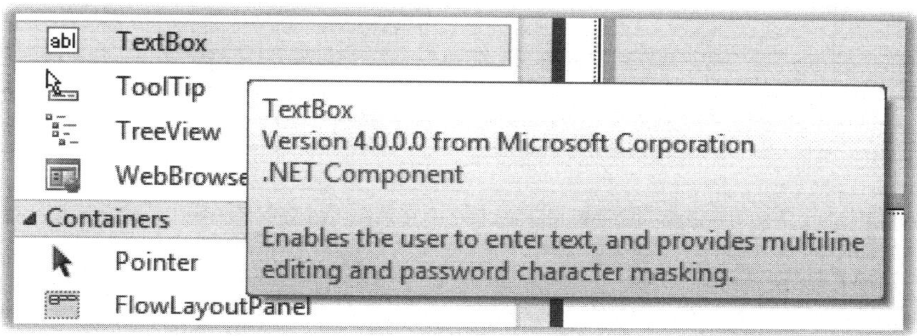

To add this control to your form, you can double-click it in the Toolbox or click and drag it from the Toolbox to the Form Design screen. You can click on the control's outline and then drag the mouse to resize or move the text box on the form.

The C# data type representing a text box in code is called **TextBox**. There are many different properties for the **TextBox** control. To view the properties, you can click on the control and then look at the Property Sheet panel. If the panel is not shown on the screen, just right-click the text box within the form and choose "Properties" from the menu. Here is a list of some of the more important properties:

Property Name	Description
(Name)	This is the name of the control. You will use this name to access the control's information in a program, so make sure this is a descriptive name that follows variable-naming rules.
Text	This is the value displayed in the control. You can use this property at design time to set the default text for the control. At runtime, you can use this property to read in the text that the user has entered, or set this value to your own string.
Enabled	This Boolean value determines whether or not the user can use this control on the form. If it is set to **false**, the text box will be grayed-out and the user will not be able to use it.
Visible	This Boolean value determines whether or not the user can see this control on the form. If this value is **false**, the text box will not appear on the form
ForeColor and **BackColor**	These properties set the foreground (text) and background colors for the control

Multiline	This property determines if more than one line of text is allowed in the control. If **false**, only one line is permitted. If **true**, the text box can be resized to hold many lines.	This is a multiple-lined text box.

There are many other properties for the **TextBox** control. To see what any of these properties do, just click on the property name and then look at the descriptive text at the bottom of the Properties panel.

If you double-click on the text box control in the form design window, the form code window will appear and a **TextChanged**() event handler function will be automatically created for you.

```
private void textBox1_TextChanged(object sender, EventArgs e)
{

}
```

This function will be called any time the user changes the text in the box. This is useful when you need to process the user input character-by-character for some reason. Or, if you need to update another area of the form to reflect the text in a text box control, you will want to know when the user has changed that text.

Using the TextBox Variable

Every **TextBox** on the form has a **(Name)** property, and that property determines a variable name for the control within your code. In the example above we used "textBox1" as the **(Name)** property. You can access all of the control's properties in code by writing "**textBox1.<property name>**".

The **Text** property is used to get or set the value in a text box. To retrieve the information a user has typed in, you can set a **string** variable equal to the **Text** property:

```
string input = textBox1.Text;   // gets current textBox1 contents
```

To set or display information in the text box control, you would just set the **Text** property to a string:

```
textBox1.Text = "Blue";         // set new textBox1 contents
```

These statements are valid from within any of your form methods, including the **TextChanged**() event handler demonstrated above and other event handlers such as button click events.

The text box control will hold only one line of text by default. If you want to change the height of the text box to hold more than one text line, you will need to find the **Multiline** property in the Property panel and change its value to **true**. Then you can click and drag the control to change its height. If you do not change this **Multiline** property, you will not be able to resize the text box's height.

If you decide to use the text box control to hold multiple lines of text, or you think the user may enter more characters than can be shown on the screen, you may want to add scroll bars to the control. Scroll bars are a set of arrows with a slider in between. A text box can contain horizontal scroll bars, vertical scroll bars or both. Horizontal scroll bars will scroll the text left and right. Vertical scroll bars will scroll up and down. Scroll bars can be enabled or disabled from the Properties sheet.

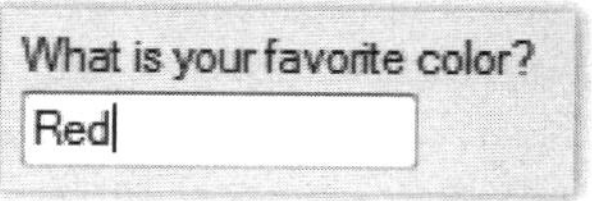

Finally, it is extremely good Windows design to use a descriptive label for any text box controls on your form. Without this, the user will not know what type of information you are expecting! So remember to drag a **Label** control from the Toolbox and position it above or to the side of the text box. Then change the **Text** property of the label with a descriptive string. You do not normally access labels from within the code at runtime. Therefore it is not usually necessary to give the label controls good variable names, because the variables will not be accessed from elsewhere in the program. If you want to change the labels while the program is running for some reason then go ahead and follow standard variable naming procedures.

Lesson Two: List Boxes and Combo Boxes

The list box control and the combo box control are useful user input controls. These controls both offer the user a choice of a list of items.

The list box control is used to display multiple items that can be selected by the user. A user can select items in the list by clicking on them. The list box can be handy when you want the user to make one or more selections from a pre-defined list of choices.

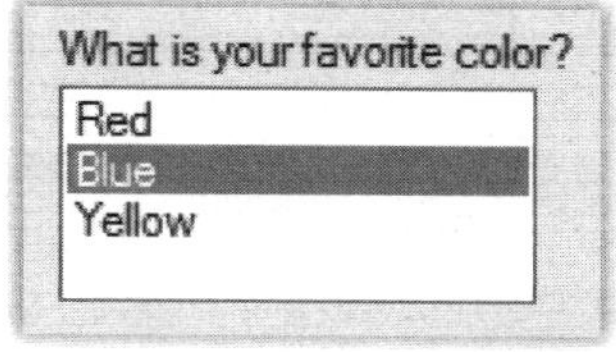

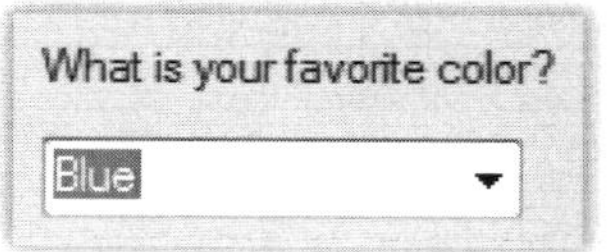

The combo box control is very similar to the list box control. Both controls allow a user to select from a list of items. A combo box, however, will only show the currently selected item in the text window. The rest of the list is hidden until the user hits a down arrow on the right. The first image shows the combo box control in its default state, while the second image shows the combo box's full drop-down list. The combo box is very useful in situations where you need to have the user select a single item from a list, but you do not have the space on your form to hold a full list box.

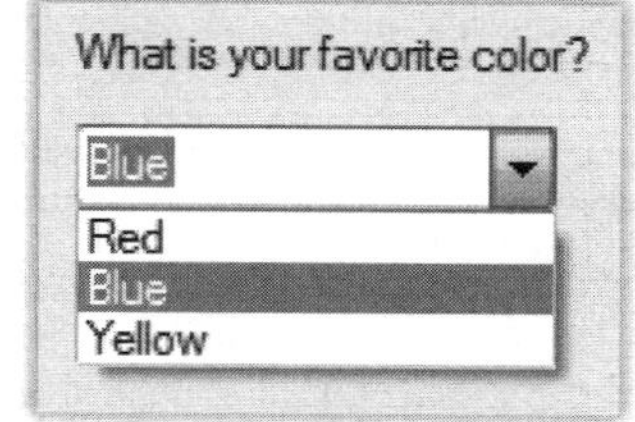

You will find the list box and combo box controls in the Toolbox under "Common Controls" just like the text box. Follow the same drag-n-drop procedure to add either control to your form.

Using the List Box and Combo Box Variables

The C# data types representing list and combo boxes in code are called **ListBox** and **ComboBox**. The list box and combo box controls on the form have a **(Name)** property that works as you might expect. Set the **(Name)** to a meaningful variable name so you can access the control variable in your code.

The list of items in a list box or combo box is set by the **Items** property. You'll note in the Property Sheet that the **Items** property is listed as a "(Collection)" with a little button to the right. To configure your collection of items, click on the "…" button to the right.

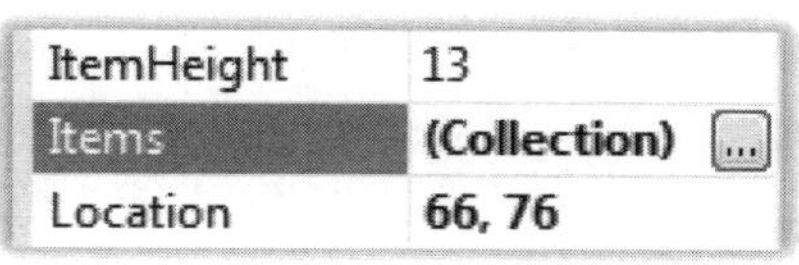

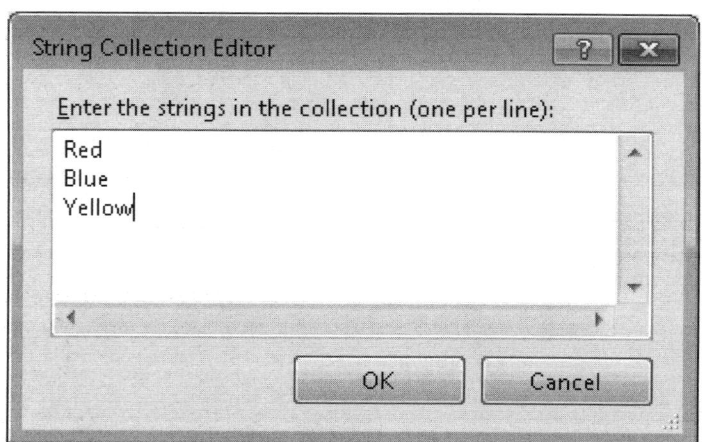

Once you click on the Collection button, a "String Collection Editor" window will pop-up on the screen. Here you can enter in as many strings as you need for your list box or combo box. Each string should be separated by hitting the enter key. When your program is run, these strings will show up in the control.

You can also programmatically set or clear the **Items** property. When you are designing a program, you may not know the list of items that you will need to put in your list box. In this case, you may need to wait until the program is running to generate the items in the list. Use the **Clear**() method on the **Items** property to remove all entries from the collection. Then call the **Add**() method to put new items in the collection.

```
listBox1.Items.Clear();            // remove all items
listBox1.Items.Add("Choice 1");    // add an item
listBox1.Items.Add("Choice 2");    // add another item
```

The items in your collection will by default appear in the order you enter them. If you wish the items to be stored alphabetically, set the **Sorted** property to **true**.

```
listBox1.Sorted = true;
```

Working with Selected Items

There are a few different ways to retrieve items that the user has selected in a list box or combo box. By default, these controls will only allow a user to choose one item at a time. The easiest method to get a single, selected item is to read the control's **Text** property. This will give you the text for the currently selected item in the list. If no items are currently selected then the **Text** property will contain an empty string (""). Similarly, you can use the **SelectedItem** property to retrieve the same value, but you have to cast the result to a **string** before assigning to a variable. Both of these statements will give you the same result:

```
string myString1 = myListBox.Text;
string myString2 = (string)myListBox.SelectedItem;
```

You can also set the currently selected item using the same properties:

```
// set the currently selected item
myListBox.Text = "Red";
myListBox.SelectedItem = "Red";
```

The items in a list box or combo box are also represented by an index value. The first item in the collection is index 0; the second is index 1, and so on. In your program, you can get or set the currently selected index by reading or assigning the **SelectedIndex** property. If nothing in the control is selected, the property will be -1.

```
// gets index of currently selected item,
// or -1 if nothing is selected.
int index = myListBox.SelectedIndex;

if (index != -1)        // safety check!
{
      // get the text selected using the index
      string selectedText = (string)listBox1.Items[index];

      // show the text we retrieved
      MessageBox.Show(selectedText);
}

// sets the currently selected item index
myListBox.SelectedIndex = 2;
```

You can use the selected index within brackets after the **Items** property to access the item text. We will discuss this "array" notation in more detail in a later chapter, but this demonstration is enough to show you how to pull text from the collection by index. Also note that the **Items** collection actually contains **Objects**, and not **strings**. So you need to cast the resulting **Object** to a **string** before storing it in a **string** variable.

Multiple Selections in a List Box

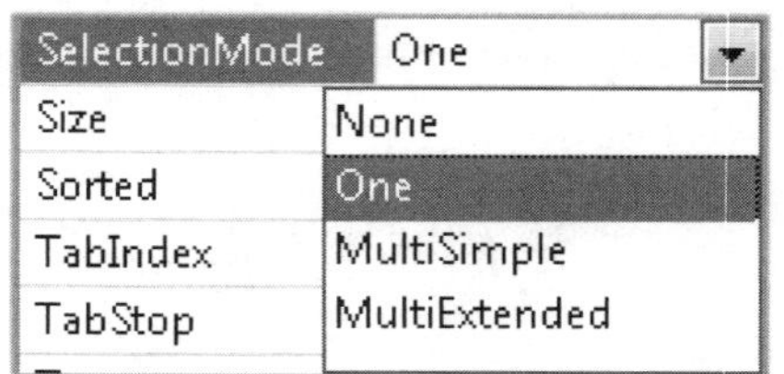

So far in this lesson we have focused on list boxes and combo boxes where a user can only pick one item at a time. This is the default setting for a list box and your only choice for a combo box! However, it is possible to create a list box that allows multiple items to be selected. To do this, you will need to change the **SelectionMode** property of the list box control from "One" to either "MultiSimple" or "MultiExtended".

The "MultiSimple" mode will allow any mouse-click or press of the space bar to toggle the selection state of the currently selected item in a list box. This means that if the item "Red" was selected in the example list box on a previous page, you could un-select it by clicking on it with the mouse or by pressing the space bar key. You can also select any other item in the list simultaneously. The "MultiExtended" mode will allow the user to select multiple items by holding down the SHIFT key and then clicking as many items as they want to select with the mouse or arrow keys.

Regardless of the multiple selection mode you choose, a slightly different technique is needed to retrieve all of the selected items. A single **SelectedIndex** or **SelectedItem** property can't represent everything the user might have selected. For any multiple-selection mode you should use two different properties to access the selected indices or selected items: **SelectedIndices** or **SelectedItems**. Both of these properties are collections just like the **Items** list. There will be one entry in the collection for each item that is currently selected, or the collection will be empty if nothing is selected.

We will discuss collections in more detail later, but the following example code should give you a good idea how to use both **SelectedIndices** and **SelectedItems**. First we examine the length of the collection to make sure at least one item is selected, and then display the first and last selected item in the collection.

```
int numSelected = listBox1.SelectedItems.Count;
if (numSelected> 0)    // if at least one is selected
{
    // get the first selected item in the list using SelectedItems
    string firstSelection = (string)listBox1.SelectedItems[0];
    MessageBox.Show(firstSelection);

    // get the last selected index in the list using SelectedIndices
    int index = listBox1.SelectedIndices[numSelected - 1];

    // get the corresponding text from the Items collection
    string lastSelection = (string)listBox1.Items[index];
    MessageBox.Show(lastSelection);
}
```

Lesson Three: Radio Buttons and Check Boxes

Radio buttons and check boxes are similar controls that allow a user to pick from a small set of options. You can find them in the Toolbox under "Common Controls" just like the other elements we have studied in this chapter. You can add them to the form and set a good variable name through the **(Name)** property in the same manner as with the other controls.

The Radio Button Control

The radio button control is used when you want the user to select only one option from a small group of items. The user can only select one radio button option at a time. For instance, in this example screen, the user can select either "Red", "Blue" or "Yellow".

Radio button controls are actually a group of controls that work together. If you place 5 radio buttons in random locations on a form, they will still work together as a group and only allow you to choose one option at a time. If you want to create multiple groups of radio buttons you will need to use a group box control, found under the "Containers" section of the Toolbox. The group box control will place a frame on the form, in which you can place related radio buttons. The radio buttons within the frame will work as a group, independent of any other radio buttons on the form. The example above shows a group box with the label "What is your favorite color?" Even if you only have one set of options on a form it's still visually appealing and consistent to always place the related radio buttons in a group box.

The C# data type representing a radio button in code is called, unsurprisingly, a **RadioButton**. To figure out which radio button in a group is currently selected, you will need to read the **Checked** property of each control's variable. If the **Checked** property is **true**, the button is selected. If it is **false**, it is not selected.

```
// determine which radio button is selected
bool isRed    = redButton.Checked;      // only one of these will be true
bool isBlue   = blueButton.Checked;
bool isYellow = yellowButton.Checked;
```

A radio button can be programmatically selected or de-selected within your code by setting the **Checked** property to **true** or **false**.

```
// select a radio button programmatically
blueButton.Checked = true;
```

Setting **Checked** = **true** would make **blueButton** the currently selected control and automatically de-select the other radio buttons in the group.

The Check Box Control

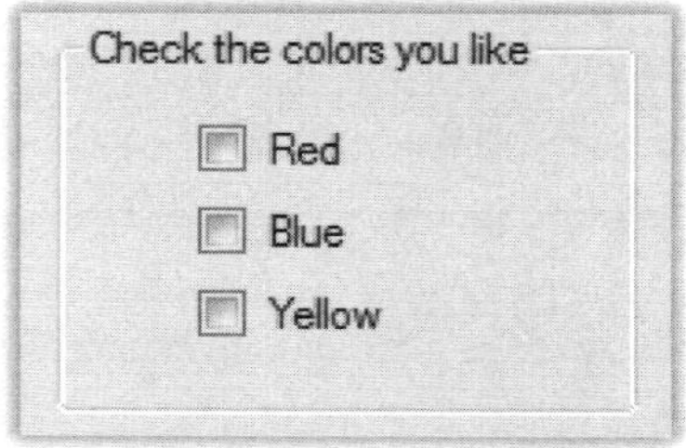

The check box control is very similar to the radio button control. Check boxes are typically grouped together and offer the user a small selection of options. The main difference is that a user can select more than one check box at a time or no check boxes at all! The check box controls are independent controls that do not ever work as a group, even though they are typically arranged in groups on the screen. Check boxes can even be placed inside of a group box control. This is mainly done as a way of visually telling the user that the check boxes contain similar options. This example shows a group box with the label "Check the colors you like". The check boxes within this group box are all independent controls.

The C# data type representing a check box in code is the **CheckBox**. To see if a check box control is selected, you read the **Checked** property on the control's variable name just like a radio button control. If the **Checked** property is **true**, the box is selected; if it is **false**, the box is not selected.

```
// determine which check box is selected
bool isRed    = redCheckBox.Checked;        // any or all of these may be true
bool isBlue   = blueCheckBox.Checked;
bool isYellow = yellowCheckBox.Checked;
```

A check box can also be selected or de-selected by setting the value of the **Checked** property to **true** or **false**.

```
// select a check box programmatically
blueCheckBox.Checked = true;
```

The above code would place a check mark in the **blueCheckBox** control.

Chapter Review

- **TextBox** controls are used to obtain text (string) input from the user.
- You should give your text box control a good **(Name)** property to control the variable name.
- Text boxes can be set to accept either single-line text or multi-line text using the **Multiline** property.
- You can read or assign the **Text** property for most controls to get or set the **string** displayed in the control.
- The **ListBox** control and the combo box control both offer the user a choice of a list of items.
- The **ListBox** control will display the possible choices as a list on the screen.
- A **ComboBox** control will display the current selection and hide the remaining items in a drop-down window.
- A **ComboBox** control is useful in an application where space is limited.
- To retrieve the currently selected item read the **SelectedItem** property of the list box or combo box control.
- A group of **RadioButton** controls can be used to make the user select one and only one option from a small set of options.
- The **RadioButton** that is currently selected will have a **Checked** property equal to **true**.
- **RadioButton** groups should be contained in a group box, especially if there are multiple unrelated groups on the form.
- The **CheckBox** control allows users to toggle a particular selection on or off.
- A **CheckBox** that is currently "checked" will have a **Checked** property equal to **true**.

Activity: Telling Tall Tales

In this activity you will create a program that allows users to write a funny story by selecting options from the controls we have learned about in this chapter.

Your activity requirements and instructions are found in the "Chapter_06_Activity.pdf" document located in your "TeenCoder\Windows Programming\Activity Docs" folder. You can access this document through your Student Menu or by double-clicking on it from Windows Explorer.

Complete this activity now and ensure your program meets the requirements before continuing!

Chapter Seven: Math Functions in C#

In this chapter you will learn all about performing simple mathematical operations in C#. We will also discuss more advanced C# math functions. Finally, you will create a graphical calculator application!

Lesson One: Math Operators (+, -, *, /, %)

Math *operators* are the symbols you use in expressions to perform some math using two operands. You are probably familiar with these operators as C# uses some of the same symbols you see on a calculator. Here is a list of the common math operators:

- addition uses the plus sign (+)
- subtraction uses the minus sign (-)
- multiplication uses the asterisk (*)
- division uses the forward slash (/)
- modulus (remainder) uses the percent sign (%)

Each operator takes two operands which can be a fixed number, a variable, or the result of evaluating a larger mathematical expression or function. You use these math operators exactly as you might expect:

```
int added = 3 + 4;          // answer is 7
int subtracted = 3 - 4;     // answer is -1
int multiplied = 3 * 4;     // answer is 12
int divided = 12 / 4;       // answer is 3
int remainder = 12 % 5;     // answer is 2
```

You can, of course, use any of the numeric data types in mathematical expressions and not just integers! The compiler will make sure all of the operands are of the same type before performing any math, making automatic casts where possible or producing a compilation error if the automatic casts cannot be made safely.

Operator Precedence

You can perform as many math operations in an expression as you would like. However, when you have multiple operators, the result can be difficult to determine. Consider the following expression:

```
int confusing = 12 + 12 / 3;
```

What is the value that is placed into the **confusing** variable? Is it 16? Is it 8? The true answer is determined by following the rules of *operator precedence*. Operator precedence determines which operators are executed first to combine operands and which ones will execute later. The rules of operator precedence in C# are:

- All of the multiplication, division, and modulus operators in an expression will execute first. If there is more than one of these operators in an expression, they are executed from left to right.
- All of the addition and subtraction operators in an expression will happen last. If there is more than one of these operators in an expression, they are executed from left to right.

Let's reconsider our confusing example and follow the operator precedence rules to find the right answer!

```
int confusing = 12 + 12 / 3;
```

Since we know division operators have a higher precedence than addition, the "12 / 3" clause will execute first resulting in a value of 4. Then we have "12 + 4" remaining which equals 16.

Now let's take a look at another example:

```
int result2 = 4 * 3  + 2 * 2;
```

We know the multiplication operations will execute before the addition. We also know the multiplications will occur from left to right. So the steps the program will take to calculate an answer are:

4 * 3 + 2 * 2	This is the original expression
12 + 2 * 2	The first multiplication from the left happens first
12 + 4	The second multiplication from the left happens next
16	Finally, the addition occurs to arrive at our result

As you can see, a complicated expression can be difficult to read. To overcome this, you can use parentheses to override normal precedence and add some clarity. Any part of an expression enclosed in parentheses is executed as a unit before combining the result with operations outside of the parentheses. This is true no matter what operator is used in the parentheses. Let's change an earlier example by adding some parentheses:

```
int result1 = (12 + 12) / 3;
```

The parentheses in this expression will completely change the result! Now the segment in the parentheses (12 + 12) is evaluated first, resulting in 24. This value is then divided by 3 for a final result of 8.

Here is another prior example that we've changed by adding parentheses:

```
int result2 = 4 * (3  + 2) * 2;
```

The addition in the parentheses will execute before the result can be used in the multiplication steps.

4 * (3 + 2) * 2	This is the original expression
4 * 5 * 2	The expression in parentheses must be resolved before being combined with others
20 * 2	The first multiplication from the left happens next
40	The second multiplication from the left happens next, giving our final result

See what a difference a single set of parentheses can make?

Shortcuts

There are many times when you want to use a variable in an expression and then store the result of the expression in the same variable. For instance, you may want to add 1 to your variable, or subtract 2 from your variable. You could code a series of statements like this:

```
int i = 5;
i = i + 1;
i = i - 2;
i = i * 4;
i = i / 2;
```

This process can get a little tedious, especially when your variable name is long. Instead, you can use a cool little shortcut by combining the math operator with the equals sign. This method will actually use the variable as the first operand in the expression. Here are the statements above, re-written with the shortcut style:

```
int i = 5;
i += 1;                 // same as i = i + 1
i -= 2;                 // same as i = i - 2
i *= 4;                 // same as i = i * 4
i /= 2;                 // same as i = i / 2
i += (4 * 3 - 2)        // same as i = i + (4 * 3 - 2)
```

Notice how much simpler the statements are with the shortcuts!

One of the most common math functions is the addition or subtraction of 1 to a variable. Since it is so common, the C# language has a built-in shortcut operator for each operation.

The increment operator is "++". When you use this operator, it will add 1 to your variable.

```
int i = 5;
i++;        // i now equals 6
i++;        // i now equals 7
```

The decrement operator is "--". When you use this operator, it will subtract 1 from your variable.

```
int i = 5;
i--;        // i now equals 4
i--;        // i now equals 3
```

Lesson Two: .NET Framework Math Functions

The .NET Framework includes an object called **System.Math**, which contains many useful math constants and functions. To use this object, just include the basic **System** namespace with the following line:

```
using System;
```

Then you can use the **Math** object functions and constants by just using the name "Math" followed by the dot operator (.) and any of the available functions and constants.

Math Constants

The **Math** object contains a couple of useful constants. The first constant, **`Math.PI`** represents the all-important value of PI (3.14159...). PI is the ratio of a circle's circumference to its diameter. This value is important for many geometric and trigonometric calculations. Another useful constant is the value of natural log base "e" (2.7182…). This value is used to calculate logarithms. The following example shows how to use one of the **Math** constants in an expression calculating the circumference of a circle from the diameter:

```
double myDiameter = 3.0;
double myCircumference = Math.PI * myDiameter;
```

Math Functions

The **Math** object contains many useful math functions. For a full list of these functions, you can check the MSDN documentation. We show the more common functions in the table below.

Function	Description
Abs(X)	Returns the absolute value of X (removes any negative sign)
Ceiling(X)	Returns the lowest integer greater than or equal to X
Floor(X)	Returns the highest integer less than or equal to X
Max(X,Y)	Returns X or Y, whichever is larger
Min(X,Y)	Returns X or Y, whichever is smaller
Pow(X,Y)	Returns X raised to the Y power
Round(X)	Returns X rounded to the nearest integer
Sqrt(X)	Returns the square root of X (which must be positive!)
Sin(X), Cos(X), Tan(X),	These trigonometric functions all operate on angles in radians
Atan(X), Acos(X), Atan(X)	These trigonometric functions all return angles in radians

Now let's take a look at some examples using these functions:

```
int positive = Math.Abs(-2);              // returns 2
double ceiling = Math.Ceiling(2.5);       // returns 3.0
double floor = Math.Floor(2.5);           // returns 2.0
int max = Math.Max(2, 5);                 // returns 5
int min = Math.Min(2, 5);                 // returns 2
double pow = Math.Pow(2, 3);              // returns 8.0
double round = Math.Round(2.4);           // returns 2.0
double sqrt = Math.Sqrt(12);              // returns 3.4641...
double sin = Math.Sin(Math.PI / 2.0);     // sin(90 degrees) returns 1.0
```

Note that some versions of the math functions take and return integers, while others take and return real numbers (**double**, **float**, etc). You can usually find a version of the function you want to use that matches your variable's data type.

Lesson Three: A Simple Calculator

Now let's use some math operators to create a simple calculator program! Start the Visual C# IDE and create a new project called "Calculator". Use the property sheet to change the **(Name)** of the form to **CalculatorForm** and the **Text** of the form to "My Calculator".

This calculator will be a simplified version of the calculator program that you probably have on your computer. We will use a label control to display the numbers the user has entered, a button for each of the numbers from 0 – 9, and then create some buttons that will add, subtract and solve the equation.

When your form is completed, it should look like the image on the right. We are using a **Label** control at the top instead of a text box. We have changed the label's **BackColor** property to "White" and its **BorderStyle** property to "FixedSingle". This makes it appear as a text box control, but will prevent the user from entering numbers directly into the control. We will add the numbers to the label as the user presses the number keys.

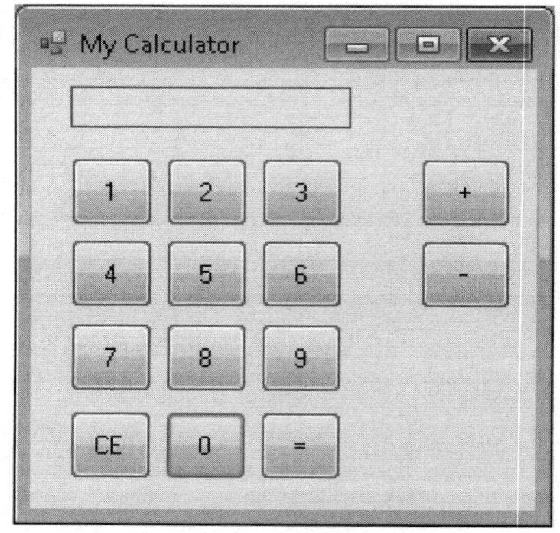

Don't forget to save your project as you go along. Use "Calculator" as the project and solution name when prompted the first time you save into your "My Projects" working directory.

To make your form look like the image shown above, complete these steps in your project now:

- Add a label control named **NumberLabel**. Set the **BackColor** property to "White" and the **BorderStyle** property to "FixedSingle". Also set the **AutoSize** property to **false** so you can drag the label box to a large enough size. Finally, clear all text from the label's **Text** property.
- Add 10 square buttons, named **Button1**, **Button2**, etc. Set the **Text** property for these buttons to be "1", "2", etc., and arrange them in the pattern that you see above.
- Add a square button named **ClearButton** with the text: "CE".
- Add a button named **AddButton** with the text: "+".
- Add a button named **SubtractButton** with the text "-".
- Add a button named **EqualButton** with the text: "=".

Next, double-click on the button for the "1" digit to create the **Button1_Click()** event handler function. In this function, add one line of code underneath the opening curly brace:

```
private void Button1_Click(object sender, EventArgs e)
{
    NumberLabel.Text += "1";
```

This appends the number "1" to the end of the text in the **NumberLabel**. Now complete similar event handler functions for the rest of your numeric buttons, adding the appropriate digit in each function.

After you have completed all 10 number button event functions, double-click on the "CE" button. This will bring up the code window with the **ClearButton_Click**() event handler. To clear the label display, add this line of code to reset the text in the **NumberLabel** back to blank:

```
NumberLabel.Text = "";
```

Now we need to write the code that will add and subtract our numbers. The first thing we will do is add two **int** variables and two **bool** variables to the top of our program. Bring up the code window, and add the following code at the top of your **CalculatorForm** class:

```
public partial class CalculatorForm : Form
{
    int firstNum = 0;
    int result = 0;
    bool addButtonFlag = false;
    bool subtractButtonFlag = false;
```

The **firstNum** variable will hold the first number the user enters, and **result** will hold the result of our calculations. The boolean variables will tell us whether the user has chosen to add or subtract the numbers. Notice that all of these variables are declared at *class* scope, meaning they are not locally defined within a function but belong to the class as a whole. These variables will therefore be accessible from any of the class functions and "live" as long as the class does.

Now you can double-click on the button with the "+" sign to bring up the code window for the "**AddButton_Click()**" event handler. The first thing we need to do is make sure that the user has entered a number. So, add an **if**() statement to verify that the contents of the **NumberLabel** control are not blank:

```
private void AddButton_Click(object sender, EventArgs e)
{
    if (NumberLabel.Text != "")
    {
```

If it is not blank, we can pull the value of the label into our **firstNum** variable, clear out the **NumberLabel**, and set the **buttonAddFlag** value to **true**. We will describe the **int.Parse**() function in a later chapter, but for now just understand that the function will convert a numeric string to an actual numeric data type!

```
        firstNum = int.Parse(NumberLabel.Text);
        NumberLabel.Text = "";
        addButtonFlag = true;
    }
```

If the value of **NumberLabel** is blank, we should tell the user to enter a number:

```
    else
    {
        MessageBox.Show("You must enter a number!");
    }
} // end of AddButton_Click
```

Now create an event handler and add the same sort of logic for the button with the (-) subtraction operation:

```
private void SubtractButton_Click(object sender, EventArgs e)
{
    if (NumberLabel.Text != "")
    {
        firstNum = int.Parse(NumberLabel.Text);
        NumberLabel.Text = "";
        subtractButtonFlag = true;
    }
    else
    {
        MessageBox.Show("You must enter a number!");
    }
}
```

Next let's add some code to our "CE" button event handler. This button will be used to clear the values in the **firstNum** and **result** variables and to clear any text from the **NumberLabel**. We will also set our button flags back to **false**. You can double-click on the "CE" button to bring up the **ClearButton_Click()** event handler and then add the following code:

```
private void ClearButton_Click(object sender, EventArgs e)
{
    result = 0;
    firstNum = 0;
    NumberLabel.Text = "";
```

```
    addButtonFlag = false;
    subtractButtonFlag = false;
}
```

Now we need to make the calculator actually perform some calculations! Double-click on the "=" button to bring up the **EqualsButton_Click()** event handler. Then add another check to make sure that the user has entered a second number:

```
private void EqualsButton_Click(object sender, EventArgs e)
{
    if (NumberLabel.Text != "")
    {
```

If the text value is not blank, then we can create a local variable called **secondNum** and pull the text from the label into the variable, like this:

```
        int secondNum = int.Parse(NumberLabel.Text);
```

Now use an **if()** statement to see if the user wants to add or subtract the two numbers. If the value of **addButtonFlag** is **true**, then we will add the two numbers. Otherwise, if the value of **subtractButtonFlag** is **true**, we will subtract the two numbers:

```
        if (addButtonFlag == true)
        {
            result = firstNum + secondNum;
        }
        else if (subtractButtonFlag == true)
        {
            result = firstNum - secondNum;
        }
```

Finally, send the value of the **result** variable back to the **NumberLabel** so the user can see the answer:

```
        NumberLabel.Text = result.ToString();
    }
}
```

That's it! Now you should have a real, working calculator program. You can only use two numbers at a time, but otherwise it's a neat little program. You'll be working with this project again in the chapter activity.

Chapter Review

- *Math operators* allow you to add, subtract, multiply, divide, and find the remainder (modulus).
- The math operator symbols are "+", "-", "*", "/", and "%".
- *Operator precedence* is the order in which multiple math operators are processed in an expression.
- The use of parentheses in an expression can change the operator precedence and make the expression easier to understand.
- Variables can be easily incremented or decremented by 1 by adding a "++" or a "--" to the end of the variable name in a statement.
- The **System.Math** object contains some useful constants, like the value of PI.
- The **System.Math** object also contains some very useful functions, like **Round**() (for rounding numbers), **Abs**() (for finding the absolute value of a number), and **Sqrt**() (for finding the square root of a number).

Activity: Divide and Multiply

In this activity you will create multiply and divide operations for the Calculator program we wrote earlier in the chapter.

Your activity requirements and instructions are found in the "Chapter_07_Activity.pdf" document located in your "TeenCoder\Windows Programming\Activity Docs" folder. You can access this document through your Student Menu or by double-clicking on it from Windows Explorer.

Complete this activity now and ensure your program meets the requirements before continuing!

Chapter Eight: Working With Strings

We previously introduced **strings** as a data type that can hold a line of text. **Strings** are very common variable types that most programs will need to use. In this chapter we take a closer look at **strings** and the methods you can use to transform, format, and convert them.

Lesson One: Common String Operations

Recall when we discussed the numeric data types that each C# type (**int**, **double**, ...) has a corresponding .NET Framework object (**System.Int32**, **System.Double**, ...) , and that the C# types and .NET framework objects can be used interchangeably. The **string** data type works the same way with a corresponding **System.String** object. The **System.String** object contains many common utility functions that allow you to easily compare, append, and retrieve information for any **string** variable.

String Properties

A very useful property on the **String** object is **Length**. The **Length** property will tell you how many characters are currently in the string.

```
string myString = "abc";
int length = myString.Length;      // length is set to 3
```

When the statements above are executed, the **length** variable will contain a value of 3, since there are 3 letters in **myString**. The **Length** property is read-only, which means you cannot set the length of a string with an assignment statement.

```
string myString = "abc";
myString.Length = 12; // ERROR:  Cannot set read-only property
```

Accessing Individual Letters in a String

Each letter in a string is given a numeric value, called an *index*, by the compiler. This value is zero-based, which means that the first letter in a string is letter number 0, the second is number 1, the third is number 2, and so on. In order to access an individual letter in a string, you can use the index value between a set of square brackets after the string variable name. So, if you wanted to read the fifth letter in a string called **myString**, you would use the following code:

```
char myLetter = myString[4];
```

String Methods

Over time a very large number of useful **string** methods have been created. The .NET Framework **System.String** object has dozens of methods to do different things. We'll describe the more common methods here and you can refer to the MSDN documentation if any more unusual methods are needed. Often a method will have a number of optional parameters that can guide the behavior.

System.String Function	Description
Equals(X) **Equals(X, StringComparison)**	Returns **true** if **string** X is equal to the current **string** object. By default this is a case-sensitive comparison. You may perform a case-insensitive comparison by specifying **StringComparison.OrdinalIgnoreCase** as the second parameter.
IndexOf(X)	Returns the index of the first instance of **string** or **char** X within the current **string**, or -1 if not found
LastIndexOf(X)	Returns the index of the last instance of **string** or **char** X within the current **string**, or -1 if not found
Replace(X,Y)	Returns a new **string** where all instances of sub-string or **char** X in the current **string** have been replaced by sub-string or **char** Y.
Substring(X,Y)	Returns a new **string** copied from the current **string** starting at index X and running for Y characters
ToLower()	Returns a new **string** where the contents of the current **string** have been converted to all lower case. The original **string** is unchanged.
ToUpper()	Returns a new **string** where the contents of the current **string** have been converted to all upper case. The original **string** is unchanged.

Now let's take a look at some examples using these functions. We will start with the following **string** variables in our examples:

```
string myString1 = "gobbledy";
string myString2 = "gook";
string myString3 = "GOOK";
```

The **Equals()** function is used to see if two strings are equal to one another. By default this function is case-sensitive. To see if two strings are equal with a case-insensitive check, add the parameter **StringComparison.OrdinalIgnoreCase**.

```
bool result1 = myString1.Equals(myString2); // result is false
bool result2 = myString2.Equals(myString3); // result is false
bool result3 = myString2.Equals(myString3,
                    StringComparison.OrdinalIgnoreCase); // result is true
```

The **IndexOf()** function is used to determine where a character or substring is in a **string**. Remember that the first character in a string is always index "0"! For instance, the following line will return a value of 1, since the letter "O" is at index 1 in **myString3**.

```
int result4 = myString3.IndexOf('O');              // result4 = 1
```

The **LastIndexOf()** function is used to find the last instance of a character in a string. This is useful when you believe there might be more than once instance of a character in a string, and you are looking for the last instance. In this example we find the last "O" in **myString3** at index 2:

```
int result5 = myString3.LastIndexOf('O');          // result5 = 2
```

You can search strings for characters (with single quotes) as demonstrated above, or entire substrings (with double quotes). For instance if we wanted to find the substring "bb" in **myString1** we could do this:

```
int result6 = myString1.IndexOf("bb");             // result6 = 2
```

The **Replace()** function creates a new string, starting with a source string and replacing all the instances of one character with another character, or one substring with another substring. The following line creates a new string, replacing all of the "o" characters with the letter "a". **myString2** itself remains unchanged!

```
string result7 = myString2.Replace('o', 'a');   // result7 = "gaak"
```

The **Substring()** function is used to pull out a segment of a string. This function will start at a given index in the string and will copy a certain number of characters. In the following code, the **Substring()** function will pull out 2 characters from **myString1**, starting at the second letter.

```
string result8 = myString1.Substring(2, 2);      // result8 = "bb"
```

The **ToUpper()** and **ToLower()** functions will create new strings from a source string, turning all of the characters to upper or lower case. The original contents of the source string are unchanged!

```
string result9  = myString1.ToUpper();            // result9  = "GOBBLEDY"
string result10 = myString3.ToLower();            // result10 = "gook"
```

Using Special Characters in a String

Escape characters allow you to put something in a string that would be hard to type in or represent otherwise. For example, tab characters, carriage returns, and linefeeds are difficult to represent in a text string. Also, some characters like the double-quote can't be entered directly because the C# language uses them to mark the beginning and end of the string. How would you write a string that contains a double quote as one of the characters? You could not output a string like this:

```
MessageBox.Show(" " ");    // this is a compile error
```

The compiler would not understand where the string stops (second quote or third?). To represent these special characters you need to use escape characters.

Escape characters start with a backslash (\) and finish with one letter. These two characters are translated by the compiler into a single character and then stored in the output string. For example, the string: "\n" is a string of length 1 that holds the "new line" character. This causes your output to skip down to the next line.

Here is a list of common escape characters and some sample usage:

Escape Character	Description	Sample Code	Output
\a	Alert – make your PC beep	**MessageBox.Show**("Bell:\a ");	**Bell: (plus beep)**
\n	New Line	**MessageBox.Show**("New line:\n#");	New line: #.
\r	Carriage Return	**MessageBox.Show**("Carriage return:\r#");	Carriage return: #
\t	Horizontal Tab	**MessageBox.Show**("Tab:\t#");	Tab: #
\'	Single Quote (')	**MessageBox.Show**("Single quote: \'");	Single quote: '
\"	Double Quote (")	**MessageBox.Show**("Double quote: \"");	Double quote: "
\\	Backslash (\)	**MessageBox.Show**("Backslash: \\");	Backslash: \
%%	Percent (%)	**MessageBox.Show**("Percent: %%");	Percent: %

Note that the "new line" and "carriage return" symbols can produce basically the same effect, which is to insert a line break and force the next character to start on a new line. Depending on how you plan to use the string, you may need to use one symbol or the other, or even both in combination like "\r\n".

Lesson Two: Formatting Strings

There are times that you will want to create a **string** based on variable parameters. You may also want to carefully guide how numbers in the string look – specifying the number of digits, decimal precision, monetary symbols, and so forth. The **System.String** object has a **Format**() method that allows you to very flexibly build a new string with variable parameters.

The syntax of the **String.Format()** function looks like this:

```
String.Format("<composite format string>", parameter0, parameter1, …);
```

The composite format string can contain a mixture of fixed text and formatting text. Each formatting text item is a numeric index surrounded by curly braces like this: {0} or {1}. The numeric index is a zero-based index and refers to a specific parameter given to the function. So {0} refers to "parameter0" and {1} refers to parameter1, and so forth. The **Format**() function will replace the numeric index in the format string with the contents of the parameters.

In the following example, the {0} refers to the first parameter **myName**.

```
string myName = "Billy";
string formatted1 = String.Format("hey there {0}", myName);
```

The resulting string contains the phrase: "hey there Billy". You can have as many formatting items and matching parameters as you would like in a **Format()** statement. The following example shows a statement with two pairs of formatting items and parameters:

```
int myAge = 18;
string myName = "Billy";
string formatted2 = String.Format("{0} is {1} years old", myName, myAge);
```

The resulting string for this example contains the sentence: "Billy is 18 years old". You can also use the same parameter more than one time in a **Format()** function statement:

```
string dance = "Boogie";
string formatted3 = String.Format("{0} {0}!",dance);
```

The resulting **formatted3** string contains the phrase: "Boogie Boogie!"

In addition to specifying the data that will be placed in a string, the formatted item (i.e. "{0}") can contain an optional format string. This format string will give you even more control over exactly how the individual items are constructed. To add a format string, append a colon (":") after the numeric index, and then add the format string before the closing curly brace. For example, "{0:F}" tells **Format()** to insert the parameter data AND format it into a floating point (decimal) format.

There are many different built-in format strings that can format numbers, date and times. We will cover the number formats here (as they are the most commonly used). For more details on the more unusual format strings, you can refer to the MSDN documentation.

Format String	Example	Description
C or **c**	**String.Format**("{0:C}", 12.4); // returns "$12.40"	Formats the number as a currency, with a dollar sign in the US or other symbols in other countries.
D or **d**	**String.Format**("{0:D}", 12); // returns "12"	Formats the integer number as a decimal string
E or **e**	**String.Format**("{0:E}", 12.4); // returns "1.240000E+001"	Formats the number in scientific (exponential) notation.
F or **f**	**String.Format**("{0:F}", 12.4); // returns "12.40"	Formats the floating point number in decimal notation
N or **n**	**String.Format**("{0:N}", 1200); // returns "1,200.00"	Formats the number to a decimal string, thousands separator (a comma in the US; other countries may use another separator).
P or **p**	**String.Format**("{0:P}", 0.12); // returns "12.00 %"	Formats the number as a percent
X or **x**	**String.Format**("{0:X}", 12); // returns "C"	Formats the number as a string of hexadecimal (base-16) digits

The actual symbols used for currency, the thousands separator and other cultural-specific text are chosen by the operating system based on your computer's cultural setting. The "**C**" or "**c**" format string may format a number into dollars, pounds, lira, etc. depending on your Windows settings. These settings can be viewed or changed in the Windows Control Panel – just look for something called "Regional and Language Options".

Many of the examples in the chart above use formatting strings to control numbers which have decimal places. If you want even more control over these numbers, you can modify the format string to specify how many decimal places are shown for a number. To do this, you just place the number of digits that you would like at the end of the format string:

```
String.Format("{0:N4}", 1200); // returns "1,200.0000"
String.Format("{0:N0}", 1200); // returns "1,200"
```

The number of digits can be specified for the "**N**", "**C**", "**P**", or "**F**" format strings.

Another (optional) feature of the format string is the alignment indicator, which is a comma followed by a number. This indicator will specify the minimum width of the output field. This can be used to easily align columns of numbers on the screen. If the specified width is positive then the text is right-aligned. If the width is negative, the text is left-aligned. If the data width is smaller than the string, the alignment indicator is ignored. The text will not be truncated to fit the specified width.

```
String.Format("#{0,5}#", "abc");     // returns "#  abc#"
String.Format("#{0,-5}#", "abc");    // returns "#abc  #"
String.Format("#{0,5}#", "abcdefg"); // returns "#abcdefg#"
```

ToString() Formatting

You can convert a numeric value to a string and format it in the same step by using the **ToString()** method with some special parameters. This method is very useful for quick and powerful number-to-string conversions. Let's take a quick look at some of these types of formatting conversions:

We will assume that we are working with the following variable:

```
double myNumber = 12.5648;
```

Here is a list of possible **ToString()** parameters that we can use on this value:

- **Fx** – Format the number to "x" number of decimal places and then convert the result to a string.
- **C** – Format the number to a currency value and then convert the result to a string.
- **Dx** – Format the number to "x" number of digits and then convert the result to a string. If the number has more digits than the "x" number, the digits will be truncated. If the number has less digits, the number will be padded with zeros at the beginning of the string.
- **P** – Format the number to a percentage value and then convert the result to a string.

Here are some examples using the **ToString()** format parameters:

```
double myNumber = 12.5648;
myString = myNumber.ToString("F2"); // myString = "12.56"
myString = myNumber.ToString("C");  // myString = "$12.56"
myString = myNumber.ToString("D3"); // myString = "012"
myString = myNumber.ToString("P");  // myString = "12%"
```

These parameters are very useful when you need to quickly format a numeric value into a string.

Lesson Three: Converting Between Strings and Numbers

There are often times when you need to convert a **string** variable to a number or a numeric variable to a **string**. The C# language makes both of these operations very easy!

To convert any data type to a **string**, you can simply call the **ToString()** method on the variable as we discussed in the last lesson. This function will return a **string** representation of whatever data is in the variable. Every data type in C# contains this very useful method, even simple integers (**System.Int32**)!

```
int myInt = 42;
string myString1 = myInt.ToString();     // myString1 = "42"

bool myBool = false;
string myString2 = myBool.ToString();   // myString2 = "False"
```

If you want more fine-grained control over the string that **ToString()** returns, you can use the format strings described in the last lesson.

```
int myInt = 42;
string myString3 = myInt.ToString("N2"); // myString3 = "42.00";
```

To convert a **string** to another data type, you can use the **Parse()** method on the data type. **Parse**() will convert an input **string** to that data type if possible.

```
string myString1 = "42";
string myString2 = "true";
int myInt1 = int.Parse(myString1);    // myInt1 = 42
bool myBool = bool.Parse(myString2); // myBool = true
```

If, for any reason, the **string** cannot be converted to the data type that you have chosen, an error will occur! If you are not sure the input **string** can be converted correctly you should consider using the **TryParse()** method instead. As you might expect from the name, **TryParse**() will attempt to convert a string just like the **Parse**() method, but errors are handled differently.

TryParse() is an example of a *static* method, which is a method you call directly on the data type without a variable instance. The syntax looks like this:

```
bool <data type>.TryParse(<input string>, out <variable to update>);
```

The data type is any of the standard types like **int**, **double**, etc. The first parameter is the input **string**. The second parameter is the variable where you want the resulting converted data to be stored. Notice the second parameter is preceded by the keyword **out**, which indicates that the function can change the parameter value. The **bool** return code from **TryParse()** will be **true** if the conversion was successful, or **false** otherwise. You can check the return code to see if the conversion was good and not have to worry about an error getting thrown on failure.

```
int myInt1;
bool success1 = int.TryParse("8675304", out myInt1);

int myInt2;
bool success2 = int.TryParse("true", out myInt2);
```

In the first case the input string is a number, so **success1** will be set to **true** and **myInt1** will contain the resulting number. In the second case the conversion was unsuccessful because the input string "true" is not an integer. So the **success2** variable will contain **false** and **myInt2** will not be changed.

Chapter Review

- The .NET Framework object for the C# **string** type is called **System.String**.
- The **Length** property on **System.String** contains the number of characters in the **string**.
- Each character in a string is represented by a numeric index, starting at 0 for the first character.
- The **System.String** object contains many useful functions for manipulating **strings**.
- The **String.Format()** method is used to create a new **string** from variable parameters.
- Formatting strings give you fine control over how variable parameters are represented in the output **string**. You can control the number of output digits, data type, monetary formats, and alignment.
- To convert any data type to a **string** value, you can use the **ToString**() method.
- To convert a **string** to another data type, you can use the **Parse**() method. If the conversion fails an error will be thrown.
- To convert a **string** to another data type without throwing an error on failure, use the **TryParse**() method instead.

Activity: Caesar's Cipher

In this activity, you will create a program that will transform a line of text using an encoding algorithm called "Caesar's Cipher" (invented by Julius Caesar himself). This algorithm is a simple substitution where one character is directly replaced by another character or set of characters.

Your activity requirements and instructions are found in the "Chapter_08_Activity.pdf" document located in your "TeenCoder\Windows Programming\Activity Docs" folder. You can access this document through your Student Menu or by double-clicking on it from Windows Explorer.

Complete this activity now and ensure your program meets the requirements before continuing!

Chapter Nine: Methods

In this chapter, we will be taking an in-depth look at the creation and use of methods (or functions). Methods are used in programs to eliminate repetitive code and to create an easy-to-follow, streamlined program.

Lesson One: Writing and Calling Methods

We have already used methods many times in this course. We created **Click**() event handler methods to process button clicks, used the **ToString**() method to translate data into strings and called the **Parse**() method to translate strings into numbers. In this lesson you will learn how to write your own methods!

A method is useful when you have a task that may need to be performed many times during a program. For instance, you may need to compute the area of a circle at several points in your program. Would you want to write the code to perform this calculation several times? Or would you want to create a single block of code that you can use over and over? The latter option is much easier to write and maintain. A *method* is a block of code that is created once and then can be called from different places in your program.

Methods Belong to a Class

In some other languages a method is referred to as a "function" or a "subroutine". In fact, these terms are nearly interchangeable. A method is really just a function that belongs to an object or class. Since all C# code belongs to a class, functions in C# are called methods. When you create a method, be sure to define it between the opening and curly braces that define your entire class, and nowhere else!

```
namespace Example
{
    // method definitions CANNOT go here, outside of a class

    public partial class ExampleForm : Form
    {
        // method definitions MUST go here, inside of a class
        public void myMethod()
        {
            // new method definitions CANNOT go here, inside another method
        }
    }
}
```

Method definitions should not be nested inside each other or outside of the class entirely. It's important to carefully manage and align your curly braces so it's easy to see where class and method bodies start and stop.

Creating and Using Methods

Here is a simple example method that will make the computer beep:

```
void makeBeep()
{
    Console.Beep();
}
```

Let's take a look at this code in more depth. The first line is the method declaration:

```
void makeBeep()
```

This line tells the compiler that we are creating a method called **makeBeep()**. The keyword **void** means that this method will not be returning any value to the calling code. The parentheses after the method name can include an optional list of parameters. The **makeBeep()** method does not have any parameters. We'll talk more about return types and parameters in the next lesson.

After the method declaration, we have a set of curly braces with one line of code inside:

```
{
    Console.Beep();
}
```

This is the *body* of the method. Any code within the curly braces will be executed every time the program calls this method. In our method, we have only one line: **Console.Beep()**. This will just make the computer beep one time and then the method will exit. Our example is very simple, but you can imagine that most functions have more complex bodies with multiple lines of code. You can also call other functions from within the function body. We will get into some more complicated methods in the next couple of lessons.

Function Naming Rules

You must follow certain rules when creating your method names. First, the method's name must consist only of lowercase or capital letters, numbers and underscores ("_"). The first symbol in your method name must always be either a letter or an underscore. Here are some examples of valid and invalid function names:

```
void myFunction();
void MyFunction();
void my_function();
void _test();
void A1();
void 1A();  // ERROR - numbers cannot be first
void A 1(); // ERROR - no spaces allowed
```

Notice that the function name **1A** is not a valid function because the name starts with a number and "**A 1**" is not valid because it contains a space.

You should always remember that method names are case sensitive. The method named **MyFunction**() is different than a method named **myfunction**(). It's not a good idea to define multiple methods in your program distinguished only by case in the name! These methods will be easily confused.

Lastly, it is easiest to read your code if you pick one naming style and stick with it throughout your program. If you decide to capitalize the first letter of every word in your method name (**MyFunction**()), do this for all your methods. If you decide to capitalize the first letter of every word except the first (**myFunction**()), be consistent. You could also decide to use all lowercase letters to name your functions (**myfunction**()) or to separate the words with underscores (**my_function**()). If you are consistent, other programmers who have to look at your code will thank you later!

Lesson Two: Method Parameters and Return Values

In the last lesson we showed you an example method with a **void** return value and no parameters. If you want to write more powerful and flexible methods, you need to learn how to use parameters and return values.

Method Parameters

It is often very useful to *parameterize*, or provide external data, to your method body. For instance, if you have a method that calculates the area of a triangle, the method will need to know the base and height length. You would use method *parameters* to give this input data to the method body. Method parameters are data that you *pass into* your method from the calling code. The definition of a method with parameters looks like this:

```
void myMethod(<data type 1> <parameter 1 name>, …)
{
    // function body here
}
```

Notice that the declaration of the function parameters looks a lot like the declaration of any other variable, except that multiple parameters are separated by a comma, not a semicolon. Each parameter has a data type (e.g. **int**) and a parameter name (which is just a variable name). You can use these parameters just like variables within the method body.

Let's look at an example method that will calculate the area of a triangle:

```
void calculateTriangleArea(double base, double height)
{
        double result = 0.5 * base * height;
        MessageBox.Show("Your area is: " + result.ToString());
}
```

The first line declares a method called **calculateTriangleArea()** that takes two parameters: a **double** variable called **base** and another **double** called **height**. Whenever this method is called, or used, from your program, you will need to provide these two parameters in order for the method to work.

You can see that our function body has only two statements: the area calculation and a **MessageBox.Show()** statement that shows the result to the user in a pop-up window. The parameters **base** and **height** are used just like any other variable in our program. Passing data into methods gives them greater flexibility.

Function Return Values

Another optional method feature is the *return value*. Return values are data that a method can return to a calling program. For instance, our **calculateTriangleArea()** function could just **return** the result instead of displaying it on the screen. This would allow us to use the result in some other calculation. To return a value, replace the **void** keyword in front with the data type that will be returned. For instance, here is our **calculateTriangleArea** method rewritten to return the result of the calculation:

```
double calculateTriangleArea(double base, double height)
{
      double result = 0.5 * base * height;
      return result;
}
```

The method return type can be any valid data type (e.g. **char**, **int**, **float**, **string**) including object references.

As always, after you declare your method, you must implement the body of your method. The difference now that we are using a return type is that the method *must* use the **return** keyword to send the result back to the calling program. When you are ready to leave your method and return to the caller, you use the **return** keyword to end your method and pass back the specified data.

A **return** statement looks like this:

```
return <expression>;
```

This is an extremely simple statement, but there are some key things to remember: First, the expression that you return must evaluate to the same data type you put in front of your method name. Don't declare a method with a return type of **int** if you are going to return a **double**. Your expression may be very easy (e.g. just a variable name) or a more complex mathematical expression that will evaluate to the correct data type.

Notice that the **result** variable in our **calculateTriangleArea**() method isn't really used for anything other than returning the data. In this case we could just **return** the expression itself and save ourselves a step. Let's look at an example of this style:

```
double calculateTriangleArea(double base, double height)
{
    return 0.5 * base * height;
}
```

Lesson Three: Calling Methods

Now that we have learned how to create methods, with or without parameters and return values, let's look at how to use these methods in a program. A statement that uses a method is said to be "calling" the method.

Calling Local Methods and Methods on Other Objects

If you are writing code within a class, and you want to call another method defined on that class, you can simply make the function call by using the function name, with opening and closing parentheses.

```
myFunction();
```

If the method is defined on some other object, then you would make that same function call by using the object reference first, then the dot (.) operator, and then the function name:

```
Object result = new Object();
MessageBox.Show("Your answer is: " + result.ToString());
```

Above we have demonstrated calling both *static* methods (like **MessageBox**.**Show**()) where you just need the name of the class, and calling *non-static* methods (like **ToString**()) where you need an actual object reference to a live object in order to call the method. We'll explore static vs. non-static concepts in detail later!

Using Return Values

If a method returns a value you may use that value in a number of ways from the calling code. Consider the following function which returns an integer (ignoring the body).

```
int myFunction(int p1)
```

What can you do with the **int** return value? Well, you may ignore it completely by simply calling the function and not saving the result:

```
myFunction(42);
```

You might also assign the result to a variable, or use the result as part of a larger expression:

```
int myData1 = myFunction(42);
int myData2 = 3 * myFunction(42);
```

You can even use the returned value as a direct input parameter to another function! Notice in the example below the **ToString**() method is called on the **int** data value returned by **myFunction** using the dot (.) operator. Then that result is combined with another **string** as a parameter to **MessageBox**.**Show**().

```
MessageBox.Show("The result is " + myFunction(42).ToString() );
```

A method that has a **void** return type cannot be assigned to a variable or used as part of an expression. Instead, it must be executed on its own line. **myFunction**() below has a **void** return type.

```
void myFunction(double param)
{
}

void callingFunction()
{
    myFunction(2.0);                  // OK
    int result = myFunction(2.0);     // ERROR - void return type
}
```

Calling Methods with Parameters

Calling a method that does not have a return value or any parameters is very simple; just place the method name with opening and closing parentheses on a statement line, followed by the semicolon.

```
myMethod();
```

Calling a method that has parameters is slightly more complicated. When you call a method with parameters, you must pass a list of values that exactly matches the number, order, and data type of the parameters as they are declared in the method itself. The values will be separated by commas. If your parameters do not match, the compiler will generate an error on that method call and your program will not build.

Each value you specify when calling a method may be a simple hard-coded value, a variable name, or an expression evaluating to the correct data type. For example, with our **calculateTriangleArea()** method, we could pass hard-coded numbers for the **base** and **height**, or we could pass a couple of **int** type variables with values assigned to them. Both of these method calls do the same thing:

```
int base = 3;
int height = 4;

calculateTriangleArea(3,4);
calculateTriangleArea(base, height);
```

Since our parameters match the declared data types (two **ints**), these method calls will compile with no errors.

Ordering of Parameters

In addition to the number of parameters, you must pay attention to the *order* of the parameters in the method. The compiler doesn't care what variable names you may pass in, it only knows the expected order of parameters. The compiler takes the first value that you pass into the method and assigns it to the first parameter. The second value that you pass is used as the second parameter and so on. Always remember that it is the *order* of the parameters that are important, not the names.

You don't need to worry about matching the names of your parameters in your functions. It's the *order* of the parameters that really matters. If your function needs a string and then an integer, make sure you pass in a string and integer in that order!

Let's take a look at an example of this key concept:

```
double divide(double dividend, double divisor)
{
      return dividend / divisor;
}
```

We have defined a simple division method. The first parameter is the **dividend** and the second parameter is the **divisor**. When calling this method, be careful not to get the parameters in the wrong order:

```
double dividend = 4.0;
double divisor = 2.0;

// This is NOT a compile-time error.  The compiler just knows you have
// satisfied the input parameter list with two doubles.  There is no
// way of knowing what you intended.  There is no matching done on the
// variable names!
double result = divide(divisor,dividend);   // WRONG ORDER!

MessageBox.Show( dividend.ToString() + " / " + divisor.ToString() +
          " = " + result.ToString() );
```

Our method requires the **dividend** to be first and the **divisor** to be second, however when we called the method above we mistakenly reversed the order! This is a common mistake because the compiler has no way to warn you. As long as the number, order, and type of the input parameters match the method, it is a valid statement. The names of variables in the calling code have no relationship to names of variables within a method!

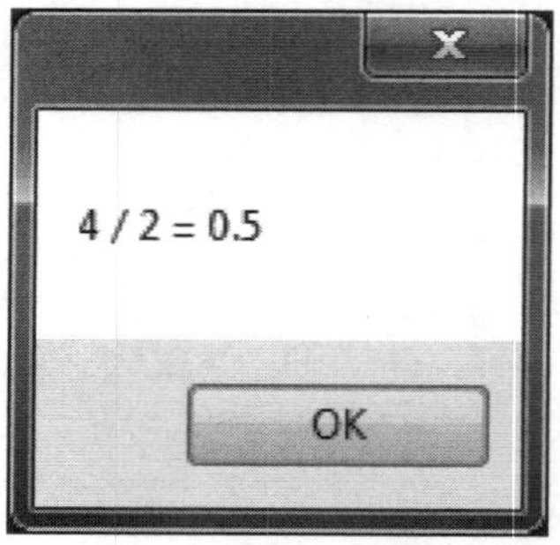

4 / 2 = 0.5

OK

In this case, the method will return unexpected results. Of course we know that 4 divided by 2 is not 0.5. We did not get a compile-time error, or a run-time error, but we observed that the program results were incorrect.

Parameters Passed by Value

One last note on calling methods with parameters: if the parameters in your method are value data types (**int**, **float**, **double**, etc.) then they are passed to your method *by-value*. When you use these values inside the method body, you are using *copies* of the value of that data. You may change the value of the copy inside the function body, but that will not change the original variable contents from the calling program, even if the variable names are the same!

For example, we will define a method called **myFunction()** that takes one parameter: **`param1`**.

```
void myFunction(int param1)
{
        param1 = 3;
        MessageBox.Show("param1 inside function = " + param1.ToString());
}
```

Then from our calling code we first define a variable **`param1`**, assign it a value, and pass that variable into the **myFunction()** method.

```
int param1 = 2;
myFunction(param1);
MessageBox.Show("param1 outside function = " + param1.ToString());
```

Now let's look at what happens to **`param1`** before and after this method is called. First we set its value as 2. We then call **myFunction()** and pass it our **`param1`** variable. Once the method has completed, we will display the value of **`param1`** again and see if it has changed. This example would give the following output:

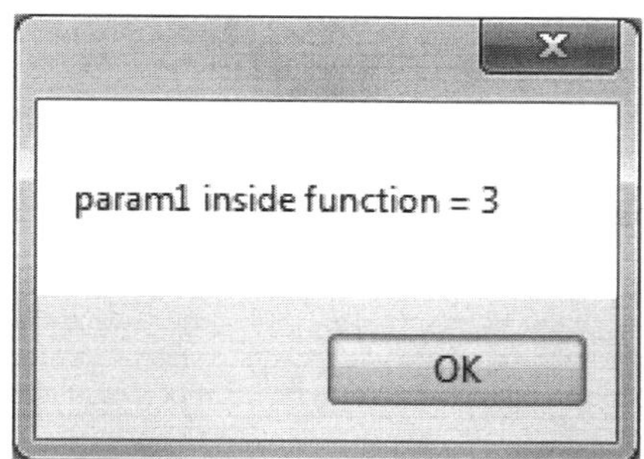

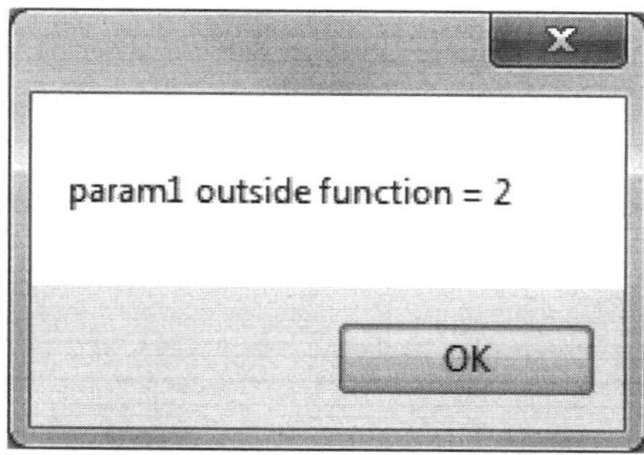

As you can see, even though the parameter **`param1`** was changed inside the method, the original variable **`param1`** outside the method was not changed.

Modifying Parameter Values

All of the function examples we have seen so far pass the method parameters "by-value" to the method body, meaning the function body actually gets a copy of the variable and cannot change the original. It is possible (and sometimes very useful) to define a method that can change the input variables from the calling code! To do this you use the **out** keyword before the data type in the method declaration. You already saw this briefly when we discussed the **TryParse()** method in the previous chapter. Let's define our own version of **TryParse()** so you can see how the **out** keyword works.

```
bool TryParse(string text, out int result)
{
        // function body goes here
}
```

Notice that we have defined the second parameter with the **out** keyword. This means that the function body is not using a copy of the input variable. Instead it is using the actual variable and any changes inside the function body will be reflected in the variable in the calling program!

```
int myResults = 0;
TryParse("42", out myResults);
```

After the method returns, **`myResults`** will have been modified inside the method body.

You can use as many **out** parameters as you like in a method. Sometimes your method may need to return far more data than a single return value can handle! **Out** parameters and normal by-value parameters can be declared in any order, though by convention the **out** parameters tend to be put last in the parameter list.

When you are implementing a method body that has received one or more **out** parameters, you are *required* to set those parameters to some value before the method returns. The compiler will show an error if you don't!

Chapter Review

- Methods are blocks of code that can be written once and then called many times in a program.
- The block of code within a method is known as the method *body*.
- Methods are also known as functions or subroutines, especially in other languages.
- A method name must start with either a letter or an underscore and contain only letters, underscores, or numbers.
- Method names are case-sensitive.
- You can call a method defined on the same class as the calling code with just the method name.
- You can call a method defined on another object by using either the object class name or object reference and the dot operator (.) before the method name.
- A method parameter is a piece of data that is passed into a method.
- A return value is a piece of data that is returned from a method to the calling program.
- The order of parameters is very important when calling a method. The parameters must be passed in the order that the method is expecting.
- Most method parameters are passed by-value, which means a copy of the data is passed and the method body cannot change the original variable.
- The **out** keyword is used before the parameter in a method to indicate the method body may change the original variable in the calling code.

Activity: What's Your Birthday?

In this activity you will create a program that implements a simple method. Your program will tell the user what day of the week they were born on, according to their birth date.

Your activity requirements and instructions are found in the "Chapter_09_Activity.pdf" document located in your "TeenCoder\Windows Programming\Activity Docs" folder. You can access this document through your Student Menu or by double-clicking on it from Windows Explorer.

Complete this activity now and ensure your program meets the requirements before continuing!

Chapter Ten: Debugging and Exceptions

In this chapter you will learn how the IDE can help you find problems in your program at runtime. You will also learn some advanced techniques for error handling within your program.

Lesson One: The Visual C# 2010 Express Debugger

A *debugger* is a program that will let you observe and analyze your program as it is running. The Visual C# 2010 Express IDE contains an integrated debugger that is very easy to use. The debugger will let you walk step-by-step through each line in your program and observe your program as it runs. This is an extremely powerful tool. While you are observing the running program, you can make sure the program is working as you expect. This includes making sure the statements are executing in the correct order and even watching the contents of your variables to make sure the data is being processed and stored correctly.

Program States

While you are running your program in the debugger your program will be in one of two states: *running* or *in break*. When your program is in a running state it is executing normally. This is not the most useful state for debugging, since the program is moving too fast to watch the statements execute or the data change. When you put your program in break mode, you are essentially *pausing* your program so that you can see exactly what values are in your variables. The debugger knows the complete state of the program, including what statement is about to be executed and what data is contained in all variables. While in break mode the debugger will highlight the statement that is *about* to be executed. The previous statement has already been executed and the one that is highlighted will be executed next.

Debugging Commands

While your program is in break mode you can use several debugging commands. These commands will allow you to execute a specific line of code, step over or into a method body, or run the program normally.

Run or Continue	If your program is not running, this command will start running your program in the debugger. If you are already debugging the program and are in a break state, this command will put the program back into the running state. The program will run until it reaches the end of the program or until a breakpoint is reached (we'll discuss breakpoints in a minute).

Step Over	This command tells the debugger to execute the currently highlighted statement, including any method calls without stepping into any method bodies. Afterwards the program will remain in break at the next statement.
Step Into	This is similar to the "Step Over" command, but if the next statement contains a method call, you will switch into the method body, still in break mode, so you can examine the method body. If your program is not yet running, executing "Step Into" will put the program in the debugger in break mode, starting at the beginning of your program.
Step Out	If you are already stepped into a method body, this command will finish executing the entire body and transfer control back to the point where the method was called. Afterwards the program will remain in break at the next statement after the method call
Stop	The "Stop" command will completely terminate your program; no more statements will be executed. You can then edit or modify your code, build, and run it again.

These commands can be found under the "Debug" menu while in break mode and have function-key hotkeys for easy access.

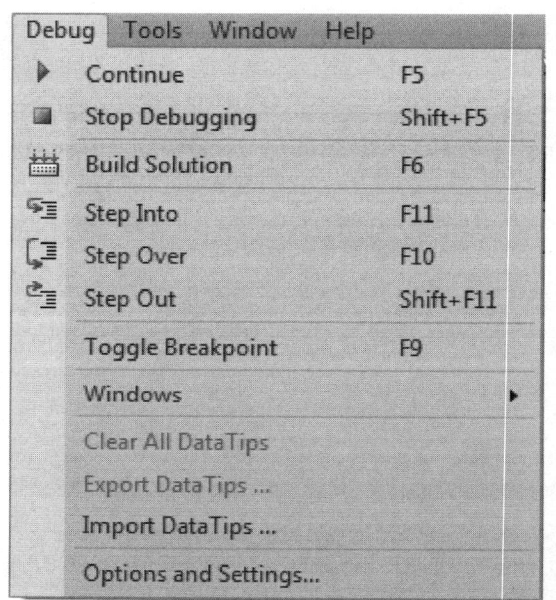

Breakpoints

A *breakpoint* is a place in the code where you want the debugger to stop and put the program in a break state. When the program is paused you can view the data in your variables at that precise point in the program.

You should always set breakpoints as close as you can to where you believe a problem exists. This will allow you to view the important data processing steps without having to wade through the entire program.

How to use the Debugger

Once you have put your program into a break state, you will be shown the code window. A yellow arrow will appear beside the next statement to be executed. At this point, you can use the debugging commands to advance the program, or you can take a look at any of the variables that are currently in use.

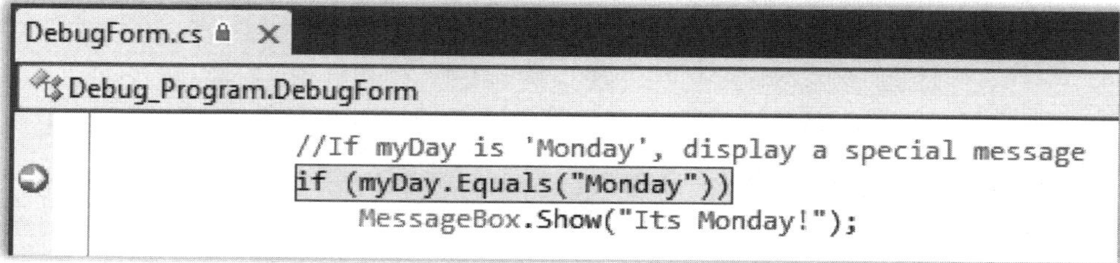

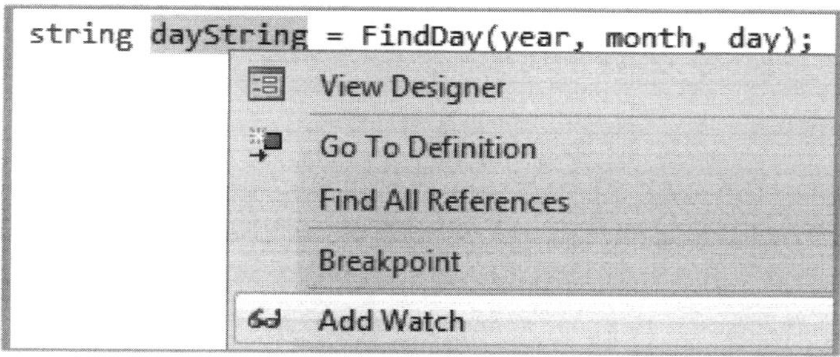

To examine the data contained in a variable, you can hover the mouse over the variable name or set a *watch*. To set a watch, right-click on the variable name and then select "Add Watch" from the menu.

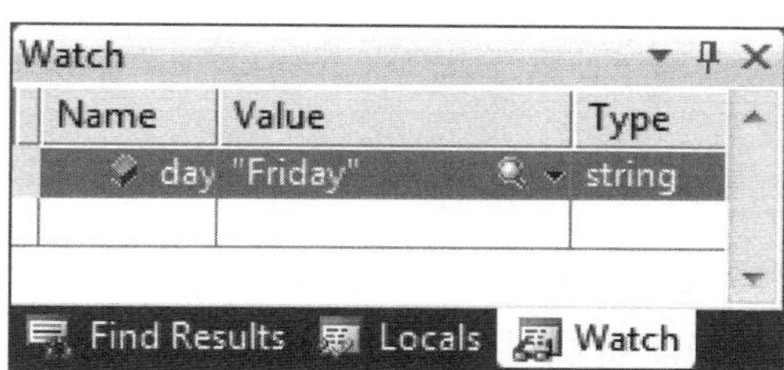

This will place the variable in the "Watch Window" at the bottom of the screen. Then you can watch the variable's value change as the lines of code are executed.

Lesson Two: Debugging Demonstration

In this lesson we will use the debugger to walk through a program. We will be using the "Debug Program" that is located in your "\TeenCoder\Windows Programming\Activity Starters" directory. Use Windows Explorer to copy this entire "Debug Program" directory from the "Activity Starters" folder to your "My Projects" folder. This program contains a single error, which we will find using the debugger.

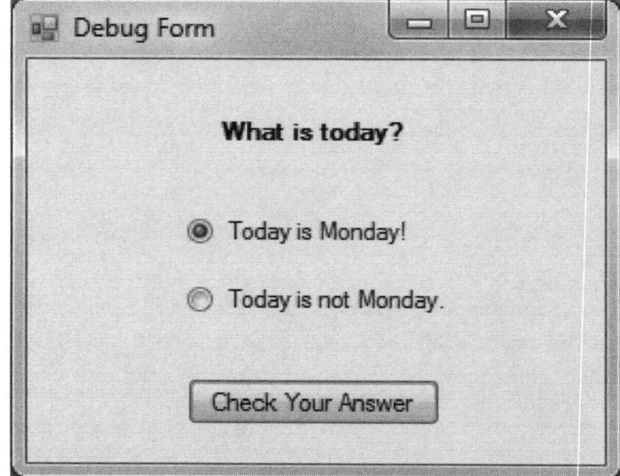

Run the Visual C# 2010 Express software and then open the "Debug Program" from your "My Projects" directory. This is a simple and somewhat silly program, but it does contain an error! The goal of the program is to ask the user if today is Monday or not, and then check their answer to see if it is correct based on the current date.

Once you have the project loaded, look at the program code. Select the "DebugForm.cs" source file and view the code. The code we're interested in can be found in the **ErrorButton_Click**() method.

```
private void ErrorButton_Click(object sender, EventArgs e)
{
    //Create a string variable
    string myDay = null;

    //Create a date/time variable and initialize to current date and time
    DateTime currentDate = DateTime.Now;

    //If the 'NoErrorRadio' button is selected
    if (NoMondayRadio.Checked == true)
        //Set myDay to the current day of the week
        myDay = currentDate.DayOfWeek.ToString();

    //If myDay is 'Monday', display a special message
    if (myDay.Equals("Monday"))
        MessageBox.Show("Its Monday!");

    else //if myDay is not Monday, just display the day
        MessageBox.Show("The current day is: " + myDay);
}
```

The program creates a string variable called **`myDay`** and a **DateTime** variable called **`currentDate`**. The value of **`currentDate`** is set to the current date and time. The program then checks to see if the radio button called **`NoMondayRadio`** is selected. If it is, the value of **`myDay`** is set to the current day of the week. Then we check to see if the current day is Monday, and we display one of two messages to the user, depending on whether or not today is Monday.

Can you tell where the error is going to occur? Let's see what happens when we run the program in the debugger. Start debugging your program by selecting "Debug → Start Debugging" from the IDE menu, or just hit the "F5" key. If you choose the "Today is Monday!" and click on the button, you will see an error:

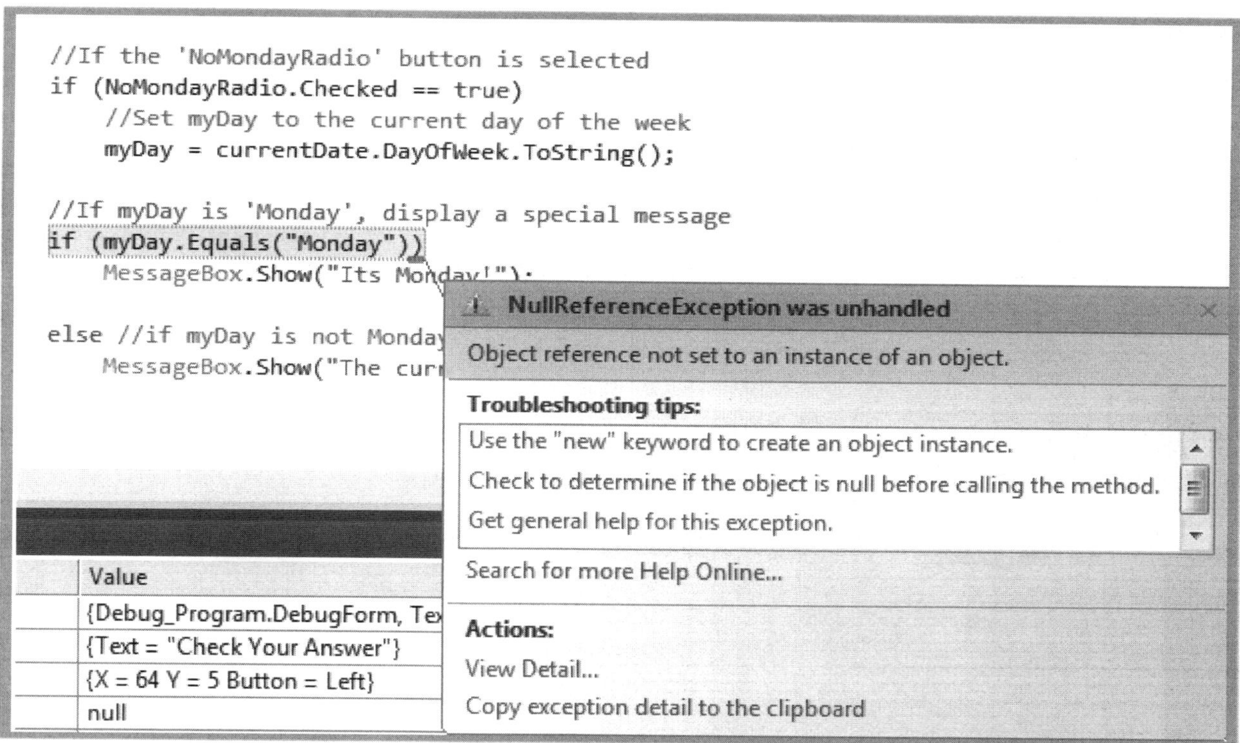

Once the program causes an error, the debugger will put the program in break mode and highlight the line of code where the error occurred. The debugger will also display some useful information about the error on the screen. In our case, the highlighted line is:

```
if (myDay.Equals("Monday"))
```

The error that has been created is called a "Null Reference Exception". The debugger even gives us a description of this error ("Object reference not set to an instance of an object") and a list of possible solutions in the "Troubleshooting Tips" section.

Let's take a look at the "Troubleshooting Tips" that we have been given. The first tip tells us that we may need to use the **new** keyword on our object. The second tip asks us to make sure the object is not **null** before we call a method on it. Since we do have an object (**`myDay`**) and we are calling a method (**Equals()**), this could be our problem. To know for sure, stop the program by clicking on the "Debug" menu and then choosing "Stop Debugging", or just hit the Shift+F5 keys together. Now place your cursor on the highlighted line and set a breakpoint. You can set a breakpoint by clicking on the "Debug" menu and choosing "Toggle Breakpoint" or by hitting the F9 key. Once you have a breakpoint set, your code window should show a red circle to the very left edge and your statement highlighted in red:

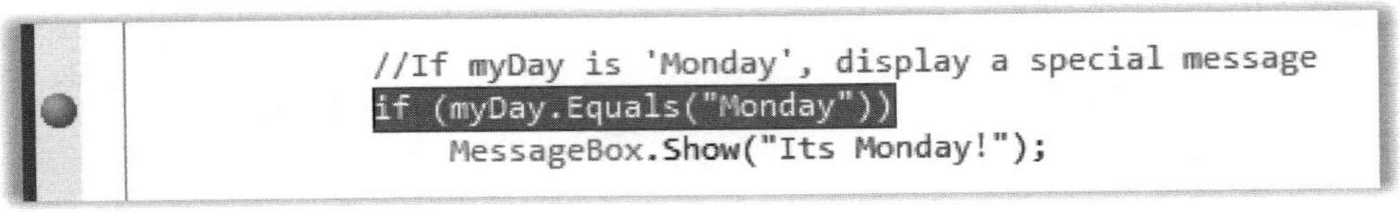

```
//If myDay is 'Monday', display a special message
if (myDay.Equals("Monday"))
    MessageBox.Show("Its Monday!");
```

Our program will now pause when it gets to the highlighted line of code. Now run the program again in the debugger and click on the "Check Your Answer" button again. The program will pause and show the code window when it gets to the breakpoint:

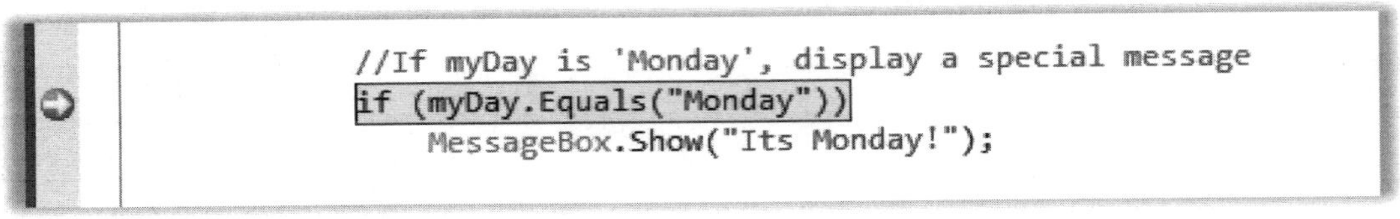

```
//If myDay is 'Monday', display a special message
if (myDay.Equals("Monday"))
    MessageBox.Show("Its Monday!");
```

The highlighted line of code *has not been executed* yet. Now we can check to see if our **myDay** variable is **null**. Hover your mouse over the word **myDay** and you will see a small pop-up window appear with the current value of this variable:

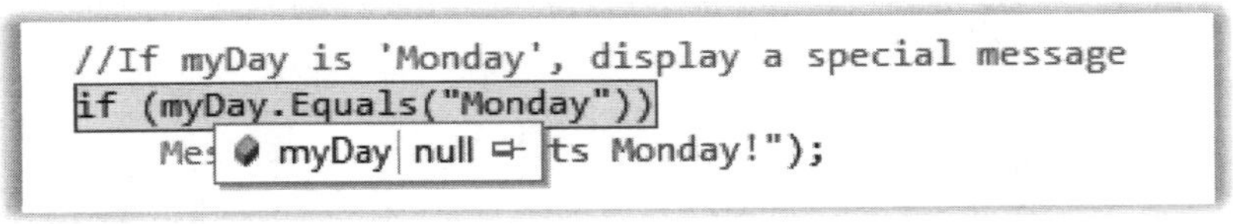

```
//If myDay is 'Monday', display a special message
if (myDay.Equals("Monday"))
    Me[ myDay | null ]ts Monday!");
```

You can also take a look at the "Locals" frame at the bottom of the code window. This frame will show all of the current values for the method's variables:

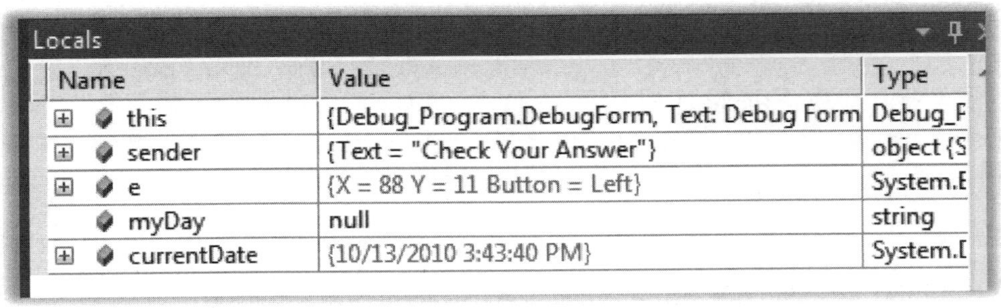

Locals

Name	Value	Type
this	{Debug_Program.DebugForm, Text: Debug Form	Debug_F
sender	{Text = "Check Your Answer"}	object {S
e	{X = 88 Y = 11 Button = Left}	System.E
myDay	null	string
currentDate	{10/13/2010 3:43:40 PM}	System.[

In both instances, the answer to our problem should be clear. The value of **myDay** is **null**! Now we can take a look at our code and try to figure out why this variable has not been initialized. If you look at the code again, you will see that we only initialize the value of **myDay** if the radio button called **NoMondayRadio** is checked.

If this radio is not checked, the value of **myDay** remains **null** and we cause an error when we try to run the **Equals**() method on a **null** variable.

To fix this error, stop debugging and remove the **if**() statement before the initialization of **myDay**. Your code should now look like this:

```
private void ErrorButton_Click(object sender, EventArgs e)
{
      //Create a string variable
      string myDay = null;

      //Create a date/time variable and initialize to current date and time
      DateTime currentDate = DateTime.Now;

      //Set myDay to the current day of the week
      myDay = currentDate.DayOfWeek.ToString();

      //If myDay is 'Monday', display a special message
      if (myDay.Equals("Monday"))
           MessageBox.Show("Its Monday!");

      else //if myDay is not Monday, just display the day
           MessageBox.Show("The current day is: " + myDay);
}
```

Now when you run the program, the error should be gone!

Debugging is a critical skill! As your programs get more complex, errors may not be obvious from code review alone. Your first response whenever a program does not behave correctly at runtime is to set a breakpoint and step through the code in the debugger. In most cases this will make the cause of the problem obvious.

Lesson Three: C# Runtime Exceptions

In some languages, when an unexpected error like "divide by zero" occurs, the whole program can crash in a spectacularly uncontrolled manner. While this is mildly entertaining, (especially when it is not *your* program that has crashed), the creators of the C# language have worked hard to eliminate this type of meltdown.

In the C# language, an unexpected error will cause (or "throw") an *exception*. Exceptions are errors that cause a program to change its normal program flow. This means that the code statements that occur after the thrown exception will not be executed. Instead, the program will pop-up a warning message on the screen. This message will appear whether you are running in the debugger or running in normal execution mode, and will describe the nature of the error. You will then have a choice of closing the program, attempting to continue to program or getting more detailed information.

Here is an example of an exception being thrown by a program:

```
int bottom = 0;
int top = 1;

// the next line raises a divide-by-zero exception
int result = top / bottom;
```

Now, of course you know that in the world of mathematics, you cannot divide any number by zero. The same is true for computer programming. Any attempt to divide a number by zero in a program will always generate an error. In our case, C# will throw an exception.

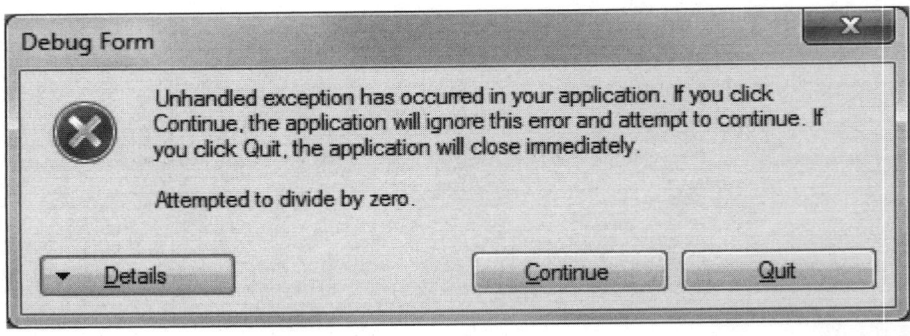

If you click on the "Details" button, you will probably see the specific location of the error. This is typically the source file name and the line number where the error occurred. This is usually a *great* debugging tool, since now you know exactly where your program went wrong. In addition, you have the error description in the popup display so you know what kind of error was generated!

In addition to the "Details" button, you have a choice of "Continue" and "Quit". If you click on the "Continue" button, your program will attempt to continue. Typically a program will not run very well after an exception is thrown, but you can always try! If you click on the "Quit" button, the program will end immediately. This is a much easier and cleaner way to end a misbehaving program. You can then either debug the program or try to run it again.

Try and Catch

An exception pop-up is not a very friendly way to inform the user of an error! Instead, the C# language has a built-in way to handle exceptions in a much gentler manner.

This method is called "try and catch". The keyword **try** is used to mark any statements that might possibly cause an exception. The statements are enclosed in a set of curly brackets that follow the **try** keyword.

```
try
{
    // any statements that could cause an exception are entered here
}
```

This block of code is followed by a **catch** block. The **catch** block is a series of statements that will be executed if an exception is thrown from within the **try** block. These statements are also enclosed in a set of curly braces. A catch block looks like this:

```
catch (System.Exception ex)
{
   // these statements will only execute if there is an exception thrown
   // in the try block above
}
```

The **catch** block will specify the type of error that it is designed to trap. Typically, this will be the **System.Exception** error, but it could be other error types as well. You can use a series of **catch** blocks to handle several different error types. However, the **System.Exception** is the most common exception and is the only error we will handle in this course.

Here is an example of a **try** and **catch** block of code:

```
try
{
  // Any Exception that happens within this try block will cause program
  // flow to immediately transfer to the beginning of the catch block.
  int bottom = 0;
  int top = 1;

  // the next line throws a divide-by-zero exception
  int result = top / bottom;
}
catch (System.Exception ex)
```

```
    {
      // get the error description from the Exception
      string error = ex.Message;

      // Display nicer error to the user
      MessageBox.Show(error, "Oops you goofed!");
    }
```

Inside the **catch** parentheses you specify the exception type like **System.Exception** and a variable name. This is just like a parameter to a function! You can use the exception variable within your **catch** block to pull some useful information. You can give the **System.Exception** error variable any name you would like in the catch statement. Short names like "e" or "ex" are conventionally used.

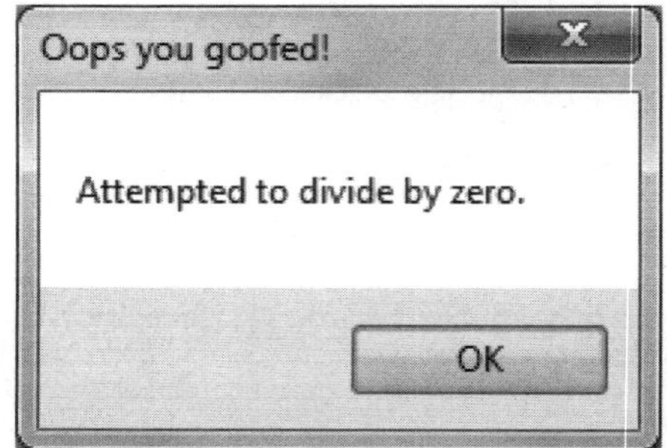

The **System.Exception** variable has a property called **Message**. This property will give you a description of the error that caused the exception. If you want to give the user some information about what caused the error, you can easily use this information in a **MessageBox** as shown above. The pop-up that will be displayed by our **catch** block is shown to the right. The **Message** value we pulled from the exception object is "Attempted to divide by zero."

The **try** and **catch** blocks are very useful whenever you have a section of code that is complicated, risky, or subject to bad user input (like a calculator program where a user could attempt to divide by zero). Wrapping these types of code blocks in **try** and **catch** blocks make error handling friendlier and debugging much easier.

Chapter Review

- Programs have two possible states in the debugger: *running* and *in break*.
- The *break* state is the most useful for debugging an application.
- A *breakpoint* is a place in the code where you can tell the program to pause when reached.
- When a program is paused, you can look at all the variables that are currently in use in the program.
- In the C# language, an unexpected error will cause an "exception".
- Exceptions will cause the program to stop and display a window explaining the error and give the user the option of closing the program.
- Exception handling allows a misbehaving program to shut down nicely.
- The C# language has a built-in way to handle exceptions from within a program.
- The **try** and **catch** statements allow a programmer to "try" a risky code section and then "catch" an exception if one occurs.
- The **try** statement is followed by a block of code that is to be "tried" by the program.
- The **catch** statement is followed by a block of code that will execute if the code in the "try" block causes an exception
- The **catch** block receives an exception object like **System.Exception**. The **System.Exception** variable has a **Message** property that contains a nice text description of the error.

Activity: Divide By Zero

When we created the "Calculator" project in Chapter Seven, we left in one hidden bug! If you run the program and try to divide any number by zero, the program will throw an exception. In this activity you will track down the problem using your debugging skills, use a **try-catch** block to catch the error and give the user a meaningful error message.

Your activity requirements and instructions are found in the "Chapter_10_Activity.pdf" document located in your "TeenCoder\Windows Programming\Activity Docs" folder. You can access this document through your Student Menu or by double-clicking on it from Windows Explorer.

Complete this activity now and ensure your program meets the requirements before continuing!

Chapter Eleven: Collections

In this chapter we will learn about data structures that allow you to easily store groups or collections of data together under one variable name.

Lesson One: Arrays

Arrays are data structures that contain a group of individual elements accessed by a numeric index. Each element of an array must have the same data type. An array can be defined for any valid data type such as **int**, **float**, **string**, or more complex objects. All of the elements in an array are kept side-by-side in a single block of memory. For an array with "N" number of elements, the index will start at 0 and run to "N-1".

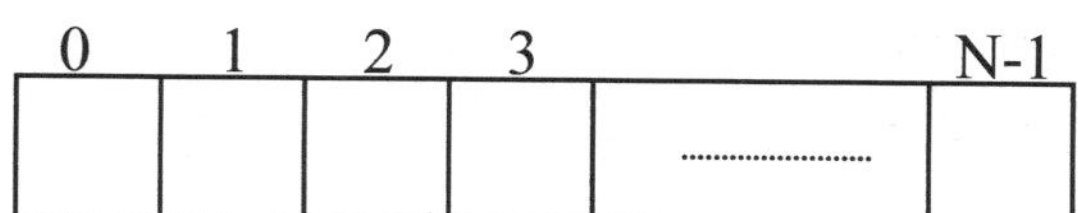

In your program arrays are represented by variable names, just like individual data types. To declare an array instead of a single variable you use square brackets after the data type like this:

```
int[] myArray;
```

Array variables are actually reference data types, even if the elements they contain are simple value types like **int**! The array variable initially contains a **null** reference and any attempt to use it before initializing will result in an error! Before using the array you will need to take an extra step and initialize the variable with the **new** keyword. The **new** keyword is used to tell the compiler to allocate (or reserve) memory for the array depending on the array size. In this example we initialize an array with 10 elements using the **new** keyword:

```
myArray = new int[10];
```

Just like any other variable, you can both declare and initialize the array in one line of code:

```
int[] myArray = new int[10];
```

Because array variables are always references, you can assign different arrays to the same variable over time. When you assign another array to a variable, all of the contents of the original array are forgotten.

```
int[] myArray = new int[10];  // start with a 10-element array
myArray = new int[20];        // replace with a 20-element array
```

In the above example, the initial contents of the **myArray** array are lost when the second line is executed.

When initializing an array, the data type after the **new** keyword must match the variable's declared type. For instance, the following would create a compiler error:

```
int[] myArray = new float[10];  // ERROR: float doesn't match int!
```

Arrays in C# are accessed by an integer index. The first element in any array is index 0. The last element is always equal to the size of the array – 1. For example, consider the following array:

```
int[] myArray = new int[3];
```

This will create a 3-element array of integers. The first element in the array is index 0, and the last element is 3-1, or index 2. To get or set the value of individual elements in the array, use the element index within square brackets after the array name like this:

```
int[] myArray = new int[3];
myArray[0] = 42;          // set 1st element = 42
myArray[1] = 641;         // set 2nd element = 641
myArray[2] = -23;         // set 3rd element = -23
int value = myArray[0]; // read the 1st element
```

C# will carefully check indexes used to access array elements when a program executes. If you try to use a bad index (an index that does not exist) the program will raise an exception at runtime.

```
myArray[3] = 100;        // ERROR – no element at index 3
```

Multi-Dimensional Arrays

An array in C# can be either one-dimensional or multi-dimensional. So far all of our examples have been one-dimensional, meaning the elements are conceptually in a line accessed by a single index. A multi-dimensional array has additional dimensions, each represented by a separate index. The same rules for zero-based index access apply to each dimension. You can create multi-dimensional arrays easily by adding a comma between the dimensions like this:

```
int[,]  myArray2 = new int[3, 3];      // 3 x 3 grid
int[,,] myArray3 = new int[2, 2, 2];  // 2 x 2 x 2 cube
```

The first array (**myArray2**) has two dimensions. A two-dimensional array can be viewed as a grid, like a tic-tac-toe board or a data spreadsheet. A 3-by-3 array will therefore have 9 total data elements. The second array (**myArray3**) has three dimensions. A three-dimensional array can be visualized as a cube, with one index in each of the dimensions. A 2-by-2-by-2 array will have 8 data elements.

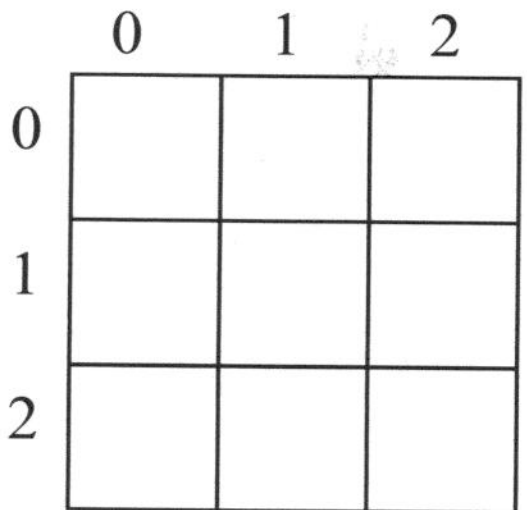

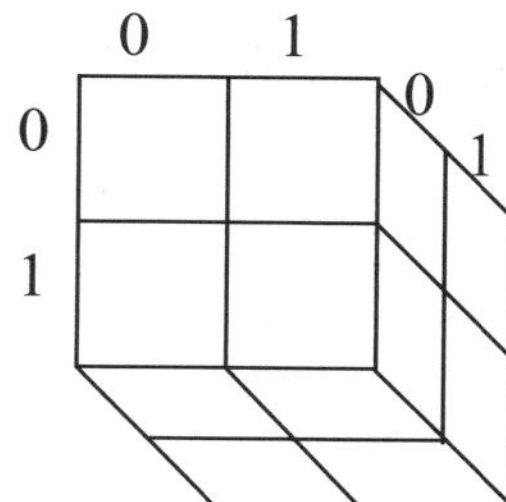

To access elements in a multi-dimensional array, use as many indexes as you have dimensions. Separate each index with a comma:

```
int[,,] myArray4 = new int[2, 2, 2];
myArray4[0,0,0] = 1562;
myArray4[0,0,1] = 12;
// etc...
myArray4[1,1,1] = 683;
```

Initializing Arrays

To initialize each element of an array when you declare it, just put the desired values in curly braces after the **new** operation. If you have multiple dimensions, separate each set of curly braces with commas.

```
int[] myArray5  = new int[3] { 50, 51, 52 };
int[,] myArray6 = new int[2, 2] { {0,1}, {2,3} };
```

You can declare and initialize an array with any number of dimensions, just extend the patterns shown above.

Array Methods

All array variables in C# belong to a .NET Framework object, just like any other built-in data type. An array in C# corresponds to the **System.Array** object. This object has several very useful functions, some of which are *static* (called through the data type itself) and some of which are called on array variables.

void Clear(**Array** arr, **int** index, **int** length)	The static **Clear**() function sets elements in the specified array to zero, **false** or **null** (depending on what type of data is in the array). The first element to be cleared is specified by the **index** parameters, and the number of elements to clear from that point is determined by the **length** parameter.
int GetLength(**int** dimension)	The **GetLength**() function will tell you how many elements are in the specified dimension of the array. Use 0 for the first dimension!
void Reverse(**Array** arr)	The **Reverse**() function will reverse the order of the elements in a one-dimensional array.

You can also read the **Length** property to obtain the number of elements in the first dimension.

Here are some example uses of these methods:

```
int[] myArray = new int[3] {1,2,3}; // myArray = {1,2,3}
int length1 = myArray.GetLength(0); // length1 = 3
int length2 = myArray.Length;       // length2 = 3
System.Array.Reverse(myArray);      // myArray = {3,2,1}
System.Array.Clear(myArray, 1, 2);  // myArray = {3,0,0}
```

Iterating Through an Array

Given an array with many elements, how can you access each of the elements? One common way to walk or *iterate* through each element is with a simple **for**() loop. We will start with the following integer array:

```
int[] myArray1 = new int[3] { 50, 51, 52 };
```

Now we can use a **for**() loop to add up all of the elements in the array and then display the result to the user:

```
int sum = 0;
for (int i = 0; i < myArray1.Length; i++)
{
        sum += myArray1[i];
}
MessageBox.Show(sum.ToString());
```

This **for**() loop will start at element 0 ("**i**" = 0)and will continue looping while the variable "**i**" is less than the length of the array. Inside the loop we access the array element at index "**i**" to perform some task (e.g. adding to a sum). Once the loop has completed, the program will show a message box on the screen with the result. Since 50 + 51 + 52 = 153, we will see "153" in the pop-up.

It is very easy to make a "one-off" mistake! This common programming error means your array index in a loop is one-value off from where you wanted it to start or stop. If your test expression was "**i** <= **myArray1**.Length", for example, your loop would go one index too far and run off the end of the array.

Lesson Two: Linked Lists

Arrays are very simple collections where all elements are stored in one contiguous memory block. However there are many other data structures that hold groups of elements in different patterns. Each data structure meets a specific need. In this lesson, we will discuss a collection called a *linked list.*

A linked list is a data structure that can be visualized as a series of elements, called *nodes*, which are connected to each other like a string of beads. Each node contains some data and one or more links to other nodes. There are two main types of linked lists: singly-linked lists and doubly-linked lists.

In a singly-linked list, each node only knows how to reach the next node in the chain:

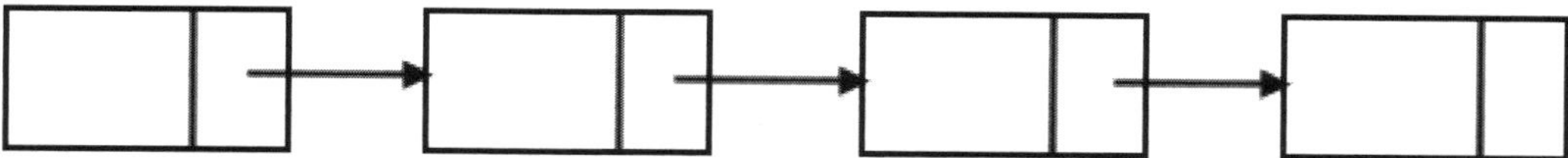

In a doubly-linked list, each node knows how to reach both the next and previous nodes:

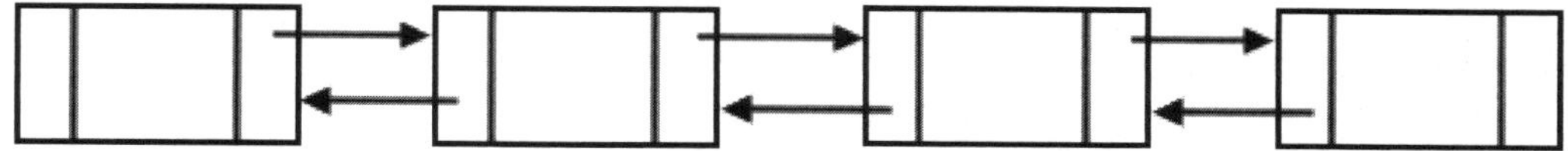

In order to "walk" through the elements in a linked list, you start with the first node in the list and then follow the *next* links until you reach the end of the list. In a doubly-linked list, you can start your "walk" from the first node or the last node and walk either forwards or backwards in the list.

So why would you use a linked list instead of an array? Arrays are perfect when you know exactly how many items of data you will need to store. However, there may be situations where you do not know the exact number of items ahead of time. This is where a linked list comes in handy. A linked list can easily grow over time by adding new nodes to the list to hold new values.

Linked lists are also handy when you need to frequently remove or add values to the list, especially somewhere in the middle. These operations are more difficult with arrays because you would have to re-allocate memory for the entire array and shift the elements around every time you removed or added an item. With a linked list, you can just insert or clip nodes out of the list as you need.

Here is what it would look like (conceptually) to add a node to a singly-linked list:

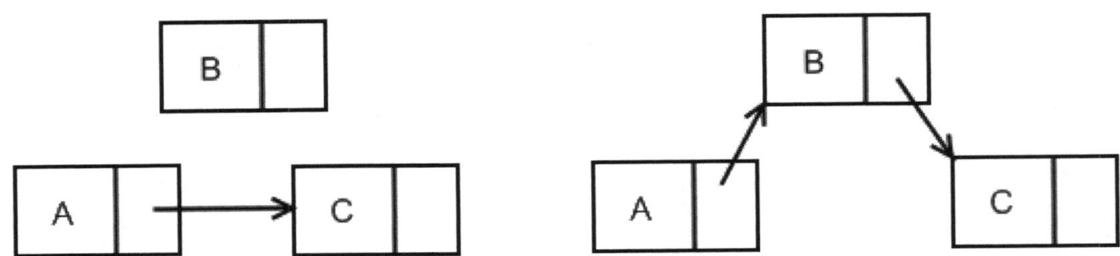

In our first image, we see the existing linked list with two items: item A and item C. We want to place item B in between A and C. To do this, we would need to set the "next" arrow on node A to point to node B. Then we need to set the "next" arrow from node B to node C. Now we have a 3 node list! If we wanted to remove node B, we would just do the opposite, clipping out B by setting the "next" arrow from A to C.

A doubly-linked list is a little bit more complicated. Here is how an insertion would look:

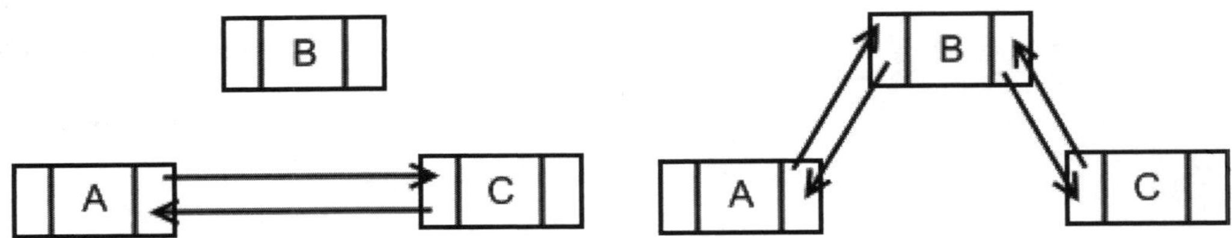

You can see the main difference is that we need two arrows: one for the **next** node and one for the **previous** node. This means that when we add node B, we set the **next** arrow from A to B and then set the **previous** arrow from B to A. We also need to set the **next** arrow from B to C and the **previous** arrow from C to B. To remove node B, we need to do the opposite, returning the arrows from A to C and vice versa.

Sometimes a linked list is not as effective as an array. What if you need to randomly access the nodes in the middle of a list? An array can access these items directly by using the specific index number into the array. A linked list, however, would have to "walk" the entire list until the desired node is reached. This will typically take more time than directly accessing a specific array element by index.

Linked Lists in C#

So now that you understand how a linked list works, let's take a look at the linked list data structure in C#. Linked lists are implemented by the following .NET Framework object:

```
System.Collections.Generic.LinkedList<T>
```

The "<T>" parameter will tell the compiler what type of data will be in your list. This data type can be anything from a simple integer <**int**> to a complex object type.

To use the **LinkedList** data type, first add a **using** statement to the top of your program like this:

```
using System.Collections.Generic;
```

Now you can simply use **LinkedList** as a data type without having to type in the **System.Collections.Generic** portion of the namespace.

Since the **LinkedList** data type is a reference type, you will need to initialize variables with the **new** keyword. For example, to create a linked list of integers called **myList**, we would use the following code:

```
LinkedList<int> myList = new LinkedList<int>();
```

Now we have a linked list of integers to work with in our program! If we wanted to add items to the front of the list, we would use the method **AddFirst**():

```
myList.AddFirst(1); // list = 1
```

Now our list has one item at the beginning of the list: the number 1.

To add items to the end of the list, we can use the **AddLast**() function:

```
myList.AddLast(4);  // list = 1, 4
myList.AddLast(5);  // list = 1, 4, 5
```

Now our list has three numbers: 1, 4, and 5.

When you want to remove items from the front of the list, you can use the **RemoveFirst**() method, like this:

```
myList.RemoveFirst();   // list = 4, 5
```

When you need to remove items from the back of the list, you can use the **RemoveLast**() method, like this:

```
myList.RemoveLast();    // list = 4
```

When you want to remove a specific value from the list, you can use the **Remove**() method, like this:

```
myList.Remove("4");     // list is empty
```

When you need to remove all items from the list in one step, call the **Clear()** method:

```
myList.Clear();          // list is empty
```

LinkedListNodes

As you can see, it's fairly easy to manage data that is on the front or back of a linked list. However, it's a bit more complicated to add or remove items from the middle of a list. To add an item to a list, you would need to walk the list until you find the correct spot for your new item. Then you will need to set the links to both the previous element and the next element in the list, like the illustrations we showed you earlier in the lesson.

The .NET Framework represents one node in the list with a helper object called **LinkedListNode**:

```
LinkedListNode<T>
```

Just like the **LinkedList** object, the **<T>** represented the data type that will be contained in the node. This object contains some very useful methods and properties for dealing with a linked list.

To retrieve the first node in a linked list, we can simply read the **First** property on the list object. To retrieve the last node in a linked list, we read the **Last** property:

```
LinkedListNode<int> firstNode = myList.First;
LinkedListNode<int> lastNode = myList.Last;
```

The **First** and **Last** properties will equal **null** if the list is empty!

The **LinkedListNode** object will allow you to easily navigate to the **Next** or **Previous** nodes in the list:

```
LinkedListNode<int> thisNode = firstNode.Next;       // second node
LinkedListNode<int> anotherNode = lastNode.Previous; // next-to-last node
```

Any time you follow a **Next** or **Previous** link past the end of the list, that **Next** or **Previous** property is **null**!

You can also use the **LinkedListNode** to add more nodes to the list, using the **AddBefore()** or **AddAfter()** methods on the **LinkedList**. Take a look at the following blocks of code. First, we will place 3 items in our list using the **AddLast()** method:

```
myList.AddLast(1);        // list = 1
myList.AddLast(3);        // list = 1, 3
myList.AddLast(5);        // list = 1, 3, 5
```

Now let's obtain the **LinkedListNode** object for the middle node (containing "3"). We can find it from the beginning or from the end of the list...either way works!

```
LinkedListNode<int> middleNode = myList.First.Next;          // "3" node
LinkedListNode<int> anotherNode = myList.Last.Previous;    // also "3" node
```

Now, we can call the **AddBefore**() method on the **LinkedList** to add a new value "before" our target node and **AddAfter**() to add a new value "after" our target:

```
myList.AddBefore(middleNode, 2);     // list = 1, 2, 3, 5
myList.AddAfter(anotherNode, 4);     // list = 1, 2, 3, 4, 5
```

To remove a node from the list, we can easily use the **Remove**() method, like this:

```
myList.Remove(middleNode);    // list = 1, 2, 4, 5
```

Lesson Three: Enumeration and ForEach

Arrays and linked lists are types of *collections*. A collection is a general term for a group of objects without describing exactly how the objects are stored internally. For the array we know the elements are stored side-by-side in a contiguous block of memory. Linked lists and other types of collections behave differently.

The .NET Framework defines a number of very useful collections and related objects in the **System.Collections** namespace. Often you will want to walk through each of the items in a collection without knowing anything about the underlying data structure. To do this you can obtain an *enumerator*, or *iterator* from the collection object. An enumerator is an object that knows how to access each element of the collection from the beginning to the end, without you knowing anything about the details of the collection.

To use an enumerator, you will first need to call a method named **GetEnumerator**() on the collection to obtain a **System.Collections.IEnumerator** object. This object will allow you to easily navigate the collection using some simple methods. Let's see how this would work with an array of integers called **`myArray1`**:

```
int[] myArray1 = new int[3] { 50, 51, 52 };
System.Collections.IEnumerator iterator = myArray1.GetEnumerator();
```

Now we have an enumerator, stored in a variable called **iterator**, which we can use to navigate our array. The enumerator initially points "before" the first element in the collection. To move to the next element in an collection, we use the **MoveNext**() method on the **iterator**. The **MoveNext**() method will return either a **true** or a **false** value. If the value is **true**, this means there are still elements left to look at in the collection. If the value is **false**, then we have reached the end of the collection.

In order to access the value at the current position in the collection, we use the **iterator** property called **Current**. The **Current** property will return the collection value currently pointed to by the enumerator.

Here is how the **MoveNext**() method could be used to walk through an entire collection. We are simply going to add up all of the integer values in the collection:

```
int[] myArray1 = new int[3] { 50, 51, 52 };
System.Collections.IEnumerator iterator = myArray1.GetEnumerator();
int sum = 0;
while (iterator.MoveNext() == true) // continue looping while elements left
{
    int i = (int)iterator.Current;    // get the current element value
    sum += i;
}
MessageBox.Show(sum.ToString());
```

This **while** loop will continue to execute as long as the return value of the **MoveNext**() method is **true**.

You will notice that we had to cast the **Current** property to an integer by using "(**int**)". The **IEnumerator** methods and properties all deal with the root **System.Object** base class, which means that the **IEnumerator** has no real idea of what data is in the collection. In this case to extract the data from the collection we should cast the **Current** property to an **int** before we can add it to our **sum**.

Enumerators are extremely flexible tools for dealing with any type of collection, including the array. You might correctly think that using enumerators for simple arrays is somewhat of a pain when compared to the simple **for**() loop. However some collections like linked lists cannot be efficiently accessed by index, so the enumerator is the best way to go!

"foreach" Loops

One final, convenient way to walk through the elements in a collection is to use a **foreach** command. The **foreach** command is available for all collections, including arrays, and will automatically walk through the collection assigning an automatically type-cast value to a variable. This technique combines the simplicity of a **for**() loop with the flexibility of an enumerator. Let's look at our summation example again, using a **foreach** loop this time:

```
int[] myArray1 = new int[3] { 50, 51, 52 };
int sum = 0;
foreach (int value in myArray1)
{
    sum += value;
}
MessageBox.Show(sum.ToString());
```

The **foreach** syntax begins the **foreach** keyword followed by a set of parentheses. Within the parentheses you first declare a variable with the same data type as the array ("**int value**"), then add the "**in**" keyword, and then add the collection or array variable name (**myArray1**). The **foreach** loop will execute once for each element in the collection.

Each time through the loop the next element in the named collection variable will be stored in the specified variable. The loop hides all the complexity around getting an **IEnumerator** object, calling **MoveNext**(), and casting the element to the correct data type! You can simply use the specified variable to do some work within your loop body. In our example we just add the **value** to our sum.

Note that you cannot *alter* the contents of a collection within a **foreach** loop! The variable receiving the collection data is read-only, so you could not (for example) attempt to set the **value** variable above equal to some other integer data.

Since a **LinkedList** is a type of collection, we can use a **foreach** loop to talk through the values in the list in exactly the same way:

```
LinkedList<int> myList = new LinkedList<int>();
myList.AddLast(1); // list = 1
myList.AddLast(2); // list = 1, 2
myList.AddLast(3); // list = 1, 2, 3

int sum = 0;
foreach (int i in myList)
{
    sum += i;
}
MessageBox.Show(sum.ToString());   // sum = 1 + 2 + 3 = 6
```

Since the **foreach** statement doesn't care what kind of collection it is using, the example works exactly the same way as the **foreach** loop we used to walk through an array!

Chapter Review

- *Arrays* are data structures that contain a group of individual elements.
- Arrays must be created with the **new** keyword, since they are reference types.
- Arrays are zero-based, which means the first element in an array is 0, the second is 1, and so on.
- Arrays in C# can be either one-dimensional (like a list) or multi-dimensional (like a grid or cube).
- The **System.Array** object has some useful functions like **Clear**(), **GetLength**(), and **Reverse**().
- One way to navigate an array is to use a **for**() loop, which accesses each element in sequential order.
- A linked list is a collection of items that are strung together like a string of beads.
- A singly-linked list is a list where each node only knows about the next node in the list.
- A doubly-linked list is a list where each node knows about the next and previous nodes in the list.
- The **LinkedList** object contains many useful methods, like **AddFirst**(), **AddLast**(), **RemoveFirst**(), **RemoveLast**(), **AddAfter**(), and **AddBefore**().
- The **LinkedListNode** object represents one node in a **LinkedList** and can be used to manually walk the list and add or remove items in the middle of the list.
- A **System.Collections.IEnumerator** is a .NET Framework object that allows programmers to use functions like **MoveNext**() and **Current** to access the elements in a collection.
- The **foreach** statement is a combination of a **for** loop and enumeration techniques.
- A **foreach** loop can be used to navigate a linked list just like an array.

Activity: Your To-Do List

In this activity, you will create a **To-Do List** program. Users can add items to the front or back of the list. They will also be able to remove items or clear the entire list. You will make the list of to-do items with a linked list.

Your activity requirements and instructions are found in the "Chapter_11_Activity.pdf" document located in your "TeenCoder\Windows Programming\Activity Docs" folder. You can access this document through your Student Menu or by double-clicking on it from Windows Explorer.

Complete this activity now and ensure your program meets the requirements before continuing!

Chapter Twelve: Object-Oriented Programming

In this chapter we will begin learning about Object Oriented Programming (OOP). OOP is a programming style and technique that can be applied to many different languages, not just C#. We will begin by describing the general concepts and leave the specific C# approach to the next chapter.

Lesson One: Object-Oriented Concepts

For a long time most computer programs were written in a *structured* programming language like "C", "Pascal", or 'FORTRAN'. A structured programming language typically produces a program that takes some input, processes it and then returns some output. The program starts at the top and executes methodically through the code until reaching the end of the program. While writing functions was supported and encouraged, the orderly management of data was more difficult.

In the 1990s, the invention of the Internet and the advent of graphical operating systems (like Microsoft Windows) changed the course of software forever. Programs needed to be more complex and more flexible. Programmers needed a way to make programs work with all kinds of data in response to more random user input. This is where *object-oriented programming* comes in handy!

So what is object-oriented programming (OOP)? OOP revolves around the creation of re-usable code *objects*. An object is something that can have both data (properties) and functions (methods) that operate on that data. Ideally, well-coded objects will be useful to many different applications and can therefore be shared between different programs.

Consider a **Circle** object. A circle is something that could be used in many applications: drawing programs, games, or any other graphics software. A **Circle** could have properties like **Size**, **Position**, and **Color** and methods like **ChangeSize**(), **MoveCircle**(), and **SetColor**(). If every program that needed to draw a circle on the screen had to create these properties and functions from scratch, we would have a lot of duplicate code! Instead, we can make a **Circle** object and share it between applications. This is object-oriented programming!

It's certainly possible to write bad programs using OOP techniques. However well-written OOP code has a number of advantages over structured programming.

Modeling Complex Systems

The OOP approach allows a programmer to implement complicated systems by breaking them down into smaller and simpler objects that work together. For example, let's say we needed to write a good representation of an "Automobile". Automobiles are very complex as a whole, but it becomes more manageable when you break it down into smaller parts like a **Body**, **Wheel**, **Engine**, etc. You can even go further and define smaller objects that work together to form a **Wheel** such as **Tire**, **Rim**, **Lug Nut**. You can keep going until the original **Automobile** object is composed entirely of very small, well-defined, easy-to-understand objects. A good rule of thumb when modeling real-world systems is to make the individual coded objects match their real-world counterparts.

Inheriting Traits

Another great benefit of OOP is a concept called *inheritance*. Inheritance allows similar objects to share common details or traits. A cat and a dog may have many physical differences, but they are both animals that have four legs, a tail, fur, and other common properties. They have behavioral similarities, like walking, eating, and sleeping. Of course there are differences too, like how they play, climb, or fetch.

We could use object-oriented programming techniques to define a general **Animal** object that contains common properties and behaviors of all animals. Then we can define another object or *sub-class* which *inherits* from the **Animal** class to create more specialized objects like **Cat** and **Dog**. These sub-classes would re-use the common functionality of **Animal** and then add special properties and behaviors for each animal type.

Hiding the Details

Another great aspect of OOP is the ability of objects to hide their internal details. These objects are often referred to as "black boxes", meaning you can't see inside them. A programmer who uses the object just interacts with the public parts of the object. The object's internal workings can be changed completely without breaking applications currently using the object, so long as the public interface is maintained.

Let's take a look at an example of a "black box" object. Let's say we created a **Random Number Generator** object. A programmer can call the method (or function) **GenerateRandNum()** to get a random number. The early versions of the **Random Number Generator** may simply return the number of milliseconds in the current time. This really is not the best way to create a random number, but it is functional and quick to implement. Later on down the road, we could change the way the random number is generated by using a more complex algorithm inside **GenerateRandNum**(). This would make the random number generator more useful and the programs that use the generator would still call the same function without knowing the difference. The object may hide any amount of internal data needed to generate a better random number. Only the code inside in the "black box" would change, while the public interface remains the same.

In computing, a "black box" has nothing to do with plane crashes. A black box is any piece of code that a programmer can use without having to know how that code works.

Lesson Two: History of OOP

The widespread use of object-oriented programming techniques did not occur until the 1990s. However, the concepts were actually pioneered back in the 1960s. In the 1960s, a company called the Norwegian Computing Center in Oslo, Norway, had a problem. They were in charge of creating simulation programs for various kinds of ships that were being built by some local ship builders. Each ship had a certain number of similarities, but also a significant number of differences. There were big ships, small ships, ships that carried cargo and ships that carried passengers. The programmers needed a way to avoid re-writing the same code for each ship simulation. In their solution they grouped the ships into different types of objects. This allowed them to re-use common code in the simulation programs. The result of their efforts was a programming language called “Simula 67”.

By the 1970s, the Simula 67 language had inspired several more object-oriented languages. The Xerox Company created the “Smalltalk” language as an educational tool in the 1970s. Smalltalk relied very heavily on OOP concepts. The “LISP” language, also developed in the 1970s, was used to write artificial intelligence programs. This language, while a bit older than Smalltalk, gained some object-oriented features in the 1970s.

The “C” language was developed at Bell Labs in the 1970s and became wildly popular in the programming community. In the 1980s, this language was extended to include object-oriented concepts and was renamed “C++”. The C++ language is extremely popular and was largely responsible for the exponential growth in object-oriented programming during this time.

The object-oriented style of programming has become very popular in the last 20 years. This leads most people to think it was recently invented, but in fact, object-oriented programming has been around since the 1960s!

By the 1990s, object-oriented programming was becoming the normal programming style, with the C++ language leading the way. However, the C++ language has some rather painful aspects, as it was developed during the earlier days of computing where very low-level details needed to be carefully managed. The “Java” language was developed in the mid-1990’s as an answer to these difficulties.

Java was developed by Sun Microsystems. It was created from the ground up as an object-oriented language. This language included many improvements over C++, including easier memory management and a flexible way of running the same program on many different combinations of hardware and operating systems.

In the 2000’s, after trying to adopt the Java language more specifically to the Windows platform (and fighting bitterly with Sun), Microsoft decided to develop their own object-oriented language from scratch. They decided to call this language “C#” (pronounced “C-Sharp”). We are using the C# language in this course! There are of course many other languages that contain OOP features. You will no doubt read about or use some of these as you continue your programming adventure.

Lesson Three: Defining an Object

In the previous lessons we introduced object-oriented programming concepts and traced the historical OOP language development. Now it's time to become a bit more formal and specific with regards to defining an actual object in code. When defining an object, there are generally three main points to consider:

Data	What variables or other objects does this object need to perform its function?
Methods	What methods (functions) are defined on the object for public use? What methods may be useful internally?
Relationships	How does this object interact with other objects? Is it similar enough in nature to other objects that they should subclass or inherit from each other?

The first step defining any object is to understand the big picture of what the object needs to represent and what it will do within your program. This can be a bit of an art form where there is no one right answer! For example, you might expect a music program to define a **Song** object which represents the different songs that can be played. Once you have the big picture in hand you can begin filling out the more detailed aspects listed above.

Data

Most objects require some sort of data. This data can consist of *properties* (variables) and possibly even other objects. For instance, if we had a **Song** object, it might have the following properties:

- **Title**
- **Artist**
- **Group**
- **Year**
- **Album Name**
- **Length**

The **Song** might possibly contain other objects, like:

- **Notes** – a list containing each of the individual notes in a song
- **Lyrics** – a list containing the words sung in the song

It is often a good idea to control the access that an external program has to an object's internal data. This keeps an external program from accidentally changing the data. Each property can be defined as *public* or *private*. Public data can be freely accessed by any external component that uses the object. Private data can only be accessed by methods on the object itself.

For example, we want to be able to set the **Year** of our **Song** object, but we don't want to give a program access to the **Year** property directly because the program might enter an invalid number. Instead, we create methods such as **GetYear**() and **SetYear**() on the object to get and set the private **Year** property. Within the **SetYear**() method we can validate that the input number is a valid 4-digit year in a reasonable range before updating the **Year** property. The **GetYear**() function will return the value of the **Year** property. In this way we have completely hidden the data within the object and an external component manages the data through the public methods!

Methods

An object will often require *methods*, or functions, that can be called in order to make the object perform some action. Object methods can be categorized as public or private just like data.

Public methods are functions that are accessible by everyone. These are often the methods that allow a program to set or change the data in an object, as in the **SetYear**() example above. Our **Song** object could have many other public methods that perform more complex tasks like **Play**(), **Stop**(), or **Rewind**().

Private methods are those methods which are only available to the object itself. These are methods that are not intended for anyone else's use. Private methods may be called by the object's public or other private methods. For instance, the **Song** object may define a private **Load**() method to read a the song contents from disk during the **Play**() method call.

Relationships

Objects don't usually exist all by themselves! They have to interact with other objects in the program. There are three main types of relationships that two objects can have with each other.

Uses-a	Object A may "use" Object B by calling the public methods defined by Object B. But Object A does not "own" Object B or "inherit" from Object B. For example, a **Trigger** object might call an **Explode**() method on a **Dynamite** object. However the **Dynamite** does not belong to (is not a part of) the **Trigger** object.
Has-a	Object A "has-an" instance of Object B as internal data. Object A owns object B by carrying it around in one of Object A's internal data variables. A **Dynamite** object might "have-a" **Fuse** object. The terms "Has-a", "Has-an", "Have-a", and "Have-an" are all equivalent.
Is-a	Object A "is-an" instance of Object B, meaning Object A inherits from or subclasses Object B. For example, a **Dynamite** object "is-an" **Explosive** object.

The definition of objects and relationships in a program is not an exact science! There are often several effective ways to accomplish the same goals. To demonstrate this, let's consider a few ways to represent Managers and Workers as objects.

We might define a **Manager** object and a **Worker** object: The **Manager** object may "use" the **Worker** objects by giving the **Workers** a command.

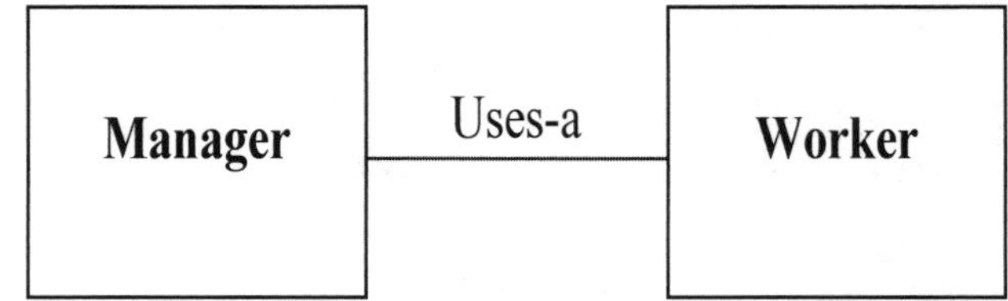

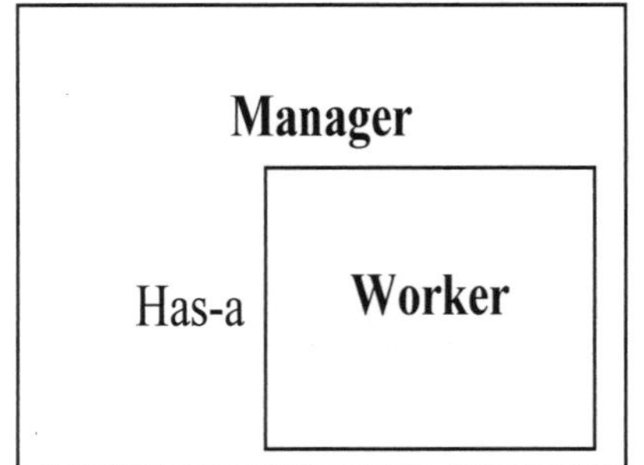

The **Manager** object may instead "have" the **Worker** objects since they all report to him or her in the company hierarchy

Or, we could define a **Person** object that contains common properties like **Name** and **Age**. Then we can define a **Worker** object that inherits from a **Person** object (all workers are people too!) and adds some job-specific features like **Title**. Then we define a **Manager** object that inherits from a **Worker** object (because all managers work too!) and adds further **Manager**-specific properties and methods that only the **Manager** needs to do.

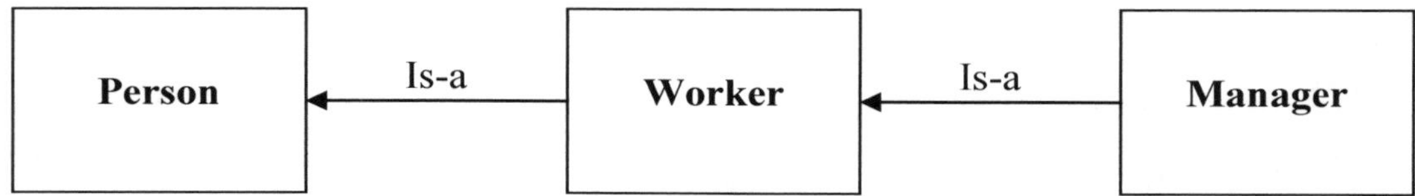

Of course we could decide that managers and workers do not have enough in common for managers to inherit from workers. So we define a **Person** object as above, but then define both **Worker** and **Manager** as inheriting directly from **Person**.

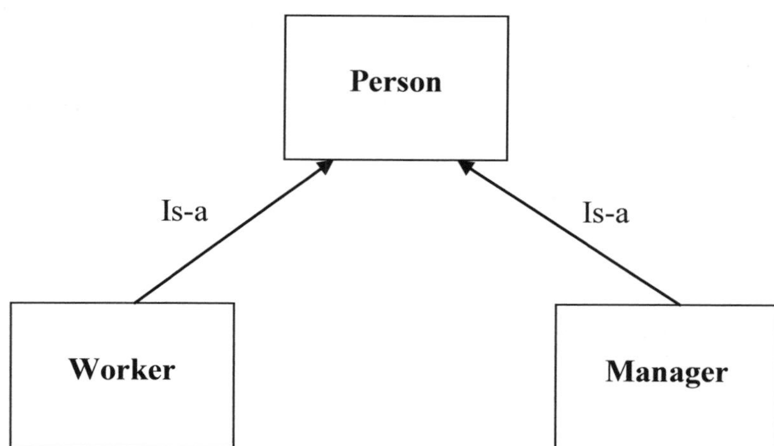

All of these approaches may be valid depending on the problem you are trying to solve!

Chapter Review

- A structured program starts its execution at the top of a program and executes predictably until the end of the program.
- *Object Oriented Programming* (OOP) is a technique built upon well-defined software objects that interact with each other.
- OOP techniques allow complicated systems to be broken down into smaller, more manageable parts.
- *Inheritance* allows similar objects to share common details.
- OOP allows programmers to hide internal implementation details inside a "black box".
- Object-oriented programming was pioneered back in the 1960s, but did not become popular until the 1990s.
- The C# language is Microsoft's latest purely object-oriented language.
- The first step in object-oriented design is to identify and define the objects in the program.
- Objects have three main aspects to consider: data, methods, and relationships with other objects.
- Object data are the *properties* (member variables) owned by the object.
- Object *methods* are the functions associated with the object.
- Object *relationships* define how the object interacts with other objects.
- With a "uses-a" relationship, two objects just interact with each other through public methods
- With a "has-a" relationship, one object owns another object
- In an "is-a" relationship, one object inherits from or sub-classes another object

Activity: Creating Songs

In this activity, you will obtain the information necessary to create **Song** objects. In the next chapter we will use this information to code a real music player that uses the **Song** objects.

Your activity requirements and instructions are found in the "Chapter_12_Activity.pdf" document located in your "TeenCoder\Windows Programming\Activity Docs" folder. You can access this document through your Student Menu or by double-clicking on it from Windows Explorer.

Complete this activity now and ensure your program meets the requirements before continuing!

Chapter Thirteen: Classes in C#

In the last chapter we introduced the concepts of Object Oriented Programming and design. In this chapter we will show you how to bring those techniques to life in C#.

Lesson One: Defining a Class

In the C# language (and in most languages), an object is referred to as a *class*. From now on, when we use the term "class", you will know that we are talking about an object in a C# program.

Classes are defined with the keyword **class**, followed by the name of the class, like this:

```
class Song
{
}
```

We have now defined a class named **Song**. The curly braces that follow the class name will contain the entire implementation of the class.

Recall that namespaces are ways to organize objects. A class may belong to a specific namespace, like this:

```
namespace MyLibrary
{
   namespace Music
   {
       class Song
       {
       }
   }
}
```

In the above example, anyone using the **MyLibrary.Music** namespace would have access to the **Song** class. You can use a simple namespace or nested hierarchy of namespaces.

If you define a class in a namespace or nested namespace, you must refer to those namespaces when you declare a class variable. It is possible to use the same class name in different namespaces, so you need to make sure the compiler understands exactly which class you want!

In order to create and use a class, you would declare a variable of the class type and use the **new** keyword to create an instance of the class:

```
MyLibrary.Music.Song mySong = new MyLibrary.Music.Song();
```

You can also add the **using** statement to avoid having to type the full namespace prefix each time:

```
using MyLibrary.Music;              // top of source file
// ...
Song mySong2 = new Song();          // somewhere within a method
```

It's important to remember that class variables are *reference* data types. The variable itself does not contain any data, it just refers to a location in memory where the class is stored. If you assign one class variable to another, you will then have two variables that refer to the same object, as the following example illustrates:

```
Song mySong1 = new Song();
Song mySong2 = mySong1;
```

At the end of this block of code, you would *not* have a copy of **mySong1** in the variable **mySong2**. Instead, both **mySong1** and **mySong2** variables point at exactly the same object in memory!

Lesson Two: Properties and Methods

In this lesson we will show you how to implement properties and methods in your C# classes. To begin, let's consider *properties*, which are variables that belong to a class. Properties can be any data type (value or reference), including instances of other classes. Properties are declared within the class definition curly braces, just like you would declare local variables inside a function. Let's add some properties to our **Song** class:

```
class Song
{
   string title;
   string artist;
   int year;
   string album;
   int length;
}
```

You can assign default values to class properties when you declare them, like this:

```
class Song
{
   string title = "Happy Birthday";
   string artist = "Mildred J. Hill and Patty Smith Hill";
   int year = 1893;
   string album = "My Party";
   int length = 30;
}
```

Each time you create a new instance of a class you get a new copy of all the properties to go along with it. The properties "live" and "die" with the class instance, so they will be around as long as you are using the object. When the instance goes away (meaning you no longer have any variable references to it in your program), all of the values and properties associated with the instance are also deleted.

Class *methods* are functions defined within a class to perform some action. All of the methods you have created so far in this course have belonged to some parent class, though it may not have been obvious if the IDE created them for you! Let's define some sample methods in our **Song** class:

```
class Song
{
   void Play()
   {
      // implement the Play method here
   }

   void Stop()
   {
      // implement the Stop method here
   }

   void Rewind(int seconds)
   {
      // implement the Rewind method here
   }
}
```

You can define any sort of method you like with different return types and input and output parameters!

Lesson Three: Public vs. Private

In the previous chapter we discussed the *public* or *private* access types methods and properties of an object. In this lesson, we will show you how use these access types in a C# class definition.

Public methods and properties are available to any program or object that is using the class. This type of access is not usually recommended for properties, since it will allow anyone to change the value of those properties directly. Public methods form your typical external interface to a "black box" class.

Private methods and properties are only available to the class itself. No outside program or class can access these methods and properties. Unless you specifically intend to allow anyone access to your properties or methods, you should always declare everything in a class as private. This helps prevent other components from accidentally interfering with the internal operations of your class.

Now let's see how to implement public and private methods and properties in the C# language. Here is the definition for our **Song** class again, but with explicit **public** and **private** keywords on the properties and methods:

```
class Song
{
    public string Title = "Happy Birthday"; // anyone can access property
    private int currentPosition = 0;        // property is internal to Song

    public void Play()
    {
        // anyone can call the Play method
    }

    private void initialize()
    {
        // only other Song functions can call initialize()
    }
}
```

Now let's take a look at some code that uses the **Song** class in a program:

```
Song mySong = new Song();

mySong.Title = "Yankee Doodle"; // OK!  title is a public property.
mySong.currentPosition = 42;    // Error!  Cannot access private property.
```

```
mySong.Play();      // Ok!  Play is a public method.
mySong.initalize(); // Error!  Cannot access private method.
```

You can see that any attempt to access a private property (like **currentPosition**) or a private method (like **initialize**()) will result in an error. Only the **Song** class can access these items from within other **Song** methods. However, any program can call the **Play**() function or use the **Title** property.

You will notice that we started the names of the private properties and methods with a lower case letter: **currentPosition** and **initialize**(). We started the names of the public properties and methods with an upper case letter: **Play**() and **Title**. Microsoft prefers this naming convention in C#, but it is not a requirement.

Protected Properties and Methods

There is one more access type for the methods and properties of a class: **protected** access. The protected access type is somewhere between **public** and **private**. **Protected** members can be accessed from within that class and from any subclasses that inherit from the class. The **protected** methods and properties class are not accessible from outside the class. We will use **protected** access later in this course.

Lesson Four: Constructors

A class *constructor* is a special method that is automatically called when the class is created with the **new** keyword. The constructor is commonly used to initialize the properties of a class. If you do not create this method in your class definition, the compiler will use a default constructor. However, if there is anything special that you would like to do when an instance of your class is created, you should create your own constructor. The name of the constructor method is always the same as the class itself. An example constructor for our **Song** class might look like this:

```
class Song
{
   public Song()    // this is the constructor method
   {
      // set a property to some default value
      Title = "Unknown";
   }
}
```

As you can see, we created a method inside of our class definition with the same name as the class itself. Our **Song()** constructor just sets the **Title** property of the song to "Unknown". Now, every time a program creates a new **Song** object the constructor will be called:

```
Song mySong = new Song();
```

If you do not define a constructor, a default constructor with no parameters and no logic within the function is automatically created by the compiler.

Constructors are particularly useful when you define parameters for the method. These parameters would be required input by the program when calling the **new** keyword and are placed between the parentheses after the class name. Constructors with parameters ensure that no instance of your class is ever created without some required data. You can define any number of constructors to initialize your class in different ways, as long as they all take different combinations of parameters.

For example, if we wanted to ensure that no one ever created a **Song** variable without providing a value for the **Title** property, we could create the following constructor:

```
public Song(string aTitle)
{
    // if this is the only constructor defined, then anyone using
    // the new keyword must provide a single string parameter.
    Title = aTitle;
}
```

With this constructor, you will have to provide a **string** parameter whenever a new **Song** instance is created:

```
Song mySong3 = new Song("Happy Birthday");
Song mySong4 = new Song();  // Error!  No parameter provided
```

Lesson Five: Static Members

All of the class properties and methods that we have used so far have belonged to specific instances of the class. In order to use any of these properties and methods, we had to create a class variable. For example, in order to access the **Title** property of our **Song** class, we had to create an instance of this class:

```
Song mySong = new Song();
mySong.Title = "My Song";
```

Static Properties

It is possible, however, to define properties and methods that belong to *all* instances of the class simultaneously! That means there is only ever one copy of the property shared by all instances of the class. This is especially useful for any property that is intended to be a *global* setting, or a setting that is used throughout the program. These types of properties and methods are defined with the **static** keyword:

```
class Song
{
   static public string Format = "MP3";
}
```

The **Format** property is now accessible without creating an instance of the class. We can easily change the format for all of the **Song** variables with just one line of code:

```
Song.Format = "WAV";
```

Now we have changed the format for every **Song** variable from "MP3" to "WAV" with just one line! Notice that you access the **static** properties of a class by using the class name itself with the dot (.) operator.

Static properties are often used to define constant values that are useful to the class in general. Let's imagine a **Note** class that defines standard values for musical note durations:

```
class Note
{
   // the following static members define the duration of
   // song notes, in milliseconds
   public static int DURATION_WHOLE = 1600;
   public static int DURATION_HALF = 800;
   public static int DURATION_QUARTER = 400;
}
```

We can now use these values anywhere we need to, even if we haven't created an instance of the **Note** class:

```
// get the duration of a whole note
int duration = Note.DURATION_WHOLE;
```

Static Methods

You can also define **static** methods for a class. There is one important thing to remember about **static** methods: these methods can only access other **static** methods and properties. In other words, these methods must work only with data that is not specific to any one instance of the class.

```
class Song
{
   static private string format = "MP3";
   static public string GetFormat()
   {
       // static methods can only access other
       // static methods and properties.
       return format;
   }
}
```

If we had tried to access any **Song Title** or **author** property within this **static** method, the compiler would raise an error since those properties are not **static** properties.

Just as with **static** properties, you call **static** methods by using the class name itself with the dot (.) operator (in our example: **Song**), not by using a variable or instance name:

```
string aFormat = Song.GetFormat();
```

Chapter Review

- Objects in C# are defined with the **class** keyword.
- An instance of a class is created by using the **new** keyword.
- A class variable is a reference variable, which means that the variable does not contain any data, it just points to an area of memory where the object resides.
- Classes may have properties and methods.
- Properties can be any data type, including other classes.
- Methods are the functions that belong to a specific class.
- **Public** methods and properties are available to any program that is using the class.
- **Private** methods and properties are only available to the class itself.
- Internal-use-only methods and properties should be declared as **private**. This keeps other users from accidentally changing the data in your class.
- A class *constructor* is a special method that is used to initialize the properties of a class when an instance of that class is created.
- The constructor is always called when a class variable is created using the **new** keyword.
- If you do not create a specific constructor for your class, the compiler will generate a default constructor.
- You can create as many constructors for your class as you would like, as long as they each have different parameters.
- **Static** properties belong to all instances of a class simultaneously.
- **Static** methods can only access other **static** methods and properties.

Activity: Your Song Player

In this activity, you will create the Song Player program that will be used to play the **Songs** that you created in the last chapter.

Your activity requirements and instructions are found in the "Chapter_13_Activity.pdf" document located in your "TeenCoder\Windows Programming\Activity Docs" folder. You can access this document through your Student Menu or by double-clicking on it from Windows Explorer.

Complete this activity now and ensure your program meets the requirements before continuing!

Chapter Fourteen: Sorting and Recursion

Sorting refers to the ordering of elements within an array or collection. In this chapter we will discuss some common algorithms used to sort numeric data.

Lesson One: Simple Sorting

Many programs require sorting of some kind. MP3 players, address books and spreadsheets all require sorting to place their songs, addresses or data elements in a particular order. Typically, the data items that you are sorting have numeric values, although you may choose to sort strings or other objects.

Let's say we have an array that contains the following numbers: { 6, 2, 7, 1, 5 }. If we sort these numbers from smallest to largest, the array would then have this order: { 1, 2, 5, 6, 7 }. Over time, many different sorting algorithms have been developed to arrange data. Each sorting algorithm can be measured in terms of its efficiency (or speed) and its computer resource requirements (e.g. memory consumption). The measurement of these factors is typically referred to as "Big O" notation.

The "O" in Big "O" notation is short for "order of" and is a rough approximation of the time and resources it would take to complete the data sorting process.

"Big O" notation is written as **O(f(n))**, where the "n" is the number of elements that need to be sorted, and f(n) is some function of that number. For instance, "O(n)" where "f(n) = n" means that the more data elements there are, the more time it will take to sort the data. This is called a "linear" sort, because there is a 1 to 1 correlation between the number of elements and the time it takes to sort the data. A "Big O" notation of "O(n^2)" would mean that as the number of data elements increases, the time it takes to sort them increased exponentially by a factor of n-squared.

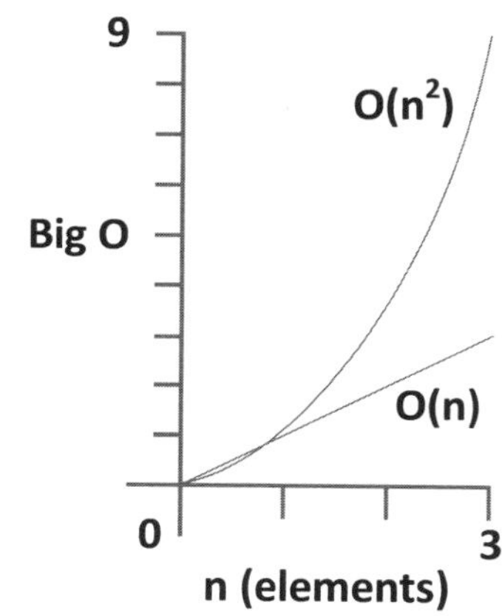

As you can see, for larger values of "n", the "O(n^2)" algorithm would take much more time than the "O(n)" function. If you had 1000 data elements (n = 1000), then "O(n)" would equal 1000, but "O(n^2)" would equal 1,000,000. That's a thousand times slower! It's important to understand "Big O" nature of the algorithm you want to use.

We will discuss two different sorting algorithms in this lesson. These are very simple algorithms and are easy to explain, but they both have an "$O(n^2)$" performance level. This means that these algorithms are good teaching tools, but are not very efficient to use in a program.

Bubble Sort

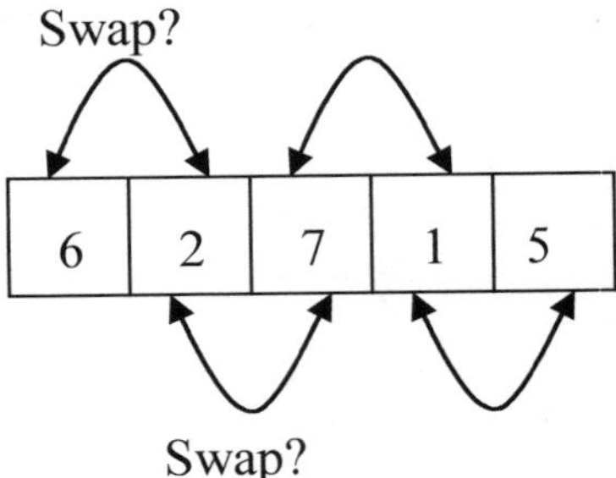

The *Bubble Sort* is the simplest of all the sorting algorithms. This sort will make multiple passes through the data elements, swapping pairs of elements that are out of order. The Bubble Sort will continue making passes over the data until all of the elements are sorted properly.

The first thing the Bubble Sort will do is compare the first and second elements in the array. If these elements are not in numeric order, they will be swapped. The sort will then move on to the second and third elements in the array. If these elements are not in numeric order, they will be swapped. This continues until the end of the array is reached. Then the sort will start at the beginning again and do the procedure all over again. The sort is complete when the algorithm can make a pass over the entire array without swapping any numbers.

Let's take a look at a Bubble Sort example using our array of numbers: { 6, 2, 7, 1, 5 }

Pass 1:

{ **6, 2**, 7, 1, 5} becomes { 2, 6, 7, 1, 5} (we swap the 0th and 1st elements)

{ 2, **6, 7**, 1, 5 } remains the same (since the 1st and 2nd elements are in order)

{ 2, 6, **7, 1**, 5 } becomes { 2, 6, **1, 7**, 5} (we swap the 2nd and 3rd elements)

{ 2, 6, 1, **7, 5** } becomes {2, 6, 1, **5, 7** } (we swap the 3rd and 4th elements)

Pass 2:

{ **2, 6**, 1, 5, 7 } remains the same (the 0th and 1st elements are already in order)

{ 2, **6, 1**, 5, 7 } becomes { 2, **1, 6**, 5, 7 } (we swap the 1st and 2nd elements)

{ 2, 1, **6, 5**, 7 } becomes { 2, 1, **5, 6**, 7 } (we swap the 2nd and 3rd elements)

{ 2, 1, 5, **6, 7** } remains the same (the 3rd and 4th elements are already in order)

Pass 3:

{ **2, 1**, 5, 6, 7 } becomes { **1, 2**, 5, 6, 7 } (we swap the 0th and 1st elements)

All remaining comparisons do not perform any swaps as they are already in order

Pass 4:

No elements are swapped in this pass, so the array is now sorted and the Bubble Sort is finished!

As you can see, this is a very simple sort to understand, but it took 4 passes through the entire array to sort 5 numbers! Just imagine what would happen if we had an array of 100 numbers!

Insertion Sort

Another simple type of sorting algorithm is the *Insertion Sort*. The Insertion Sort only requires one pass through the array, but it still takes a good deal of time to complete.

The Insertion Sort begins with the second element in the array (index 1). That element is removed from its original slot and "walked" from the beginning until it finds a number greater than itself. The value is then inserted before that greater element, sliding all other elements down to make room. Then the Insertion Sort repeats starting with the third element (at index 2) and continues until all elements have been processed.

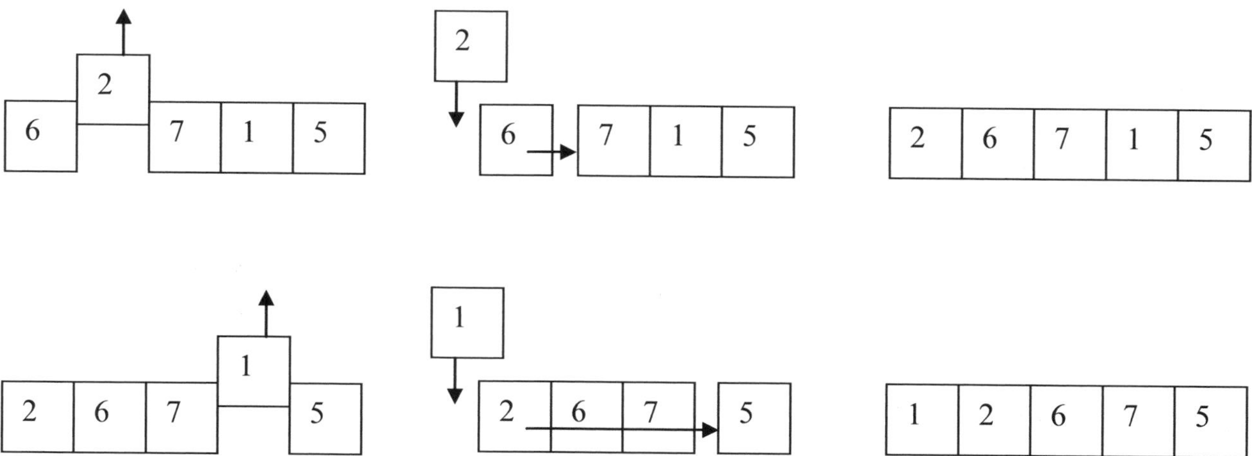

In the example above we start with the element at index 1 and compare it to the beginning element. "2" is less than "6", so we insert "2" in the array before the "6", and slide the "6" value down in the array to the slot vacated by the "2". Next we repeat the operation starting with the element at index 2. The "7" happens to be in the right spot, so the Insertion Sort will not have to move anything around (not shown). Next we repeat with the element at index 3. The "1" will be inserted prior to the "2", sliding down the remaining elements to make room. You can imagine a similar procedure for the "5" in the last element.

Here is the complete single-pass Insertion Sort for our example array, starting with the following values:

{ 6, 2, 7, 1, 5 }.

Pass 1:

> { 6, **2**, 7, 1, 5 } becomes { 2, 6, 7, 1, 5 } where the 2 is inserted in front of the 6
>
> { 2, 6, **7**, 1, 5 } stays the same, since the 7 is greater than all values before it
>
> { 2, 6, 7, **1**, 5 } becomes {1, 2, 6, 7, 5 } where the 1 is inserted in front of the 2
>
> { 1, 2, 6, 7, **5** } becomes {1, 2, 5, 6, 7 } where the 5 is inserted in front of the 6

After you make one complete pass through the data you have a completely sorted set! Even though the list is sorted after only one pass, Insertion Sort is still not a very efficient sorting algorithm. This is mainly due to the number of times that you have to slide a bunch of elements down in the array. As you can imagine, a linked list would be a more efficient data structure for the Insertion Sort. You can easily remove and insert items within the list just by rearranging the **Previous** and **Next** links...no copying or sliding necessary!

Lesson Two: Recursion

You are by now familiar with calling functions from other functions in your code.

```
public void functionA()
{
    // some logic, including a call to functionB()
    functionB();
}

public void functionB()
{
    // do something useful
}
```

There are a number of interesting programming tasks (including sorting) that can be effectively addressed by having a function call *itself* instead of some other function! This technique is called *recursion* and it looks something like this:

```
public void functionC()
{
    // some logic, including a call to functionC()
    functionC();
}
```

Now, clearly the **functionC** shown above is bad news because there is no way for **functionC()** to ever stop calling itself! In all *recursive* functions you will need to have some exit logic that will allow the recursive function calls to end, otherwise the computer eventually runs out of memory.

So how do recursive functions work? Let's consider the following example:

```
public string insertStars(string input)
{
    if (input.Length == 0)
        return ""; // quit recursing when our input is empty

    // break the input string in 2 parts - the first character and the rest
    char first = input[0];
    string remainder = input.Substring(1, input.Length - 1);

    // return a string containing a star, the first character of the
    // input string, and the result of recursively calling insertStars()
    // on the remainder of the input string.
    return " * " + first + insertStars(remainder);
}
```

The **insertStars()** function is recursive, since it calls itself from within the function body. What are the exit criteria that will prevent infinite recursion? The recursion will stop when the input string length reaches 0.

Now we need some code that will call our recursive function initially:

```
string result = insertStars("Hello");
MessageBox.Show(result);
```

Here we have called our **insertStars()** function and passed in the value: "Hello". When the function is complete, we will output the result using a message box. But what does this recursive function do? Envisioning the stack of function calls in a recursive algorithm can sometimes be challenging. It's important to understand that each call to the function has its own inputs and outputs. Let's visualize a series of steps, where each step is either a function call or function return. We have numbered the steps in the order that they occur in the program (down the first column then up the second one)!

Step	Function call	Step	Return value
1	insertStars("Hello")	12	" * H * e * l * l * o"
2	insertStars("ello")	11	" * e * l * l * o"
3	**insertStars**("llo")	10	" * l * l * o"
4	**insertStars**("lo")	9	" * l * o"
5	**insertStars**("o")	8	" * o"
6	**insertStars**("")	7	""

As you can see, the **insertStars**() function calls itself recursively, trimming the input string by one character each time, until the input string is blank. Then, as the bottom-most functions return, the upper functions are able to build up the result string and then return it to the top-most function. The result is the following string:

" * H * e * l * l * o"

Each time the recursive function is called, the function body represents a new scope with its own copy of any local variables. When the recursive function returns, you go back to the previous scope where the recursive call was made and continue processing normally from that point.

Now you're probably thinking: "Great! If I ever need to add stars to a string this is the way to go!" Of course, our example is pretty silly, but there are many valid uses for a recursive function. One common usage would be the traversal of the files and directories on a hard drive. Imagine these files and directories as a giant tree where subdirectories are branches and files are the leaves. A recursive algorithm could follow the branches to the end, and then back up and search other branches. Recursive functions can also be used when writing an algorithm to find your way through a maze, sort data, or compute the exponential powers of a number.

Let's take a look at a common example that uses a recursive function to raise a number to a specific power. In this function, "X" is raised to the "Y" power, or X^Y. If you know your algebra, you will recall that X^Y can also be written as $X * X^{Y-1}$ or $X * X * X^{Y-2}$, etc. This expansion works really well in a recursive function, like this:

```
public double power(double X, int Y)
{
    if (Y == 0)
    {
        // this is our recursion terminating condition
        return 1.0;  // any number to the 0 power equals 1.0
    }

    // recursively call power() to get X to the Y-1 power
    return X * power(X, Y - 1);
}
```

Our **power()** function calls itself to calculate successively smaller values for X^{Y-1} until finally we reach X^0, which is just 1.0 in all cases (that's our loop termination condition). Consider the following code:

```
double result2 = power(3.0, 4);
MessageBox.Show(result2.ToString());
```

We will be raising the number 3 to the 4th power (or 3^4), which will return the value 81. How does it work? Let's take a look at the individual steps:

Step	Function call	Step	Return value
1	**power**(3.0, 4)	10	3.0 * 27.0 = 81.0
2	**power**(3.0, 3)	9	3.0 * 9.0 = 27.0
3	**power**(3.0, 2)	8	3.0 * 3.0 = 9.0
4	**power**(3.0, 1)	7	3.0 * 1.0 = 3.0
5	**power**(3.0, 0)	6	1.0

If recursion is so great, why isn't it used more often? Well, there are some drawbacks to consider:

- It can take quite a bit of computer memory to hold the nested scopes of the recursive function calls.
- You need to be very careful to avoid an infinite recursion. You must always remember to include a termination condition in a recursive function. If you don't, your computer could run out of memory, which will cause a "Stack overflow error".
- Recursion can be difficult to visualize and implement properly!

Nonetheless, recursion is a powerful tool when used properly, and certain categories of programming problems are well-served with a recursive solution.

Lesson Three: Recursive Sorting

The sorting algorithms that we used in Lesson One were simple, but not very efficient. In this lesson, we will take a look at a much more efficient sorting method: the *Quick Sort.*

Quick Sort Concepts

The Quick Sort algorithm uses recursion to obtain a better "Big O" efficiency rating. The rating of the Quick Sort in the best case is "O = n * log(n)". For larger values of "n", the function "n * log(n)" does not grow nearly as quickly as "n^2" which is your "Big O" rating for the Bubble and Insertion Sorts.

The Quick Sort method works by using a "divide and conquer" approach to sorting data. This means that a large amount of data is progressively broken down into a series of smaller problems until the pieces are so small that they can be sorted very easily.

The first step is to see if there are any elements in the list. If there are no elements, there is nothing to sort. In addition, if there is only one element in the list, then the list is already sorted, so there is still nothing to do!

The second step is to choose a "pivot" point in the list. This can be any element in the list, but for simplicity's sake, most programmers choose the first value in the list as the "pivot" point. The next step is to arrange the elements in the array so that all of the values that are less than the "pivot" point value are to the left of the pivot, and all of the values that are greater than the pivot value are to the right. Any value that is equal to the pivot value can be placed on either side. This step is often called "partitioning", since the data is being "partitioned" or divided into smaller groups. Once this step is completed, the pivot point value is in its correct position in the list. This gives us a smaller set of values on the left and right of the pivot point which now need to be sorted.

To sort the smaller sections to the left and right of the pivot point, we treat them each as another list. We pick a pivot point (again choose the first value for simplicity) and then place all the values that are less than that value on the left and all the values that are more on the right. This process continues over and over until all of the items in the entire list are sorted as a series of trivial-length (0 or 1 element) partitions.

In the example below we start with our familiar array containing {6, 2, 7, 1, 5}. Since 6 is the first in the list we choose that as the first pivot and rearrange the array so that the smaller {2, 1, 5} values are to the left and the {7} is to the right. We then split the array into smaller pieces, where the left side {2, 1, 5} itself needs to be sorted. We choose the left-most value again {2}, and partition again so that the smaller {1} is to the left and the larger {5} is to the right. Then after a final partition we are left with only trivial-sized one-length arrays that can be combined in the correct order to get {1, 2, 5, 6, 7}.

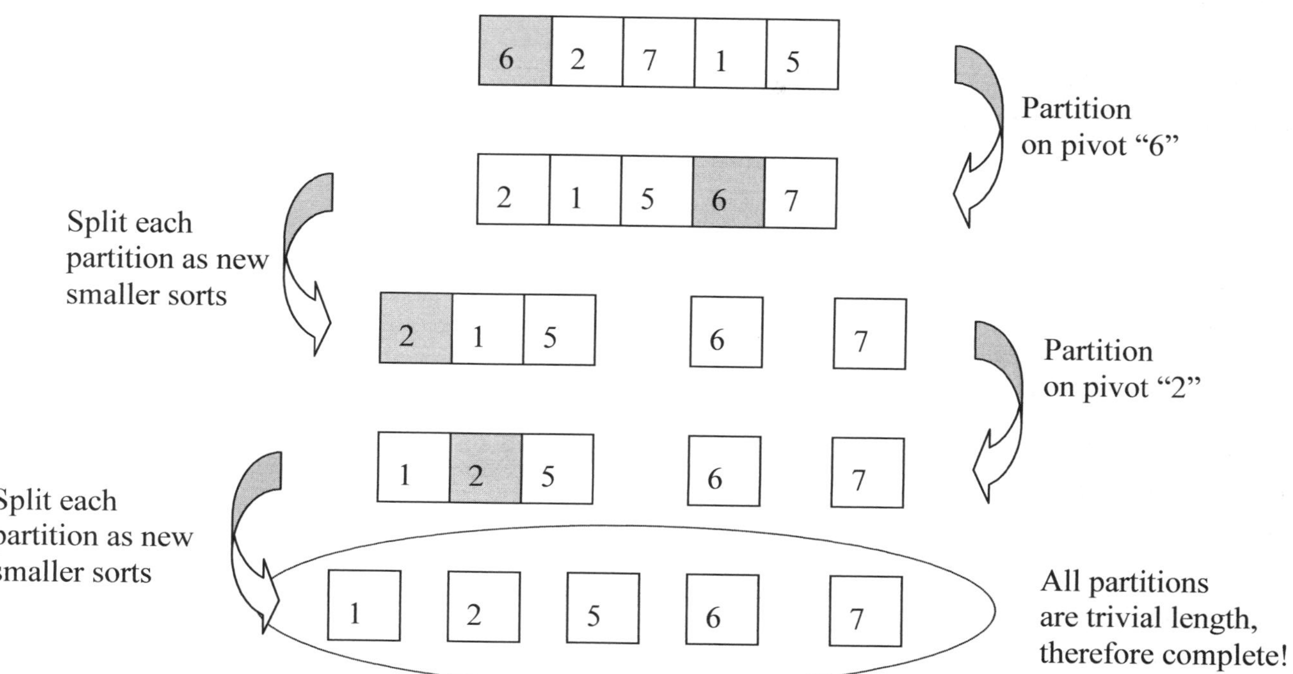

Of all of the steps in the Quick Sort algorithm, the partitioning step takes the most effort. The goal of this step is to move elements around in the array in the most efficient manner possible. Above we freely moved elements around within the array, but it is important to do this without making multiple copies of the array in memory (since that will slow down the process).

Quick Sort in C#

Our C# Quick Sort algorithm will operate on an array without making any copies of the array data. We are going to use recursion to define a method to sort an input array (or some smaller fragment of the array). The method definition looks like this:

```
void sortData(int[] target, int leftBound, int rightBound)
```

The array to be sorted is the first **target** parameter. However, we're only sorting the portion of the array defined by the **leftBound** and **rightBound** index parameters! To begin the sort we will define our familiar starting array and pass the **target** into the **sortData**() method. The initial **leftBound** and **rightBound** parameters are 0 and **target**.Length - 1 to cover the entire array.

```
int[] target = { 6, 2, 7, 1, 5 } ;
sortData(target, 0, target.Length - 1);
```

Now, what's going on inside the **sortData**() method? Here is the entire implementation with inline comments:

```
void sortData(int[] target, int leftBound, int rightBound)
{
    // We are sorting the target array "in place", meaning we aren't making
    // any copies of the memory.  Therefore we are using the leftBound and
    // rightBound variables to keep track of which little section of the
    // array this iteration of the sortData() function is operating on.

    // Step 0 - if the input array bounds cover 0 or 1 element,
    // it is trivially sorted already so just return.
    if (leftBound >= rightBound)
        return;

    // Step 1 - choose any value from the initial list as the "pivot".
    // For simplicity we'll choose the first (leftmost) value.
    int pivot = target[leftBound];

    // Step 2 - "Partition" the array such that all of the values less than
    // the pivot value are to the left of the pivot, and all of the values
    // greater than the pivot go to the right.  Values equal to the pivot
    // can go on either side.

    // Start with two indexes...one "i" initialized to the leftmost array
    // position, and one "j" initialized to the rightmost array position.
    int i = leftBound;
    int j = rightBound;

    // while our left index has not crossed over the right index
    while (i <= j)
    {
        // Increment "i" while the ith element is less than pivot value.
        while (target[i] < pivot)
        {  i++; }

        // Decrement "j" while the jth element is greater than pivot value
        while (target[j] > pivot)
        {  j--; }

        // If, at this point, i <= j (meaning they haven't crossed),
        // then swap the elements at those positions
```

```
            if (i <= j)
            {
                int temp = target[i];
                target[i] = target[j];
                target[j] = temp;

                // Then increment i and decrement j by one so move to the next
                // values for comparison, and continue through the loop again
                i++;
                j--;
            }
        }

        // After partitioning,
        // all values less than pivot are to the left of the "i" position and
        // all values greater than pivot are to the right of the "i" position.

        // Step 3 - Recursively quick sort each side of the array
        // if anything non-trivial remains
        if (leftBound < (i - 1))
        {
          // recursively quick sort the left fragment of the array
          sortData(target, leftBound, i - 1);
        }

        if (i < rightBound)
        {
          // recursively quick sort the right fragment of the array
          sortData(target, i, rightBound);
        }
    }
```

In your "\Activity Starters" directory there is a sub-directory called "Quick Sort". This directory contains a solution file called "Quick Sort.sln". This project contains an example of a Quick Sort in C#. The code examples shown here are taken from this project.

If you would like to see this algorithm in action, open up the Quick Sort solution and step through the program as if you were debugging the program. Place a breakpoint at the top of the **sortData()** method and set a "Watch" on the variable named **target**. Now you can use the "Step Over" command to go through the program line-by-line and watch as the algorithm sorts the data.

The Quick Sort method may be a bit difficult to understand without a visual example. The following diagram shows the Quick Sort steps in our example array: { 6, 2, 7, 1, 5 }.

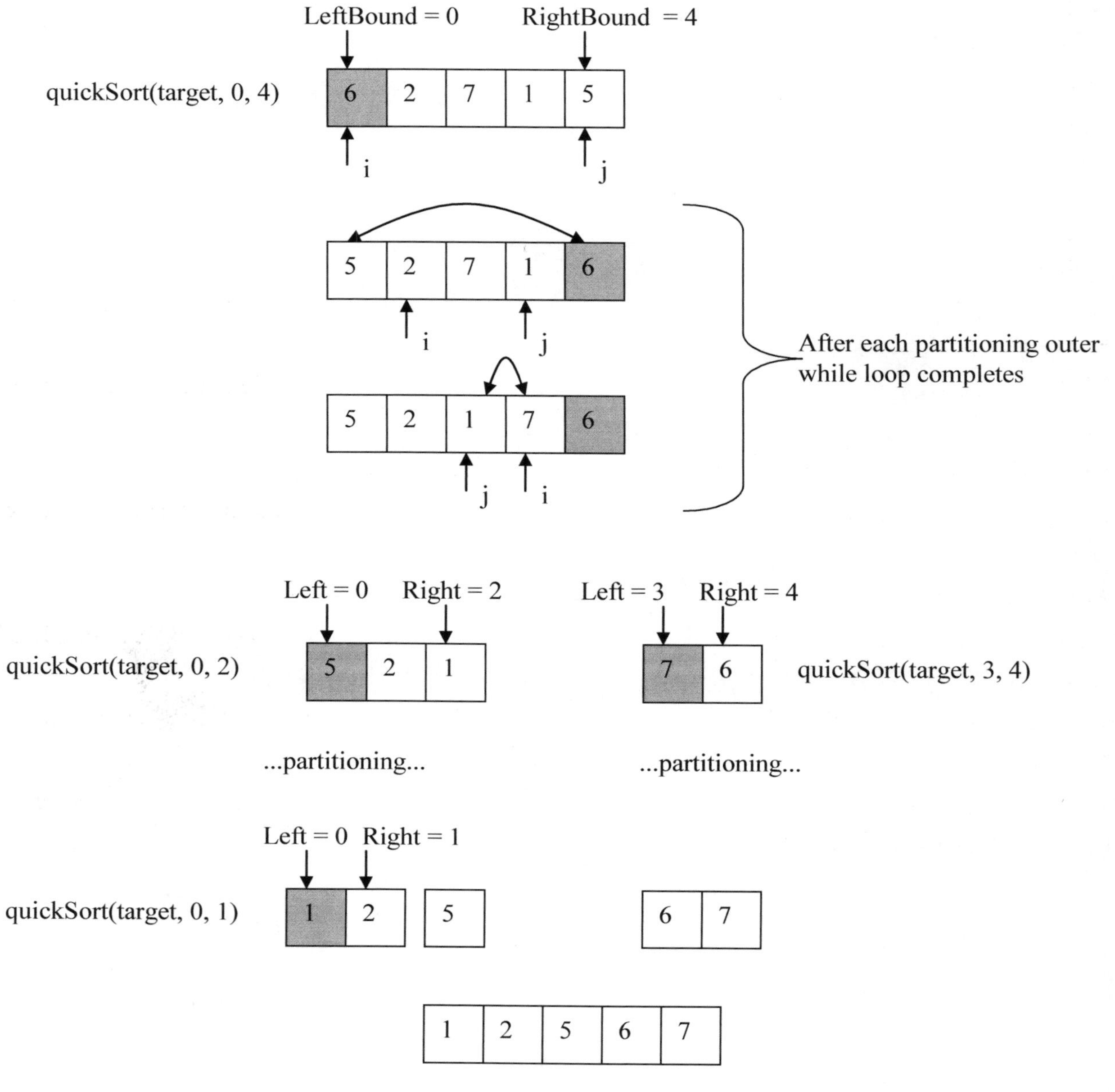

At the end, our initial array has been sorted: { 1, 2, 5, 6, 7 }.

As you can tell, it may be difficult to visualize and write a recursive sorting algorithm. However the improved speed and efficiency are certainly worth it!

Chapter Review

- *Sorting algorithms* are used to order data.
- "Big O" (the "O" is for "order-of") notation is used to represent the resources required for an algorithm based on the number of elements.
- "Big O" notation is written as "O(f(n))", where the "n" is the number of elements that need to be sorted, and f(n) is some function of that number.
- Two simple sorting algorithms are the Bubble Sort and the Insertion Sort.
- These sorting methods have an efficiency of "$O(n^2)$". This means that as the number of data items increases, the amount of computing resources increases exponentially.
- *Recursion* occurs when a function calls itself in a program.
- A recursive function must have some sort of exit condition that allows will stop it from calling itself. Without this, the recursion will continue infinitely.
- Each recursive function call creates an entirely new local scope with new copies of local variables.
- The Quick Sort is a sorting method that uses recursion to sort data items.
- The Quick Sort breaks the sorting task down into smaller and smaller pieces, until the individual pieces are simple to complete.

Activity: The Number Sort

In this activity, you will create a program that will sort numbers using the Insertion Sort algorithm.

Your activity requirements and instructions are found in the "Chapter_14_Activity.pdf" document located in your "TeenCoder\Windows Programming\Activity Docs" folder. You can access this document through your Student Menu or by double-clicking on it from Windows Explorer.

Complete this activity now and ensure your program meets the requirements before continuing!

Chapter Fifteen: File Input and Output

Many programs store data in files on the computer's hard drive. Having the ability to read and write files to disk opens up many interesting possibilities to the programmer and can provide nicer features for the user.

Lesson One: Using Files in a Program

Reading and writing to files is often referred to as *file input and output* or "file I/O". Visual C# file I/O functions are kept in the .NET Framework **System.IO** namespace, so you will include this namespace at the top of every source file that will read and write to files.

```
using System.IO;
```

Now we can easily use all of the features in the **System.IO** namespace without having to prefix the object names with "System.IO".

File Extensions

A file *extension* is the last part of the filename after the period. You are probably already know about different file extensions such as .EXE (executable program), .PDF (document), .WAV (audio file), and .JPG (image).

Typically, you should use the appropriate file extension on any data file you create in a program. A text file should have a ".TXT" extension, a music file should reflect its internal format as an "MP3" or "WAV", and an image file should have a "JPG", "GIF", or other image file extension. However, file extensions do not guarantee that the file contains a specific type of data. For instance, you can create a text file and then save it with a ".JPG" extension. This does not mean that the file is now magically an image file! In fact, if you tried to open this file in an image editing program, you would likely get an error. It is up to the file creator to save a file with the correct extension.

Directory Objects

A directory is a virtual space where groups of files or other directories can be organized. In the Windows operating system, a directory is usually called a "folder". The .NET Framework contains several useful objects for dealing with files and directories on a computer. The first object we will discuss is **System.IO.Directory**. This object is responsible for the methods that will create, move, and navigate directories and sub-directories on a computer's hard drive.

Here are some of the more commonly-used methods in the **Directory** object. All of these methods are **static** methods, meaning you call them directly on the **Directory** data type and not an instance of a **Directory** object.

Method	Description
`string GetCurrentDirectory()`	This method will return the current program's working directory. If you create a file in your program without specifying a directory, this is where your file will be created.
`string[] GetFiles( string path)`	This method will return an array of **strings** that contains all of the filenames within a specific directory.
`string[] GetDirectories( string path)`	This method will return an array of **strings** that contains all of the subdirectory names within a specific directory.
`string[] GetLogicalDrives()`	This method will return an array of **strings** that contains the names of all of the logical hard drives that are available on the computer. These names will be formatted as "<drive letter>:\", like "C:\".
`DirectoryInfo CreateDirectory( string path)`	This method will allow you to create a new directory along the specified path. Any missing intermediate subdirectories are also created!
`void Delete( string path)`	This method will delete a specific directory from the computer. In order for this method to work, the specified directory *must* be empty.
`bool Exists( string path)`	This method will return **true** if the specified directory exists, or **false** otherwise.
`void Move( string sourceDirName, string destDirName)`	This method will move a directory (and all contained files and subdirectories) to a new location on the hard drive.

Many more **Directory** methods exist to perform other folder-related tasks! See the MSDN documentation on the **Directory** object for details.

Here is a simple block of code which demonstrates some uses for the **Directory** object:

```
// This statement will get the current directory name
string currentDirectory = Directory.GetCurrentDirectory();

// If the "c:\MyDir" directory does not exist
if (Directory.Exists("c:\\MyDir") != true)
    // create the missing directory
    Directory.CreateDirectory("c:\\MyDir");
else
    // delete the existing directory
    Directory.Delete("c:\\MyDir");
```

File Objects

A *file* is a data block (or series of bytes) stored on a hard drive. Files have a name (filename), location (directory), and other properties. The .NET Framework contains a **System.IO.File** object which can be used to copy, delete, or manage the files on a computer. Like the **Directory** object, all **File** methods are **static**.

Here are some of the more commonly-used **File** methods:

Method	Description
`void Copy(string sourceFileName, string destFileName)`	This method will copy an existing file to a new directory location. The filename may be different in the new location.
`void Delete(string path)`	This method will delete the specified file from the computer.
`bool Exists(string path)`	This method will return **true** if the specified file exists on the computer, or **false** otherwise.
`void Move(string sourceFileName, string destFileName)`	This method will move a file to a new location on the computer. The filename may be different in the new location.

Here is a simple block of code which demonstrates some uses of the **File** object:

```
// Create a string to hold the name of our file
string filename = "C:\\MyDir\\test.txt";

// If the file exists on the computer
if (File.Exists(filename))
{
    // Copy the file to a new file, called test2.txt
    File.Copy(filename, "c:\\MyDir\\test2.txt");

    // Delete the old file
    File.Delete(filename);
}
```

Windows Paths

A Windows "path" is a string representing a directory structure and optional filename, such as "C:\myfolder\myfile.txt". Notice that a single back-slash character (\) is used to separate each folder and file within the path. However, recall from Chapter Eight that when typing quoted strings in C#, the back-slash character itself is an escape character that signals the start of some special character! In order to represent one back-slash in a quoted string, you therefore need to use **two** back-slashes like this: "\\". So in your C# code, our example path would be written "C:\\MyDir\\myfile.txt".

Lesson Two: Reading and Writing Text Files

Programs frequently store file data in text format. In this lesson we will learn how to read and write text files.

StreamWriter

To create a text file we will use an object from the **System.IO** namespace called **StreamWriter**. A **StreamWriter** will allow us to open a file and then write lines of text to the file. To create a new **StreamWriter** object variable we will use the **new** keyword. The only parameter to the constructor is the name of the file we want to create:

```
StreamWriter myFileWriter = new StreamWriter("c:\\myFile.txt");
```

This will create a file named "myFile.txt" in the "c:\" directory. You can also just use the filename such as "myFile.txt" and the file will be saved in the program's current working directory. So far we have simply hard-coded the target filename, but in a later lesson we will show you a convenient, built-in dialog to allow the user choose the file name and location.

Now that we have opened our file the **StreamWriter.WriteLine**() function will write a single line of text:

```
myFileWriter.WriteLine("My Information");
```

We can make repeated calls to **WriteLine**() for each line of text that we want to write to the file. When done, we must **Close**() the file to ensure the contents are completely written to disk:

```
myFileWriter.Close();
```

That's really all there is to writing lines of text to a file: just three simple lines of code!

StreamReader

When we want to read file data into our program, we use a **System.IO.StreamReader**, which is conceptually very similar to a **StreamWriter**. To create a new **StreamReader** object we will use the **new** keyword. The only parameter to this constructor is the name of the file we want to read:

```
StreamReader myFileReader = new StreamReader("c:\\myFile.txt");
```

Now we are ready to read lines of text from our file. There are two different methods which can be used to read data from a text file: **ReadLine** () and **ReadToEnd**(). The **ReadLine**() method will read one line of text at a time. The **ReadToEnd**() method will read the entire contents of the file into a string all at once.

The **StreamReader.ReadLine**() method looks like this:

```
string stringFromFile = myFileReader.ReadLine();
```

This will place a line of text from our file into the variable **stringFromFile**. If **stringFromFile** is set equal to **null** after **ReadLine()** returns, then there is no more information in the file.

The **StreamReader.ReadToEnd**() method looks like this:

```
string stringFromFile = myFileReader.ReadToEnd();
```

Now the **stringFromFile** variable will contain the entire file from the current read point to the end.

When done with the **StreamReader**, call the **Close**() method to release the file resources.

```
myFileReader.Close();
```

Here is a longer example where we create a new file, write several lines of text, then read them back and print out the results for confirmation:

```
// open new file called myFile.txt
StreamWriter myFileWriter = new StreamWriter("myFile.txt");

// write out 4 lines of text
myFileWriter.WriteLine("My text file");
myFileWriter.WriteLine("Go high");
myFileWriter.WriteLine("Go low");
myFileWriter.WriteLine("and away we go!");

// close the file
myFileWriter.Close();

// open existing file called myFile.txt
StreamReader myFileReader = new StreamReader("myFile.txt");

// create a variable to hold lines of text we read from a file
string myLine;
```

```
// loop over all lines of text in the file
do
{
    // read next line of text
    myLine = myFileReader.ReadLine();

    // if we got something
    if (myLine != null)
    {
        // display line of text to the user
        MessageBox.Show(myLine);
    }
} while (myLine != null);     // continue until ReadLine returns null

myFileReader.Close();         // all done!
```

If you ran this code then you would see a file called "myFile.txt" created in the directory with your executable (.exe) program. You can edit the text file with Windows Notepad or any other text editor and see these lines:

```
My text file
Go high
Go low
and away we go!
```

Those same lines of text would be displayed by the **MessageBox** when the file is read back in the **do** loop!

To read the entire "myFile.txt" file in one step, you could use the **ReadToEnd**() method, like this:

```
// open existing file called myFile.txt
StreamReader myFileReader = new StreamReader("myFile.txt");

// create a variable to hold the text we read from a file
string myFileText;

// retrieve the entire contents of the file
myFileText = myFileReader.ReadToEnd();

// show the user the contents of the file
MessageBox.Show(myFileText);
```

The **`myFileText`** variable will hold the entire contents of the text file.

Lesson Three: Reading and Writing Binary Files

A *binary* file contains data written as a series of bytes that may not represent textual information. A binary file is useful when you want to store data in "raw" form, literally copying the bytes from memory into the file.

You probably use binary files every day without realizing it! Binary file examples include executables (".EXE"), image files (".JPG") and audio files (".MP3" files). If you were to try to open any of these types of files in a text editor, you would see apparently random gibberish like this:

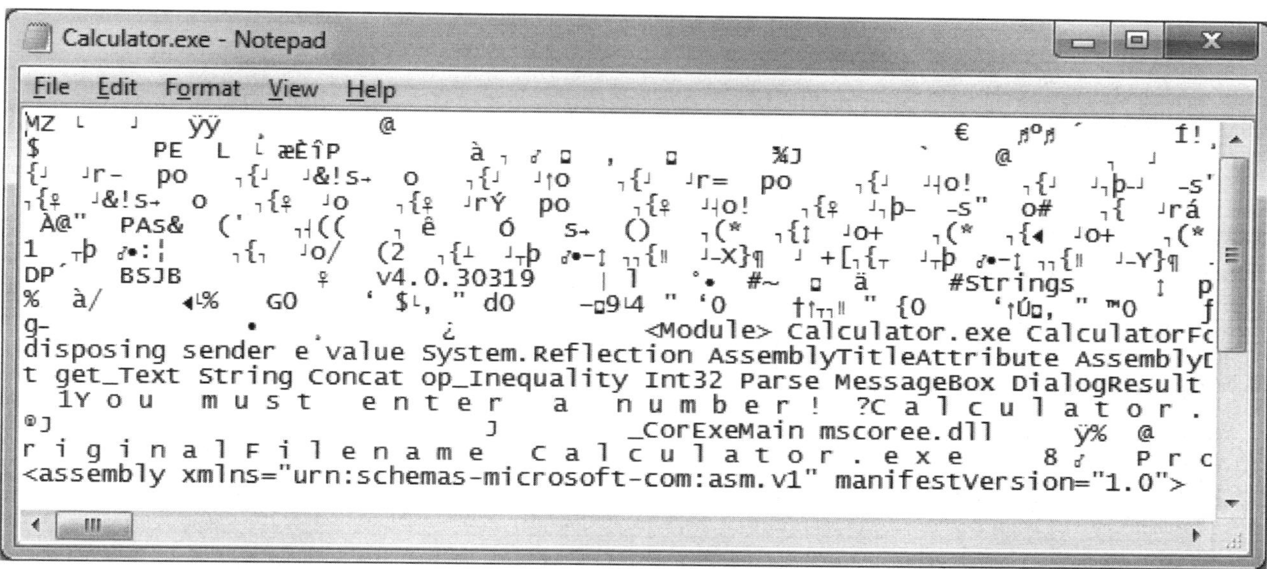

This data is not really human-readable, but the right computer programs can understand the binary format.

BinaryWriter

To create a binary file, we will use another object from the **System.IO** namespace called **BinaryWriter**. A **BinaryWriter** will allow us to open a file and then write binary data to the file. Initializing a **BinaryWriter** variable is a bit more complex than the **StreamWriter**. We still use the **new** keyword, but instead of a simple filename string we need to pass in the result of calling the **File.Open**() method like this:

```
BinaryWriter myBinWriter = new BinaryWriter(
                              File.Open("c:\\myFile.dat", FileMode.Create));
```

This will create a file named "myFile.dat" in the "c:\" directory. You can also just use the filename such as "myFile.dat" and the file will be saved the program's current working directory. We picked the extension ".DAT" as shorthand to represent "data". You can use any extension for your binary files, but you don't usually want to use a ".TXT" extension, since this data is not readable text, nor do you want to re-use a well-known extension like ".MP3" unless your binary data is actually in that format!

Now that we have opened our binary file, let's write some data! First, we will define some data to write to the file. For example purposes, we will use these variables:

```
int myInteger = 45;
double myDouble = 23.5;
string myString = "Hello!";
```

The **BinaryWriter** object uses the **Write**() function to write a variable to the file:

```
myBinWriter.Write(myInteger);
myBinWriter.Write(myDouble);
myBinWriter.Write(myString);
```

Notice that we do not have to specify what type of data is being written to the file. The **Write**() method takes many different data types and the compiler will automatically call the correct one to match the input data. You will need to call one **Write**() function for each piece of data that you want to store in the file.

Finally, when you are done writing binary data to the file, close the file with this statement:

```
myBinWriter.Close();
```

Our example code would create the file called "c:\myFile.dat". If you were to open that file in a text editor like Notepad, you would see garbage characters on the screen – possibly mixed in with recognizable characters from any string data. All of the data has been written in binary form.

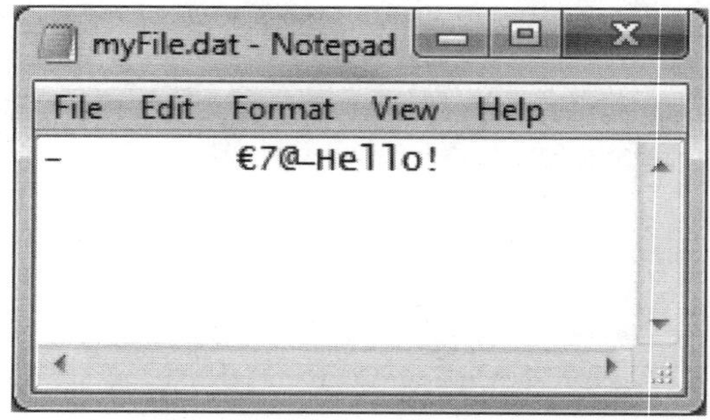

BinaryReader

Once we have created a binary file and written some information to it, we need to know how to read the data back into a program. We can retrieve the data with a **System.IO** object called **BinaryReader**. This object is initialized in a manner similar to **BinaryWriter**. Notice we use **FileMode.Open** instead of **FileMode.Create**.

```
BinaryReader myBinReader = new BinaryReader(
                        File.Open("c:\\myFile.dat", FileMode.Open));
```

Now we are ready to read the data from our file. This process is a bit more complicated than reading text from a file. Since many different types and lengths of data can be stored in a binary file, we need to specify the data type we are reading each time we try to extract a piece of data.

The **BinaryReader** object contains many different "Read" methods to handle the built-in data types:

Method	Description
`bool ReadBoolean()`	Reads and returns a **bool** data type from the file.
`byte ReadByte()`	Reads and returns a **byte** data type from the file.
`char ReadChar()`	Reads and returns a **char** data type from the file.
`decimal ReadDecimal()`	Reads and returns a **decimal** data type from the file.
`double ReadDouble()`	Reads and returns a **double** data type from the file.
`int ReadInt32()`	Reads and returns an **int** data type from the file.
`single ReadSingle()`	Reads and returns a **single** data type from the file.
`string ReadString()`	Reads and returns a **string** data type from the file.

Recall in our previous example we wrote an **int**, **double**, and **string** in that order. We would read that data from the file back into our variables *in the same order*, like this:

```
myInteger = myBinReader.ReadInt32();
myDouble  = myBinReader.ReadDouble();
myString  = myBinReader.ReadString();
```

Finally, when you are done reading binary data from the file, close the file with this statement:

```
myBinReader.Close();
```

Here is a longer example where we create a new file, write some binary data, and then read the data back:

```
// open new file called myFile.txt
BinaryWriter myBinWriter = new BinaryWriter(
                             File.Open("myFile.dat", FileMode.Create));
int myInteger = 45;               // create our variables
double myDouble = 23.5;
string myString = "Hello!";

myBinWriter.Write(myInteger);   // Write the data to our file
myBinWriter.Write(myDouble);
myBinWriter.Write(myString);
myBinWriter.Close();  // close the file

myInteger = 0;      // clear the data from our variables
myDouble = 0.0;
myString = "";
// open existing file called myFile.dat
```

```
BinaryReader myBinReader = new BinaryReader(File.Open("myFile.dat",
                                             FileMode.Open));
// read the data back into our variables
myInteger = myBinReader.ReadInt32();
myDouble  = myBinReader.ReadDouble();
myString  = myBinReader.ReadString();

myBinReader.Close(); // all done with the file

// Show the data in a message box
MessageBox.Show("myInteger: " + myInteger.ToString());
MessageBox.Show("myDouble:  " + myDouble.ToString());
MessageBox.Show("myString:  " + myString);
```

If you run this code you would see the message boxes appear with the correct data. There would also be a file called "myFile.dat" created in the directory next to your executable (.exe) program. If you try to edit this file with a text editor, you will only see the gibberish characters representing binary data.

Lesson Four: SaveFileDialog and OpenFileDialog

For all of the previous examples we used a specific filename hard-coded into our source files. This is not always ideal since it will only allow us to work with one file at a time. What if we wanted to let the user select a filename? In this lesson we will learn how the user can choose a target file name and location.

You have no doubt saved and loaded many files through other applications such as a word processor. You likely used a nice dialog pop-up that allowed you to browse through the directories on your hard drive and select a target filename. We could create that form ourselves, but it's quite a bit of effort. Fortunately the .NET Framework already has a nice little control that will handle all of this for us!

Save File Dialog

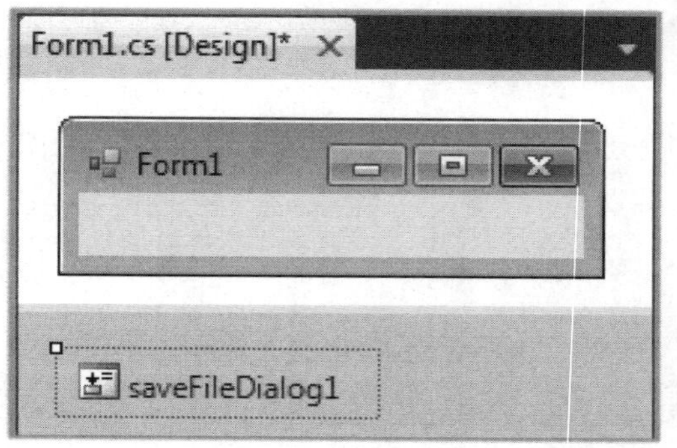

Look at the Toolbox from the form designer in the IDE. You should see a control named **SaveFileDialog** under the heading "Dialogs". If you add this to your form, the control will show up at the bottom of your design screen. Why did it show up at the bottom of the design window and not on the form itself? The dialog controls are not like a button or a text box that you will be able to see on your form when you run your application. The dialog controls are complete Window forms that you can call from your program, without having to design them at all! When you add one of these dialogs to your program, you are just adding the ability to call these pre-designed forms at some point in your program. Depending on your version of Windows, the "Save As" pop-up will look something like this:

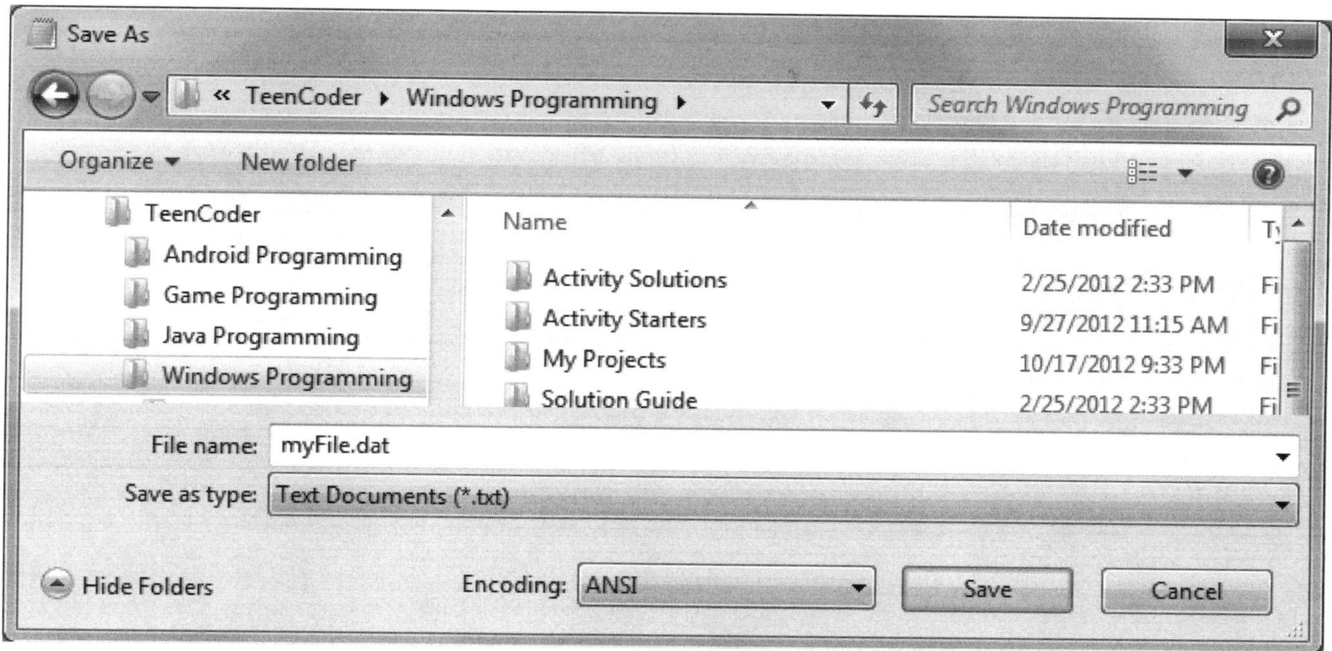

Once you have the **SaveFileDialog** control added to your form, you can view and change the properties for the control in the Property Sheet, just like any other control.

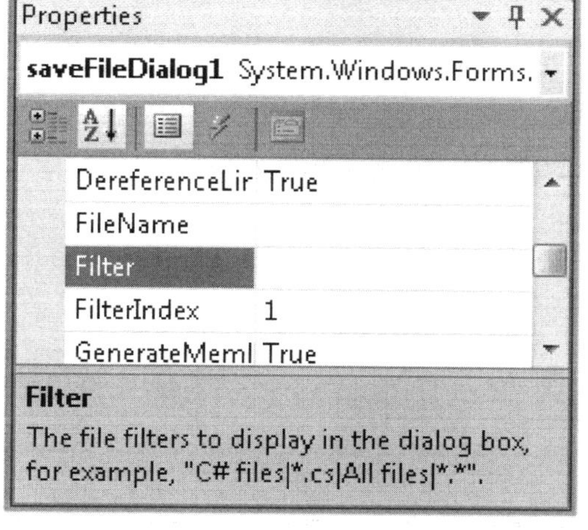

You may notice that the default pop-up "Save as type" field is empty. This field serves as a filter that only allows file names of certain extensions to be displayed in the dialog. For instance, if we only wanted to show ".TXT" files, we can set a filter in the **SaveFileDialog**. Right-click on the **SaveFileDialog** control in your form and then look at the properties window. You should see a property called **Filter**. Here is where we can tell the **SaveFileDialog** what files we want to show to the user.

For a simple text file, we can add the line: "Text Files|*.txt".

This line will tell the dialog two things: First, it will add an item to the "Save as type" drop-down list box that says 'Text Files'. Second, we tell the dialog that the "Text Files" end with ".txt". These two items are separated with the bar character "|", which is located above the "\" character on your keyboard. If we wanted the user to choose other types of files, we could add items to the filter by adding more file types and extensions in the Filter field as shown below.

"Text Files|*.txt|Other Text Files|*.text|All Files|*.*"

We have now put three items in our "Save as type" drop down list box:

- "Text Files", with an extension of "*.txt"
- "Other Text Files", with an extension of "*.text"
- "All Files", with an extension of "*.*"

Now that we have added the **SaveFileDialog** control to the form, and configured the **Filter** to show our desired file extensions, we can easily use the dialog from within our program. To show the dialog on the screen, we just call the **ShowDialog()** method on the **SaveFileDialog** control variable. We will also need to create a variable that will tell us whether the user clicked the "OK" button or the "Cancel" button on the file dialog. The **ShowDialog()** method returns the data type **DialogResult** to represent the user's button choice. This is a special data type which will contain the value **DialogResult.OK** or **DialogResult.Cancel**.

Once we get an OK result we can read the **SaveFileDialog.FileName** property to get the file name chosen by the user. Here is some sample code, assuming **SaveFileDialog1** is the control variable name:

```
// show the SaveFileDialog and allow the user to pick a target filename
DialogResult saveResult = SaveFileDialog1.ShowDialog();

// if the user clicked the OK or Save button
if (saveResult == DialogResult.OK)
{
   // create new file using the FileName property from the SaveFileDialog
   StreamWriter myFileWriter = new StreamWriter(SaveFileDialog1.FileName);

   // continue writing to your file as in the previous example...
}
else
{
   // Code to be executed if Cancel button was clicked
}
```

Once you make the call to **ShowDialog()**, your program's control has been handed over to the **SaveFileDialog** window. The next statement is not executed until the user clicks either the "Save" or "Cancel" button to close the **SaveFileDialog** window. We then receive the **DialogResult** and can see if the user chose a file or clicked the "Cancel" button.

Open File Dialog

When the user wants to load a file from the hard drive we may want them to pick a target file. Fortunately we can use a control called the **OpenFileDialog** control to let the user pick the directory and filename. The

OpenFileDialog control can be found in the Toolbox, just under the **SaveFileDialog** control. If you add this to your form, the control will show up at the bottom of your design screen, just like the **SaveFileDialog** control. You can then use the **OpenFileDialog** from your code using the control variable name.

You can filter the filenames that are shown to the user in the **OpenFileDialog** just like the **SaveFileDialog**. If you click on the **OpenFileDialog** object and then look at the properties sheet, you will see the **Filter** property. This filter works exactly like the **Filter** property for the **SaveFileDialog**. Adding a filter to select your files is often very important, since you want to make sure that the program is going to try and load information from the correct file type. If we try to open and read text data from some other random file type such as an executable file (.EXE), we would create errors in our program.

Using **OpenFileDialog** is almost identical to **SaveFileDialog**. You will call the **ShowDialog()** function to display the pop-up and then check the results to see if they hit the "Open" or "Cancel" button. Once you get an OK result then read the **OpenFileDialog.FileName** property to get the file name chosen by the user. In this example we assume your control variable name is **OpenFileDialog1**.

```
// show the OpenFileDialog and allow the user to pick a target filename
DialogResult results = OpenFileDialog1.ShowDialog();

if (results == DialogResult.OK) // if the user clicked the OK / Open button
{
    // open new file using the FileName property from the OpenFileDialog
    StreamReader myFileReader = new StreamReader(OpenFileDialog1.FileName);

    // continue reading file as specified in the previous example
}
else
{
    // Code to be executed if Cancel button was clicked
}
```

Once you make the call to **ShowDialog()**, your program's control has been handed over to the **OpenFileDialog** window. The next statement is not executed until the user clicks either the "Open" or "Cancel" button on the **OpenFileDialog** window. When either of these buttons is clicked, the **OpenFileDialog** window closes and we can check the **DialogResult** to see if the user chose a file or not.

That's all the file handling skills you need to load and save a file! You now know how to create new files and write out some data, how to open existing files to read in data, and how to let the user conveniently choose the file names for the "Load" and "Save" operations within the program.

Chapter Review

- The .NET Framework contains the **System.IO** namespace, which hold useful objects for file and directory management.
- A *directory* is a virtual space where groups of files or other directories can be organized.
- The **Directory** object in the **System.IO** namespace allows you to query hard drives, directory structures, rename, move, and delete directories.
- A *file* is a block of data or series of bytes stored under a filename in a directory on a PC hard drive.
- A file extension consists of the letters that follow the period in a file name. (For example, in the file name "myText.txt", the extension is "txt".)
- File *extensions* are used to describe the file contents.
- The **File** object in the **System.IO** namespace has many useful methods and properties for creating, writing, reading, and deleting files.
- A **StreamWriter** object in the **System.IO** namespace is used to write text data to a file.
- A **StreamReader** object in the **System.IO** namespace is used to read text data from a file.
- A **BinaryWriter** object in the **System.IO** namespace is used to write binary data to a file.
- A **BinaryReader** object in the **System.IO** namespace is used to read binary data from a file.
- The **SaveFileDialog** is a pre-built dialog that can be used within a program to allow the user to specify which file name and location to use for saved data.
- The **OpenFileDialog** is a pre-built dialog that can be used within a program to allow the user to specify which file name and location to use for loading data.
- Once these dialogs have been called, the program gives control over to the dialog window. When the dialog window is closed, the control falls back to the program.

Activity: Your Own Notepad

In this activity, you will practice your file input and output skills by creating your own note editor program.

Your activity requirements and instructions are found in the "Chapter_15_Activity.pdf" document located in your "TeenCoder\Windows Programming\Activity Docs" folder. You can access this document through your Student Menu or by double-clicking on it from Windows Explorer.

Complete this activity now and ensure your program meets the requirements before continuing!

Chapter Sixteen: Inheritance and Polymorphism

One of the greatest features of object-oriented programming is the ability of one class to *inherit* shared behavior and data from another class. This powerful concept promotes code re-use and careful definition of common traits.

Lesson One: Base Classes and Derived Classes

In order to use class inheritance, you first need to define a *base* class. Any class which inherits from a base class is called a *derived* class or *subclass*. Base classes usually provide some common properties and methods that are useful to an entire category of objects. A derived class will then expand on these capabilities.

Throughout this chapter we will develop a set of base and derived classes that will be used as part of your final project. For your final project you will write a chess game! You may already be familiar with chess, but we will review the basic rules first and then get started with our class development.

The Game of Chess

Chess is a board game that is played between two players. The game board is checkered with 64 black and white squares arranged in an eight-by-eight grid. Each player has sixteen playing pieces: a king (**K**), a queen (**Q**), two rooks (**R**), two knights (**K**), two bishops (**B**) and eight pawns (**P**). One player has all white pieces and the other player has all black pieces. The object of the game is to "checkmate" the opponent's king. A "checkmate" occurs when a player's king is under imminent attack and there is no possible way to remove it from danger in the next move.

Each type of chess piece follows certain rules for movement and capturing opponents. The starting location for all pieces is shown on the right, with the black pieces on top and the white on the bottom. For programming purposes we will identify each square with a column and row integer coordinate pair from 0 through 7. For instance, the black king starts at "4, 0".

	0	1	2	3	4	5	6	7
0	**R**	**K**	**B**	**Q**	**K**	**B**	**K**	**R**
1	**P**	**P**	**P**	**P**	**P**	**P**	**P**	**P**
2								
3								
4								
5								
6	P	P	P	P	P	P	P	P
7	R	K	B	Q	K	B	K	R

Creating a Base Class

We would like to define a set of objects to represent the different types of pieces in the chess game. We know pieces have some things in common and some things that each does differently. It's possible to approach our object design in different ways – there is no one right answer. We will start simply with a base class called **ChessPiece**. We know that all chess pieces on the board share certain common properties:

- Name
- Player (Black or White)
- Current Location (Column and Row)

Thinking ahead, we suspect that we'll want to display some descriptive text about each piece, so we'll define the following common method on the base class:

string GetDescription() – returns a descriptive string about the chess piece.

In C#, we could implement the **ChessPiece** base class as follows:

```
// the following enum allows us to identify chess piece as black or white
public enum PlayerType
{
    BLACK,
    WHITE
}

class ChessPiece
{
    public string Name;                // "Pawn", "Rook", etc.

    public PlayerType Player;          // BLACK or WHITE
    public int Col;                    // 0 - 7
    public int Row;                    // 0 - 7

    public string GetDescription()
    {
        if (Player == PlayerType.BLACK)
            return "Black " + Name;
        else
            return "White " + Name;
    }
}
```

Within our chess game we might then create an instance of a **ChessPiece** like this:

```
ChessPiece piece1 = new ChessPiece();
```

Now, this is a nice starting point – our chess program can manage all chess pieces in a common way by setting the **Name**, **Player**, **Col**, and **Row** properties.

Abstract Methods

We know that chess pieces all behave differently when they move. When a user tries to move a piece the chess program will want to determine if it's valid move. So, let's add another method to our **ChessPiece** class. This new method will tell us if a move to a target square is valid for a particular chess piece.

```
public bool CanMoveToLocation(int targetCol, int targetRow)
```

To implement this method, we will need to know some specific information about the chess piece type and how it can move on the board. Since movement logic will be different for each chess piece, we are going to define this method in the **ChessPiece** class, but *not actually implement it* yet! One of the derived classes must implement it instead. We use the keyword **abstract** in front of the method definition to indicate the method is defined in the base class but must be implemented by a derived class. Instead of curly braces and a method body after the parameter list, just end the method definition with a semicolon.

```
abstract public bool CanMoveToLocation(int targetCol, int targetRow);
```

Once you declare any method in a class to be **abstract**, you will also need to mark the overall class as **abstract** too by adding the **abstract** keyword in front of the class name. To make it clear that our class is now an **abstract** class, we will also change the name from **ChessPiece** to **AbstractChessPiece**.

```
public abstract class AbstractChessPiece
{
        public string Name;                 // "Pawn", "Rook", etc.

        public PlayerType Player;           // BLACK or WHITE
        public int Col;                     // 0 - 7
        public int Row;                     // 0 - 7

        // This method is defined but not implemented by AbstractChessPiece.
        // Each derived class will have to implement its own version.
        abstract public bool CanMoveToLocation(int targetCol, int targetRow);
```

```
        public string GetDescription()
        {
            if (Player == PlayerType.BLACK)
                return "Black " + Name;
            else
                return "White " + Name;
        }
}
```

Abstract classes cannot be created with the **new** keyword, because they are not completely implemented! If you did try to create this class with the **new** keyword, the compiler would generate an error:

```
    AbstractChessPiece piece2 = new AbstractChessPiece();  // ERROR:
                           // because AbstractChessPiece is declared as abstract!
```

Creating Derived Classes

So how do we use our **AbstractChessPiece** class? To use this class, you must derive a subclass from it. Let's define a new derived class called **Pawn** that inherits from **AbstractChessPiece**:

```
    class Pawn : AbstractChessPiece
    {
        // Implement the abstract method defined in the base class.
        override public bool CanMoveToLocation(int targetCol, int targetRow)
        {
            // implementation details go here
            return false;
        }
    }
```

To create a derived class place a colon ":" character between the name of the derived class and the name of the base class. Recall from our object-oriented discussion that base and derived classes have an "is-a" relationship. In our example, a **Pawn** "is-an" **AbstractChessPiece**.

To implement an **abstract** method in a derived class you need to repeat the method definition again and add the **override** keyword in front. Then implement the method body normally. From a derived class method we are able to access any of the **public** or **protected** methods and properties on the base class as if they were declared on the derived class. However a derived class cannot access any **private** methods or properties on the base class!

Any derived class that fully implements all of the **abstract** methods from the base class is called *concrete*. A concrete derived class can now be created with the **new** keyword because all methods are implemented. Our **Pawn** class is ready to be used in a program:

```
Pawn piece3 = new Pawn();
piece3.Player = PlayerType.BLACK;
piece3.Name = "Pawn";
piece3.Col = 3;
piece3.Row = 1;
string description = piece3.GetDescription();
```

By now, you can probably imagine that a chess program might define a class for each of the different pieces, all derived from the base class **AbstractChessPiece**.

Complex Class Hierarchies

While we will stick to simple two-level class hierarchies for our remaining programs, it is possible to create a deeply nested class structure. One class can derive from a parent and in turn serve as the base class for another more specialized object.

You can find many examples of multi-level class hierarchies in the .NET Framework. For example, each time you design a form, you are actually using **Form** object which is derived from the following hierarchy of classes:

```
System.Object
  System.MarshalByRefObject
    System.ComponentModel.Component
      System.Windows.Forms.Control
        System.Windows.Forms.ScrollableControl
          System.Windows.Forms.ContainerControl
            System.Windows.Forms.Form
```

If you want to see additional details of this object hierarchy, you can check out the MSDN documentation for these classes.

Lesson Two: Using References to Base and Derived Classes

When you create a variable of a class data type, you can of course assign an instance of that class to the variable. If your variable type happens to represent a base class, you can also assign an instance of any class *derived from* that base type to the variable!

```
Pawn piece3 = new Pawn();
AbstractChessPiece piece4 = new Pawn();
```

In the first line, we declare the variable **piece3** as a new instance of the **Pawn** class. This means that the variable **piece3** must always point to some instance of the derived class **Pawn**. In the second line we declare variable **piece4** as an **AbstractChessPiece**, but can still assign a **Pawn** (or any other piece derived from **AbstractChessPiece**) to **piece4**.

When to Use Derived Class References

If you want to use a method or property on a derived class that is not available on the base class, then you should declare your variable to be of the derived class type. That way the C# compiler knows how to use those items specific to the derived class. For instance, if there was something special on the **Pawn** class that you want to use, you should declare a variable of the **Pawn** type and not **AbstractChessPiece**. Let's consider an example! We know that pawns have a special ability to move two squares on the first move in the game of chess. In order to determine if our **Pawn** class object has moved yet, we can define a method just for the **Pawn** class like this:

```
class Pawn : AbstractChessPiece
{
    // this is the concrete implementation of the abstract method
    // defined in the base class
    override public bool CanMoveToLocation(int targetCol, int targetRow)
    {
        // implementation details go here
        return false;
    }

    // this special method is available only to pawns
    public bool IsFirstMove()
    {
        // implementation details go here
        return false;
    }
}
```

We have created a method called **IsFirstMove()** which is defined only for a **Pawn** object. This means that any **Pawn** variable can use the new method, but a variable of type **AbstractChessPiece** would have no knowledge of the method.

```
Pawn piece3 = new Pawn();
AbstractChessPiece piece4 = new Pawn();
bool firstMove3 = piece3.IsFirstMove(); // OK!
bool firstMove4 = piece4.IsFirstMove(); // ERROR!
```

As you can see, if we try to use the **IsFirstMove()** method on the **piece4** variable, the compiler will generate an error because **AbstractChessPiece** doesn't know about the method. But what if we know for sure that **piece4** is really a **Pawn**? In this case, we can temporarily treat it as a **Pawn** and access the **IsFirstMove()** method by using the *casting* technique previously described for the built-in data types. *Casting* means changing a variable or reference to another data type. We can cast a class reference to another class type by putting the new class type in parentheses before the variable name in a program statement, like this:

```
AbstractChessPiece piece5 = new Pawn();
Pawn piece6 = (Pawn)piece5;                      // cast to Pawn type
bool firstMove6 = piece6.IsFirstMove();          // OK!
bool firstMove5 = ((Pawn)piece5).IsFirstMove();  // also OK!
```

First we demonstrated a step-by-step approach where **piece5** was cast to a **Pawn** and stored in a **Pawn** variable for later use as a **Pawn**. A shorter approach is shown last where we make the cast and a **Pawn** function call all on one line. Use parentheses to surround the results of temporarily casting **piece5** to a **Pawn**, and then call the **Pawn** method without actually creating a **Pawn** variable.

You can cast up an object hierarchy (*upcasting*) by casting a derived reference to a base data type. You can also cast down an object hierarchy (*downcasting*) by casting a base data type to a derived class. Notice that *upcasting* is guaranteed to work because the compiler knows in advance that a derived class inherits from the base class. However, *downcasting* will cause an error if you attempt to cast a base class to a derived type, and the actual object is not of that derived type! For instance, you could always safely cast a **Pawn** reference to an **AbstractChessPiece**. But if you cast an **AbstractChessPiece** to a **Pawn**, and the object is actually a **Rook**, you will cause an error at runtime!

When to Use Base Class References

So why would we want to declare a variable as the base class and not the specific derived class? By declaring **piece4** as an **AbstractChessPiece**, the variable is able to hold any sort of object that is derived from **AbstractChessPiece**. This variable can hold a **Pawn** object, or a **Rook**, or a **Queen**, etc. You can then use all of the public methods and properties on the **AbstractChessPiece** without really knowing about the derived type. If the user attempts to move a piece to a certain location, we don't actually need to know what the piece is. Simply call the **CanMoveToLocation**() method, which we declared as **abstract**, and the correct method on the actual derived data type will be called automatically!

```
AbstractChessPiece piece4 = //some valid chess piece...Pawn, Rook, etc.
bool validMove = piece4.CanMoveToLocation(3,2);
```

We have just demonstrated the concept of *polymorphism*. Polymorphism means you can use an object as a *generic* type and it will actually behave differently, according to its *actual* type. Class hierarchies naturally implement polymorphism through the abstract methods defined in derived classes. This feature is one of the most powerful aspects of C# and other object-oriented programming languages! We will make good use of polymorphism in our final project.

Lesson Three: Virtual Base Methods

In the previous lessons we discussed how to create base and derived classes and how to implement **abstract** methods in derived classes. But what if the base class implements a method that works for most derived classes, but not all? What if some of the derived classes want the method to work differently but others just want to use the base class implementation?

We can solve this problem by implementing the method on the base class first. We then mark this method as **virtual** (instead of **abstract**) which allows individual derived classes to choose whether or not to override the base class implementation with another version.

For example, let's add a **virtual** method called **CanCaptureLocation**() to our **AbstractChessPiece** base class. This method will return **true** if the piece can capture an opponent piece that is in the target location.

```
abstract class AbstractChessPiece
{
    // this abstract method is defined but not implemented
    abstract public bool CanMoveToLocation(int targetCol, int targetRow);

    // this virtual method is implemented but may be overridden later
    virtual public bool CanCaptureLocation(int targetCol, int targetRow)
    {
        // most chess pieces capture the same square they can
        // normally move to, so just re-use that method by default.
        return CanMoveToLocation(targetCol,targetRow);
    }
}
```

In most cases a chess piece can capture an opponent directly in a square it could normally move to, so the base class implements the **CanCaptureLocation**() method by simply returning the result of the method **CanMoveToLocation**(). However, **Pawns** capture opposing pieces by moving *diagonally* on the board. This is *not* a direction they can normally move if the target square is empty.

So how can we allow the **Pawn** class to override this method? We need to do two things: first, we add the **virtual** keyword to the front of the method in the base class. This keyword tells the compiler that derived classes are allowed to override this method. Then we can use the **override** keyword in our implementation of this function in the **Pawn** class definition. This tells the compiler to use the Pawn's **CanCaptureLocation**() method for any instance of the **Pawn** class.

```
class Pawn : AbstractChessPiece
{
    //this override method will replace base version for Pawn objects.
    override public bool CanCaptureLocation(int targetCol, int targetRow)
    {
        // implement the Pawn's version here.
        return false;
    }
}
```

Now let's say we have defined a **Rook** class, which is just like a **Pawn**, except the **CanCaptureLocation**() method will *not* be overridden:

```
class Rook : AbstractChessPiece
{
    // implementation details here
}
```

Now, consider the following code:

```
AbstractChessPiece piece5 = new Pawn();
AbstractChessPiece piece6 = new Rook();

// the Pawn's overridden method will be called here for the Pawn
bool validMove5 = piece5.CanCaptureLocation(3,2);

// the original base method will be called for the Rook, because
// we didn't override the method for Rook objects
bool validMove6 = piece6.CanCaptureLocation(3,2);
```

In both cases above our class variable was an **AbstractChessPiece**, which could hold a **Pawn**, **Rook**, or any other derivative of **AbstractChessPiece**. When you call a method through a base class reference, C# is smart enough to figure out which version to call based on the actual type of the object. In the case above, the compiler will select the overridden method **CanCaptureLocation()** for the **Pawn** object stored in **piece5** and the base class method **CanCaptureLocation()** for the **Rook** object in **piece6**.

Lesson Four: The "Object" Base Class

In the C# language, all objects inherit from a single root base class call **System.Object**. This base class contains a small handful of common methods and properties. The most interesting and useful is the **ToString()** method. The **ToString()** method returns a human-readable string representation of the object.

Here is an example showing how **ToString()** would work on a simple object:

```
Object o = new Object();
MessageBox.Show(o.ToString());
```

This code creates a variable named "**o**", which contains a member of the **Object** class. When we use the **MessageBox.Show()** function with the **ToString()** method on our "**o**" variable, we get "System.Object" as the output.

We don't typically use simple **System.Object** variables directly in most programs. However, since **ToString()** is marked **virtual**, and all classes are derived from **System.Object**, we can always make better use of the **ToString()** method to display more descriptive data. The built-in data types such as **int** and **double** are secretly derived from the **Object** class, so you can call the **ToString()** method on any numeric variable.

You may find it useful to override the **ToString()** method so your object will produce better human-readable text. For instance, the default **ToString()** method on the **Pawn** class doesn't give very interesting results:

```
Pawn piece3 = new Pawn();
piece3.Player = PlayerType.WHITE;
piece3.Name = "Pawn";
piece3.Col = 3;
piece3.Row = 1;
MessageBox.Show(piece3.ToString());
```

We would get a window on the screen that contained just "Chess.Pawn" as the output of the default **ToString**() method. That's not very descriptive or informative at all!

Let's override the **ToString**() method in our **AbstractChessPiece** class, like this:

```
abstract class AbstractChessPiece
{
    override public string ToString()
    {
        if (Player == PlayerType.BLACK)
            return "Black " + Name + " at (" + Col + "," + Row + ")";
        else
            return "White " + Name + " at (" + Col + "," + Row + ")";
    }
}
```

Now we'll call the **AbstractChessPiece ToString**() method again:

```
Pawn piece3 = new Pawn();
piece3.Player = PlayerType.WHITE;
piece3.Name = "Pawn";
piece3.Col = 3;
piece3.Row = 1;
MessageBox.Show(piece3.ToString());
```

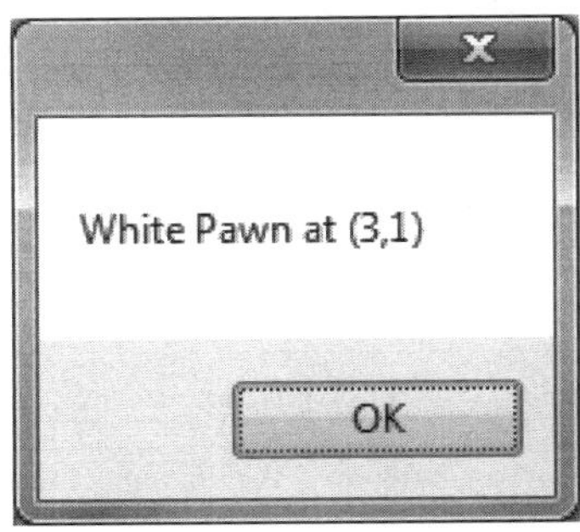

Our overridden **ToString**() method will produce a much more useful description! It is often a good idea to override the **ToString**() method on your classes to provide better information, especially if you want to use the method to create some class-specific text to show the user. You can get a good description of an object from a base class reference, even if the reference actually holds some derived class (polymorphism at work again).

Lesson Five: Using Base Features from Derived Classes

In our previous lesson, we discussed how to override the **virtual** methods of a base class. However, there may be times when you will want to both override a base class method and yet still have access to that base method from the derived class when needed. When this is the case, you can reference the base class version of a method by using the **base** keyword in front of the method call in your code.

Let's look at an example of this scenario with our **Pawn** class. We decide that the default **ToString()** method on the **AbstractChessPiece** class is okay, but needs a little sprucing up. So on our **Pawn** object we'll override **ToString()** again:

```
class Pawn : AbstractChessPiece
{
    override public string ToString()
    {
        // use the base class version of ToString() and add extra text
        return base.ToString() + " - PAWNS RULE!";
    }
}
```

You will notice that inside the **Pawn**'s **ToString()** implementation we still used the **AbstractChessPiece** version as well by calling **base.ToString()**. We just added another string to the end of the base string to make our feelings on chess pawns very clear!

Now when we call **ToString()** on our **Pawn** object:

```
Pawn piece3 = new Pawn();
piece3.Player = PlayerType.WHITE;
piece3.Name = "Pawn";
piece3.Col = 3;
piece3.Row = 1;
MessageBox.Show(piece3.ToString());
```

We will get a window that shows the **Pawn ToString()** method has combined both the base class **ToString()** results with some extra text.

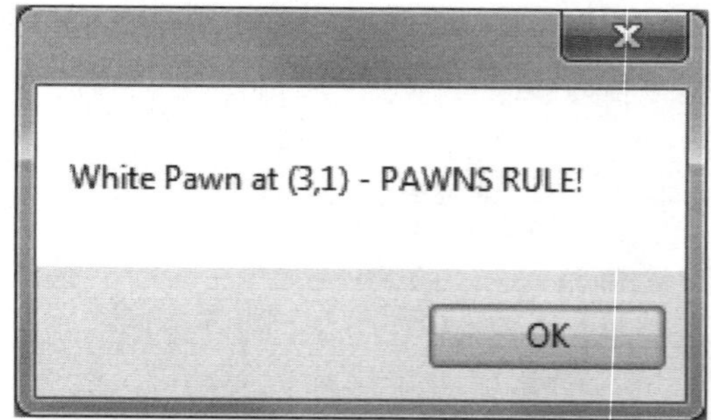

Calling Base Constructor Methods

Now you know how to call a normal base class *method*, but how would you call a particular version of a base class *constructor*? Let's say we decided not to allow an **AbstractChessPiece** to be created without specifying the piece's name and owning player right up front in the constructor. To do this, we would create a constructor for this **AbstractChessPiece** that demanded those two parameters:

```
abstract class AbstractChessPiece
{
    public string Name;              // "Pawn", "Rook", etc.
    public PlayerType Player;        // BLACK or WHITE

    public AbstractChessPiece(string newName, PlayerType newPlayer)
    {
        Name = newName;
        Player = newPlayer;
    }
}
```

Now, if we were to create a new instance of our **Pawn** class (which is derived from the **AbstractChessPiece** class, we would have a problem. The constructor for the **Pawn** class does not specify either the name or player for the chess piece. The following code would generate a compiler error:

```
// this calls the Pawn's default constructor, which doesn't help
// call the AbstractChessPiece constructor with parameters!
Pawn piece8 = new Pawn();  // ERROR
```

To fix this error we need to define a constructor for the **Pawn** class that will call the **AbstractChessPiece** constructor with the required parameters. To call the base class constructor, we need to create a constructor for the **Pawn** that can supply the required parameters to the base. We need to make an explicit call to the base constructor from the **Pawn** constructor by adding a colon and the keyword **base** with the required parameters in parentheses, like this:

```
public Pawn() : base("Pawn", PlayerType.WHITE)
{
    // Pawn constructor logic here
}
```

This will cause the base class constructor (the **AbstractChessPiece** constructor in this example) to be executed *before* any of the derived class constructor (the **Pawn** constructor) logic within the brackets is executed.

Now we can safely create a **Pawn** class again without any errors:

```
Pawn piece8 = new Pawn();  // OK
```

Of course, we know that all pawns are not white! A better **Pawn** constructor would also demand to know what player owns the piece and pass that information along to the **AbstractChessPiece**:

```
public Pawn(PlayerType player) : base("Pawn", player)
{
    // Pawn constructor logic here
}
```

We can hard-code (or pre-fill) the first parameter to the base constructor as "Pawn" since we know we are creating a **Pawn** object from the **Pawn** constructor. We also take the **PlayerType** input parameter from the **Pawn** constructor and pass it directly into the base class constructor. Now we can create **Pawns** for the desired player and fully initialize the base class:

```
Pawn piece9 = new Pawn(PlayerType.BLACK);
```

As you might imagine, the constructors for **Rooks** and all other chess pieces would look similar, except they should substitute their own names as the first parameter.

Chapter Review

- *Inheritance* means one class can re-use and extend the properties and methods of another class.
- A *base* class is a class from which other classes can inherit.
- A *derived* class is a class that inherits from a base class.
- An **abstract** method is declared in the base class but has no method body. The derived classes will be responsible for implementing methods with the **override** keyword.
- Any class with **abstract** properties or methods must be defined as an **abstract** class
- *Polymorphism* means you can use an object through a base reference and it will behave differently according to its actual derived type.
- *Casting* is used to change references to another data type.
- A **virtual** method is implemented by the base class and overridden by a derived class, if necessary.
- In the C# language, all objects inherit from the root **System.Object** class.
- The **System.Object** class has several useful methods that are available to all derived classes.
- A commonly used **System.Object** method is **ToString**(), which will return a string (text) representation of the object.
- The **ToString**() method can be overridden by any derived class. This is usually a great way to format the text representation of your object.
- To call a base method or property from within a derived class, you can simply use the **base** keyword before the method or property.
- To call the base constructor with useful parameters, use the **base** keyword at the end of your derived class constructor function header.

Activity: Creating the Chess Pieces

In this activity you will start writing the some of the code that will be used for the final project! Your chess program will rely heavily on the **AbstractChessPiece** hierarchy we used as a running example in this chapter. It's time to start filling out the details for real!

Your activity requirements and instructions are found in the "Chapter_16_Activity.pdf" document located in your "TeenCoder\Windows Programming\Activity Docs" folder. You can access this document through your Student Menu or by double-clicking on it from Windows Explorer.

Complete this activity now and ensure your program meets the requirements before continuing!

Chapter Seventeen: Final Project

You've learned quite a bit about C# and Windows programming throughout this course. Now it's time to put these concepts to work in your final project! In this chapter you will create a graphical chess game for two players. You may already be very familiar with chess, but we'll briefly review the rules in the first lesson.

Lesson One: The Game of Chess

Chess is a two-player game that uses a standard 8 x 8 grid of squares as a game board. The grid contains a checkerboard pattern of light and dark squares. One player has 16 black pieces, and one player has 16 white pieces. Each player starts the game with their 16 pieces arranged in two rows on their side of the board. There are six different types of playing pieces: eight "Pawns", two "Rooks", two "Bishops", two "Knights", one "Queen" and one "King". Each player takes turns moving pieces across the board. The object of the game is to *checkmate* the opposing King by making it impossible for the opponent to make a move without the King being subject to capture.

Your chess board and player pieces will look like the screen shot shown to the right. Each piece is represented by the first character of its name. Note the King is underlined like this (K) so you can tell it apart from the Knight.

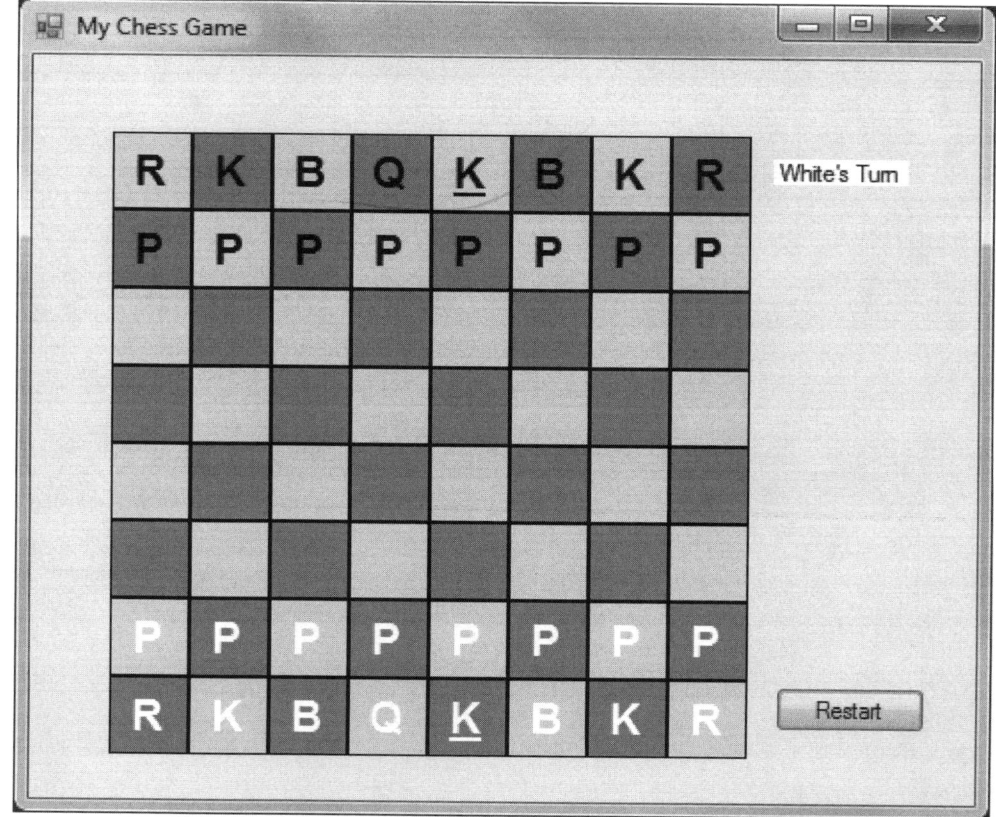

Each chess piece can move across the board in different ways, so let's review each behavior now.

Pawns

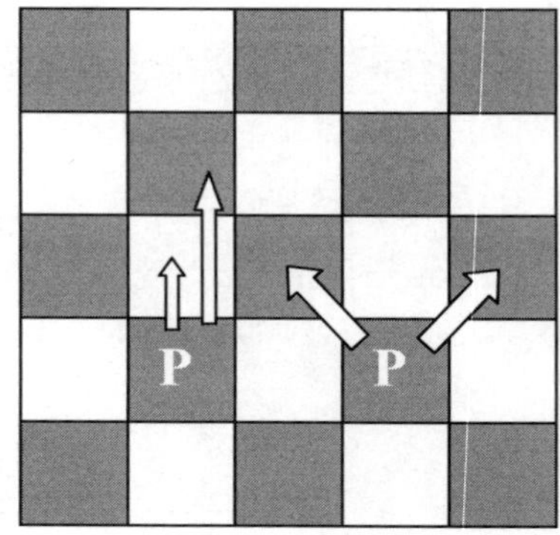

The first time a Pawn is moved on the board, it can be moved one or two spaces in the forward direction. After the first move, they can only move a single space at a time. A Pawn captures an opposing piece by moving one diagonal space forward. Pawns are the only pieces that have different rules for normal moves and capturing moves. The example shows the Pawn piece on the left can move to either of the spaces that are indicated if they are empty. The Pawn piece on the right can capture an opponent in either of the two forward diagonal spaces.

Rooks

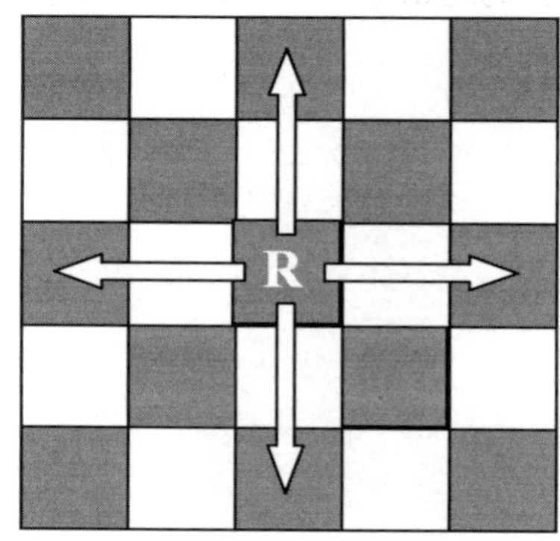

A Rook can move any number of squares straight forwards, backwards, left or right. Rooks cannot jump over any other piece in the way. If there is an opposing piece in their path, the Rook can stop in that square and capture the piece (by removing it from the board).

Bishops

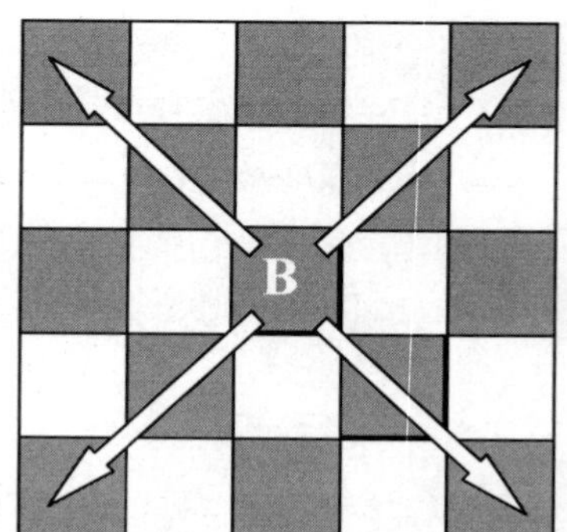

Bishops can move any number of squares in a diagonal direction. Bishops cannot jump over any other piece in the way. If there is an opposing piece in their path, the Bishop can stop in that square and capture the piece (by removing it from the board). Each player has two Bishops, one starting on a black square and one starting on a white square. Since it can only move diagonally, a Bishop will always be on the same color square as the square the piece started on!

Queen

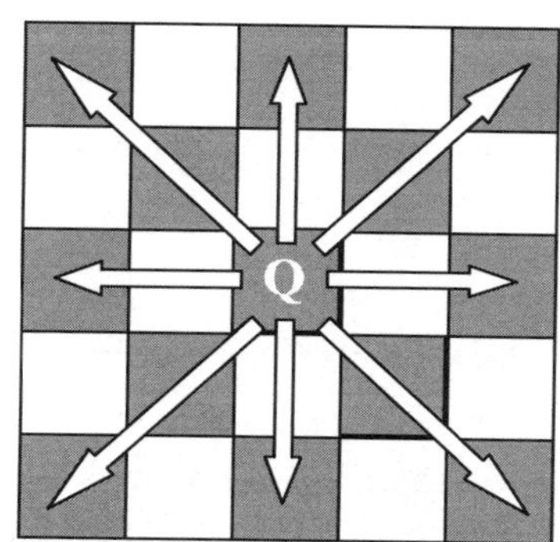

The Queen piece combines the movement of the Rook and Bishop pieces. The Queen can move any number of squares diagonally or forwards, backwards, left or right on the board. The ability to make all of these moves makes the Queen the most powerful piece on the chess board. Queens cannot jump over any pieces in the way and will capture opponents just like the Bishop and Rook.

King

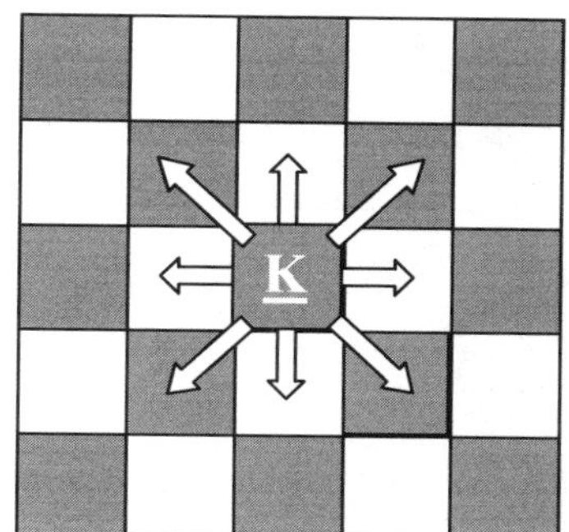

The King can only move one space in any direction. Otherwise, it captures opponents and is blocked by pieces of the same color just like the Bishop, Rook, and Queen.

Knights

The Knight is the only piece that "hops" over other pieces to land in its target square. The Knight moves across the board in an "L-shaped" pattern. This means that a Knight can move two spaces in one direction and then one space in a perpendicular direction, or one space in one direction and two spaces in a perpendicular direction. Knights do not capture any pieces that are on the squares that it "hops" over. Only opposing pieces that are on the target square are captured. In the example diagram, the arrowheads lie on the target squares for this Knight piece.

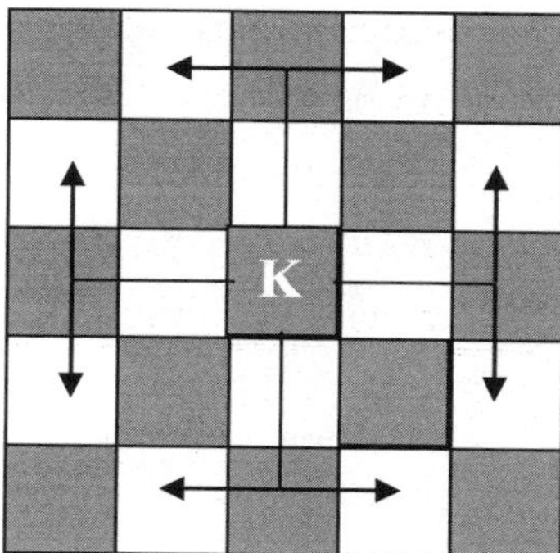

Except for the Knight, no piece can hop or skip over another piece to reach a destination square. All pieces can "capture" (or remove from the board) an opposing piece when their move ends on that opposing piece's square. No chess piece can land on or capture pieces of their own color!

Winning the Game

The object of the game is to "checkmate" the opponent's King. When a King piece is in danger of being captured, he is said to be "in check". When a King is in check, the player **must** get the King out of check on the next move! When a King cannot possibly escape capture by his opponent's next move, he is said to be "checkmated" and the game is over.

Advanced Rules

There are some more advanced chess rules like "Castling" and "Pawn Promotion". For the sake of simplicity, we will not be implementing these advanced rules in the final project. However you are welcome to implement the advanced rules on your own.

Lesson Two: The Starter Project

As you can imagine, writing a computer game like chess from scratch can be a tricky task. Therefore we have provided a starter project with some aspects of the game already in place. The starter project contains the following components:

- The **ChessForm** graphical design
- The **ChessForm** game data variables
- The **ChessBoard** object, which represents the 8x8 game board and tracks all of the player's pieces

In this lesson we will review the **ChessForm** and **ChessBoard** components that we provide for you. It is important to understand how the game is designed and what utilities are available to complete your portion of the project.

To begin, copy the "\TeenCoder\Windows Programming\Activity Starters\Chess" folder to your "My Projects" working directory using Windows Explorer. Once you have copied this directory, you can open the solution for the project by selecting the "Chess.sln" in the IDE. Go ahead and open the solution in the IDE now so you can follow along in the code as we explore the different components.

Note that the project will not initially compile without errors until you follow some steps specified later in this lesson. For now just review the code without attempting to compile!

The ChessForm

The main screen is called the **ChessForm**, found in the "ChessForm.cs" file. It looks pretty simple in the Form Design screen!

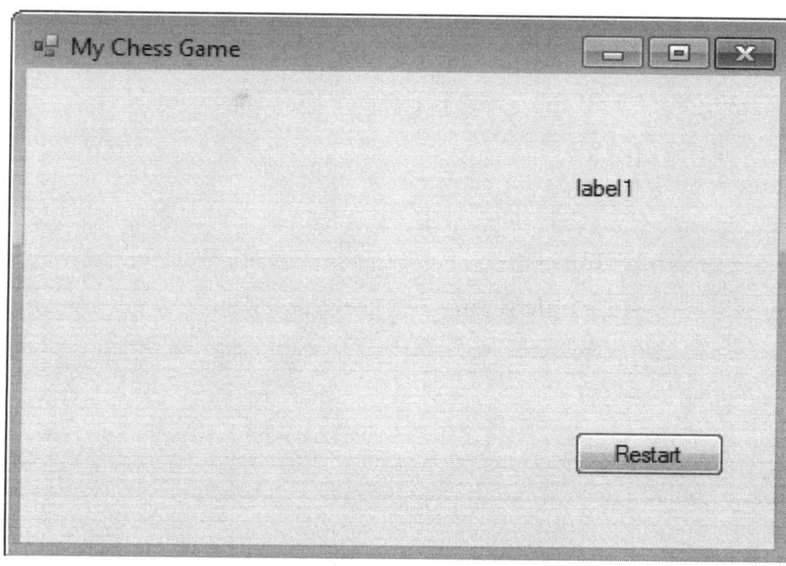

There are initially only two elements on the form: a label named **`LabelPlayer`** and a button named **`ButtonRestart`**. The label will be used to display the current player's turn (Black or White). When the "Restart" button is clicked, the game board should be reset to the initial state with all the pieces back where they started. The 8x8 square grid will be formed by **Button** controls added by the **ChessBoard** object.

The **ChessForm** also contains all of the data necessary to implement the game:

```
// The following variables encompass all of the game data
private ChessBoard gameBoard;
private ChessSquare selectedSquare;
private PlayerType currentPlayer;
```

You are already familiar with the **PlayerType** enumeration specified at the top of the "ChessPiece.cs" file:

```
// the following enum identifies a chess piece as black or white
public enum PlayerType
{
    BLACK,
    WHITE
}
```

The **ChessBoard** and **ChessSquare** objects are new to you and are more fully described later in this lesson.

The following methods are fully implemented on the **ChessForm** in the starter project:

ChessForm()	The constructor creates a new **ChessBoard** object, assigns it to the **`gameBoard`** variable, and then calls **initializeGame**().

void gameSquare_Click()	This method is called when a player clicks on any square on the game board. It identifies which square was clicked and then calls **handleClick**() to determine what happens with the user input.

The following **ChessForm** methods are defined but not implemented. You will be responsible for finishing them as we move through the project!

void initializeGame()	This method is called to start a new game. It will set the current player to White, clear the game board of any prior pieces, and create new, correctly positioned pieces on the game board for each player.
void setPlayer()	This method will update the **`currentPlayer`** variable and adjust the **`labelPlayer`** display to reflect the current player's turn.
void changePlayer()	This method will switch the current player from Black to White or White to Black.
void handleClick()	This method encapsulates much of the game logic! When the user clicks on a square we need to determine if they are selecting a piece they own, moving a previously selected piece, and so forth.
void buttonRestart_Click()	This method should simply call **initializeGame**() to start a new game.

Now that you have a good feel for the main **ChessForm** object, let's take a closer look at the new **ChessBoard** and **ChessSquare** objects that make up the rest of the game data.

The ChessBoard Object

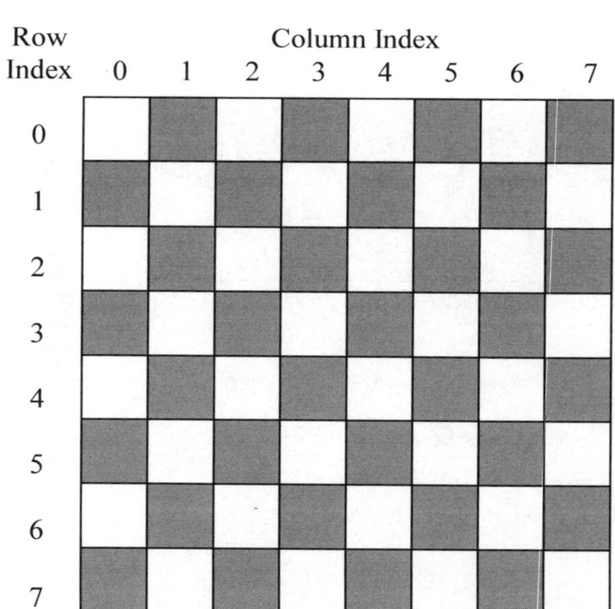

The **ChessBoard** object is fully implemented for you, so you don't have to modify it at all. This object will track each of the 8x8 squares on the game board grid and provide several utility methods to let you access the squares.

Each square on the board is uniquely represented by a column and row index from 0 - 7. For instance, the upper-right square has column = 7 and row = 0, which may be written as "(7, 0)".

The individual squares are actually **ChessSquare** objects stored in an 8x8 array. Each **ChessSquare** contains a Button control to receive mouse clicks.

The **ChessBoard** implements a number of public functions that you will use during game development:

void ClearSquares()	Remove all chess pieces from all squares
void AddNewChessPiece(**int** col, **int** row, **AbstractChessPiece** piece**)**	Assigns the specified chess piece to the square located at the target column and row
ChessSquare GetSquare(**int** col, **int** row**)**	Returns the **ChessSquare** object located at the target column and row
ChessSquare GetClickedSquare(**string** buttonName**)**	Returns the **ChessSquare** object identified by the specified button name
LinkedList<ChessSquare> **GetDiagonalSquares(** **int** col1, **int** row1, **int** col2, **int** row2**)**	Returns a list of **ChessSquares** on a diagonal line between (col1, row1) and (col2, row2)
LinkedList<ChessSquare> **GetStraightSquares(** **int** col1, **int** row1, **int** col2, **int** row2**)**	Returns a list of **ChessSquares** on a straight line in any direction between (col1, row1) and (col2, row2)
LinkedList<ChessSquare> **GetSquaresUp(** **int** col1, **int** row1, **int** col2, **int** row2**)**	Returns a list of **ChessSquares** on a straight line "up" between (col1, row1) and (col2, row2)
LinkedList<ChessSquare> **GetSquaresDown(** **int** col1, **int** row1, **int** col2, **int** row2**)**	Returns a list of **ChessSquares** on a straight line "down" between (col1, row1) and (col2, row2)
AbstractChessPiece **MoveChessPiece(** **ChessSquare** selectedSquare, **ChessSquare** clickedSquare**)**	Performs all of the operations necessary to move a chess piece from the selected square to the clicked square. Returns the piece from the target square that was captured, if any, or **null** otherwise.
bool TestMoveForCheck(**PlayerType** currentPlayer, **ChessSquare** selectedSquare, **ChessSquare** clickedSquare**)**	Tests to see if a potential move from the specified player from selected square to clicked square would leave the player still in check. Returns **true** if still in check, or **false** otherwise.
bool IsInCheck(**PlayerType** player**)**	Tests to see if the indicated player is currently in check. Returns **true** if in check, or **false** otherwise.

The ChessSquare Object

The **ChessSquare** object represents one square on the chess board. Each **ChessSquare** has the following public properties:

```
public int Col; // the col index 0-7 identifying this square
public int Row; // the row index 0-7 identifying this square

// identify the current chess piece, if any, on the square
public AbstractChessPiece ChessPiece;
```

The **Col** and **Row** variables contain the 0-7 column or row index of the square on the overall 8x8 game board grid. The **ChessPiece** variable contains a reference to the piece that is currently on the square, if any. If there is no piece on the square then the **ChessPiece** value is **null**.

The **ChessSquare** object also contains a **Button** and other logic necessary to draw the square and chess piece (if any) on the form with the right color, font type, and button size. Each graphical square is represented by a **Button** object on the form. You won't have to worry about the details of how exactly the graphical operations take place in order to complete the project. But, if curious, you can review the code for details.

The **ChessSquare** contains the following public methods that you will use while completing the project:

void Select()	Sets the square to a "selected" state, meaning the square is drawn with a thick yellow border
void Unselect()	Sets the square to an "unselected" state, meaning the square is drawn with a normal black border
SetChessPiece(AbstractChessPiece piece)	Places the specified **piece** on the square, updates the piece's **Col** and **Row** properties, sets the square's font and color based on the player that owns the piece
void RemoveChessPiece()	Removes any chess piece previously on the square and resets the button's text to an empty string (removes the piece abbreviation).

The **ChessBoard** and **ChessSquare** objects are located in the "ChessBoard.cs" file. You will not need to make any modifications to that file, but can refer to the function definitions for any detailed questions about how the objects behave.

Activity One: Starting Your Chess Project

In this activity you will add your "ChessPieces.cs" source file from the last chapter into the Chess project and ensure the entire project compiles without errors.

Your activity requirements and instructions are found in the "Chapter_17_Activity1.pdf" document located in your "TeenCoder\Windows Programming\Activity Docs" folder. You can access this document through your Student Menu or by double-clicking on it from Windows Explorer.

Complete this activity now and ensure your program meets the requirements before continuing!

Activity Two: Initializing the Game

In this activity you will:

- Complete the **ChessForm.setPlayer**() method
- Complete the **ChessForm.initializeGame**() method
- Complete parts of the **ChessForm.handleClick**() method

Your activity requirements and instructions are found in the "Chapter_17_Activity2.pdf" document located in your "TeenCoder\Windows Programming\Activity Docs" folder. You can access this document through your Student Menu or by double-clicking on it from Windows Explorer.

Complete this activity now and ensure your program meets the requirements before continuing!

Activity Three: Finishing handleClick()

The goal for this activity is to allow the current player to move the selected piece anywhere on the board (with no movement restrictions). Players will be notified when pieces have been captured.

Your activity requirements and instructions are found in the "Chapter_17_Activity3.pdf" document located in your "TeenCoder\Windows Programming\Activity Docs" folder. You can access this document through your Student Menu or by double-clicking on it from Windows Explorer.

Complete this activity now and ensure your program meets the requirements before continuing!

Activity Four: Moving Pawns

It's time to start enforcing real chess movement and capture rules on our pieces. In this activity you will:

- Complete the **ChessForm.buttonRestart_Click**() method
- Complete the **Pawn.CanMoveToLocation**() method
- Complete the **Pawn.CanCaptureLocation**() method

Your activity requirements and instructions are found in the "Chapter_17_Activity4.pdf" document located in your "TeenCoder\Windows Programming\Activity Docs" folder. You can access this document through your Student Menu or by double-clicking on it from Windows Explorer.

Complete this activity now and ensure your program meets the requirements before continuing!

Activity Five: Moving Other Pieces, Testing for Check

In this lesson you will finish up the movement logic for the remaining chess pieces. Fortunately they are not as specialized as the **Pawn**! You will implement the **AbstractChessPiece.CanFollowPath()** method as a utility to be used by the rest of the derived classes. You will then implement the **CanMoveToLocation()** method on the remaining pieces.

Your activity requirements and instructions are found in the "Chapter_17_Activity5.pdf" document located in your "TeenCoder\Windows Programming\Activity Docs" folder. You can access this document through your Student Menu or by double-clicking on it from Windows Explorer.

Complete this activity now and ensure your program meets the requirements before continuing!

Wrap-up and Extra Credit

Congratulations! You have now finished your final project. Successful completion demonstrates a solid understanding of what it takes to complete a moderately complex, graphical Windows program using object-oriented programming techniques.

You now have a simple two-player chess game. Sharp chess players will notice that we have not implemented some features such as checkmate detection, castling, and pawn promotion. For extra credit or your own satisfaction you are encouraged to implement any or all of these features based on your understanding of the overall program flow and game data. Some modification to the **ChessBoard** object may be required depending on the approaches you take. Have fun!

What's Next?

Congratulations, you have finished the *TeenCoder™: Windows Programming* course! If you are interested in a career in computers, the concepts and skills you learned are a solid foundation for further study.

The next course in the TeenCoder™ C# series is *TeenCoder™: Game Programming*. In the game programming course you will build on your C# and Windows programming skills to learn the fine art of writing your own computer games! We also offer a TeenCoder Java series that will teach you to write Java programs and Android smart-phone applications.

Our two KidCoder™ series for 4th+ grade students focus on other programming topics. The KidCoder Visual Basic series gives you some of the same graphical Windows capabilities in an easy-to-use language. The KidCoder Web Design series will teach you simple HTML, CSS, and JavaScript techniques so you can build your own websites.

We hope you have enjoyed this course produced by Homeschool Programming, Inc. We welcome student and teacher feedback at our website. Please also visit our website to request courses on other topics or see what new courses are available!

http://www.HomeschoolProgramming.com

Index